Building Your Finances God's Way

A financial discipleship study

Orlando, Florida
407-331-6000 www.compass1.org

Thank You!

A special thank you to:

Dan & Lynn Nicewander

Jim Whorton

Brad Jack

Dan Schilling

Peter Briscoe

Jennifer Winborn

for using your gifts to help "build" this study!

American Bible Society helped fund the original production of this study. We are grateful to serve together to encourage meaningful Bible engagement.

COMPASS®
-finances God's way
A FINANCIAL DISCIPLESHIP MINISTRY™

Concepts and portions of this text have been taken from the Navigating Your Finances God's Way study by Howard Dayton, © 2011

A Message from Howard

I am so thankful that you have decided to participate in the Building Your Finances God's Way financial discipleship study. The Lord has used the principles you are about to learn in the lives of millions of people around the world, and we are excited about what He will teach you through these six chapters.

This financial discipleship study is designed to be taught in several ways:

As a one-on-one study

In a group of 3-4 people

In a small group of 12 people or less

We recommend these group sizes based on the ways Jesus taught and spent time with his disciples.

Warning - it's going to be different!

What you learn in this study will often seem radical and revolutionary because it's so different from the way most people view their finances. But what you learn will transform your relationships and your financial statement - for the better. I can guarantee that, because you will be learning what the Lord of the universe knows is best for you.

God expressed it this way in Isaiah 55:8-9: *"'My thoughts are not your thoughts, neither are your ways my ways,' declares the Lord. 'As the heavens are higher than the earth, so are my ways higher than your ways'"* (NIV).

God has His ways, and they are the best ways. But they're not always the commonly accepted ways in our culture. God has paths for us to walk, and they are amazing. But they're not always the paths that most people follow.

God's ways of having stable finances are very different from the way most people think and act. But they are so much higher - so much better - than most people can even imagine.

As you look at what God has to say about finances, my prayer for you is that you will enjoy a growing intimacy with Jesus and with one another!

Table of Contents

Modified Inductive Study Method

This study uses a modified inductive study method to engage people in God's word. This method includes making observations on a passage of Scripture and then drawing conclusions based on those observations. Compass financial discipleship studies utilize four key components: prayer, observation, interpretation, and application.

> ***Prayer - Ask for Guidance.*** Pray for the Holy Spirit's guidance as you begin reading passages of Scripture. Ask for clarity and insight as you engage in God's word.
>
> ***Observation - What Does the Text Say?*** Pay close attention to what the text actually says. Gather facts like an investigative reporter. Answer questions to help you observe the facts: Who? What? When? Where? How? Why? Take note of any key words or phrases that stick out to you.
>
> ***Interpretation - What Does the Text Mean?*** What is the author's intent in this passage? What is one principle or lesson God is communicating through these words? What does the author seem to want you to wrestle with or learn? What are your life experiences related to the meaning of the passage?
>
> ***Application - How Do I Apply the Text?*** How can I apply the heart of this message to my life and finances?
>
> ***Compass Commentaries.*** At the end of each chapter are the Compass Commentaries. These commentaries are there to give you additional insight into the scripture verses for each day's homework.

Please note - The daily Scripture verses used in this study are taken from the ESV version of the Bible unless otherwise noted. Please feel free to use a different Bible version if you desire.

Again, we are very grateful you are participating in the Building Your Finances God's Way financial discipleship study. I pray that the Lord will bless you in every way as you learn His way of handling money.

Howard Dayton

Howard Dayton

Founder, Compass – finances God's way

Study Requirements

Through years of practice and experience, we have learned that people benefit most from this study when they are faithful to complete the following steps.

1. Homework. The homework will take about 20-30 minutes each day to complete. Space is provided in the workbook to answer the questions. A married couple will use separate workbooks.
2. Scripture memory. Memorize an assigned verse from the Bible for each chapter and individually recite the verse at the beginning of class. This will help you remember the most important principles - not just for a few weeks but for years to come.
3. Application worksheets. Complete a practical exercise, such as a debt list.
4. Prayer. Everyone prays for the other group members each day. Answers to prayers are one of the most encouraging parts of the small group experience.

If an individual is unable to complete the requirements for a particular chapter, we recommend that he or she attend but refrain from participating in the discussion. This accountability helps us to be faithful. And the more faithful we are, the more benefits we receive from the study.

Attendance. Everyone should attend at least 5 of the 6 meetings. Please notify one of the facilitators in advance if you anticipate missing a meeting or arriving late. The meetings are designed to begin and end on time.

Group Discussion Agenda

Please note: All time frames are meant to be used as an approximation to help you finish the group discussion in two hours. Times may vary based on group size.

1. ***Open the group discussion in prayer.***
2. ***Everyone individually recites the memory verse (10 minutes).***
3. ***Discuss the daily homework (100 minutes).***

    Review the Day One Homework.

    Have someone from the group read the Bible verses for that day's homework. After reading the verses, begin the group discussion.

    Have everyone answer the Observation questions.

    After the Observation questions have been answered, have everyone answer the Interpretation questions.

    After the Interpretation questions have been answered, have everyone answer the Application questions.

    After the Application questions have been answered, repeat the process for the next day's homework.

    Day Six

    Have each person answer the discussion questions from the Day Six homework.

4. ***Take prayer requests and have participants note them in their prayer logs (10 minutes).***
5. ***Have one person close the group discussion in prayer.***

Helpful Discussion Tips:

If you have a large group or are have trouble finishing your meetings in a two-hour time frame . . .

1. You can speed things up by making sure each participant answers all the questions from a section of homework before moving on to the next person. For example, on the Day One - Interpretation questions, have one person answer all Day One - Interpretation questions before the next person shares their answers for the same questions. Repeat this process with the Observation and Application questions.

2. Ask study participants to write their prayer requests for the Prayer Log prior to the meeting. This can save considerable time sharing prayer requests for the Prayer Log at the end of each group discussion.

3. You may choose to omit reading the Bible verses for each day's homework and move directly to answering the questions related to those verses.

Compasstools.org

Compasstools.org is your one-stop shop to find any of the online tools for this study.

You will find all sorts of great online tools to help you on your financial discipleship journey including:

> *The Building Your Finances God's Way videos*
>
> *Electronic application worksheets- they do all the calculations for you!*
>
> *Audio Notes*
>
> *Online calculators*
>
> *Memory verse tools*
>
> *See their Story videos*
>
> *Example application worksheets for each chapter*
>
> *Additional Tools for the Journey and more!*

The Financial Discipleship App

The Financial Discipleship App has some great features that are designed specifically for this study.

> *A mobile 30-Day tracking tool to help you track your expenses when you are on the go! You'll learn more about this in Chapter 4 of the study.*
>
> *A really great prayer tool that allows you to create groups, add prayer requests and more.*

Download on the App Store

GET IT ON Google Play

The Compass Vision, Mission & Values

Our Vision:

To see everyone, everywhere faithfully living by God's financial principles in every area of their lives.

Our Mission:

Equipping people worldwide to faithfully apply God's financial principles so they may know Christ more intimately, be free to serve Him and help fund the Great Commission.

Core Values:

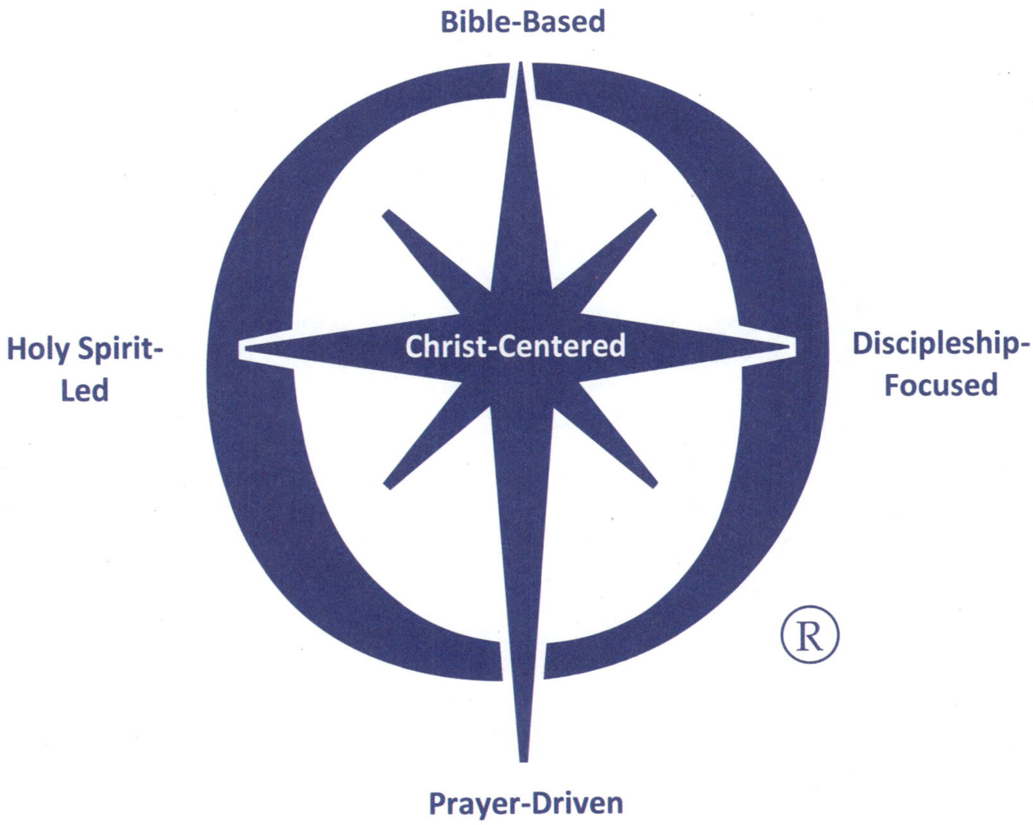

Chapter 1:

The Foundation

*All tools, videos, resources and electronic applications for this chapter can be found at **compasstools.org***

THIS CHAPTER'S MEMORY VERSE:

1 Chronicles 29:11-12

DAILY HOMEWORK:

Day One – God's Word

Day Two – God's Ownership, begin working on the Personal Financial Statement

Day Three – God's Provision

Day Four – God's Control

Day Five – Our Part, begin working on The Deed

Day Six – Watch the Build Your Finances God's Way video, Read the Notes, answer the discussion questions

BEFORE YOUR GROUP MEETING:

1. Memorize 1 Chronicles 29:11-12, TLB. To prevent confusion when reciting the verses in a group setting, please memorize the version shown below.

> *"...Everything in the heavens and earth is yours, O Lord, and this is your kingdom. We adore you as being in control of everything. Riches and honor come from you alone, and you are the ruler of all mankind; your hand controls power and might and it is at your discretion that men are made great and given strength." (1 Chronicles 29:11-12, TLB).*

2. Complete the Daily Homework.

Each day's homework is designed to take 20-30 minutes to complete.

1 - DAY ONE

Homework

God's Word

PRAYER

Pray for the Holy Spirit's guidance as you begin reading passages of Scripture. Ask for clarity and insight as you engage in God's word.

SCRIPTURE READING

Read 2 Timothy 3:14-17

"But as for you, continue in what you have learned and have firmly believed, knowing from whom you learned it and how from childhood you have been acquainted with the sacred writings, which are able to make you wise for salvation through faith in Christ Jesus. All Scripture is breathed out by God and profitable for teaching, for reproof, for correction, and for training in righteousness, that the man of God may be complete, equipped for every good work." (ESV)

Read Isaiah 55:8-12

"For my thoughts are not your thoughts, neither are your ways my ways,
declares the Lord. [9]For as the heavens are higher than the earth, so are my
ways higher than your ways and my thoughts than your thoughts. [10]For as the
rain and the snow come down from heaven and do not return there but water
the earth, making it bring forth and sprout, giving seed to the sower and bread
to the eater, [11]so shall my word be that goes out from my mouth; it shall not
return to me empty, but it shall accomplish that which I purpose, and shall
succeed in the thing for which I sent it. [12]For you shall go out in joy and be led
forth in peace; the mountains and the hills before you shall break forth into
singing, and all the trees of the field shall clap their hands." (ESV)

OBSERVATION

What are these passages saying about...

God's Word?

God's thoughts?

1 - DAY ONE

Homework

SCRIPTURE READING

Read 2 Timothy 3:14-17

"But as for you, continue in what you have learned and have firmly believed, knowing from whom you learned it and how from childhood you have been acquainted with the sacred writings, which are able to make you wise for salvation through faith in Christ Jesus. All Scripture is breathed out by God and profitable for teaching, for reproof, for correction, and for training in righteousness, that the man of God may be complete, equipped for every good work." (ESV)

Read Isaiah 55:8-12

"For my thoughts are not your thoughts, neither are your ways my ways,
declares the Lord. 9For as the heavens are higher than the earth, so are my
ways higher than your ways and my thoughts than your thoughts. 10For as the
rain and the snow come down from heaven and do not return there but water
the earth, making it bring forth and sprout, giving seed to the sower and bread
to the eater, 11so shall my word be that goes out from my mouth; it shall not
return to me empty, but it shall accomplish that which I purpose, and shall
succeed in the thing for which I sent it. 12For you shall go out in joy and be led
forth in peace; the mountains and the hills before you shall break forth into
singing, and all the trees of the field shall clap their hands." (ESV)

INTERPRETATION

Why is it important to study and apply the Scriptures?

How can the Bible change the way we think and act?

How have you experienced God's word impacting your life?

APPLICATION

How can you apply the principles of these passages to your finances?

HOWARD'S HIGHLIGHTS

God wants the best for you

It's important to understand that the biblical truths and cautions addressed to us are intended for your good. God loves you with an unfathomable love.

John 15:9 says, "Just as the Father has loved Me, I have also loved you." Imagine the depth of love God the Father has for God the Son. In the same way, He loves you! And just as a loving earthly father desires a close relationship with his children, so our heavenly Father hungers for such a relationship with each of us. God knows very well that money can present a potential barrier to this intimate relationship with Him.

"It is important to realize every time God says, 'You shall not,' He is simply saying, 'Don't hurt yourself,' and when He says, 'You shall,' He means 'help yourself to happiness.' God only wants for us what we would want for ourselves if we were smart enough to want it." – Pastor Adrian Rogers

God's Economy

God's economy and the way most people view money are in sharp contrast. This should not surprise us. *Isaiah 55:8-9 reads, "'For My thoughts are not your thoughts, neither are your ways My ways,' declares the Lord. 'For as the heavens are higher than the earth, so are My ways higher than your ways, and My thoughts than your thoughts.'"* God's ways are not only different, they are so much better than our practices! The most significant difference is that in God's economy, the living Lord plays the dominant role. He is central. As elementary as it appears, this distinction has profound implications.

Because God has chosen to be invisible and to operate in the unseen supernatural realm, most people view financial decisions based on the Bible as an illogical leap of faith.

You might be surprised to learn just how much the Bible says about money. More than 2,350 verses relate to handling money and possessions, including fifteen percent of everything Jesus said!

PRAYERS FOR TODAY

This prayer section is for personal use and isn't meant to be part of the group discussion.

For you...

For your family and friends...

For those in your group...

1 - DAY TWO

Homework

God's Ownership

PRAYER

Pray for the Holy Spirit's guidance as you begin reading passages of Scripture. Ask for clarity and insight as you engage in God's word.

SCRIPTURE READING

Read Psalm 50:7-15

"Hear, O my people, and I will speak;
O Israel, I will testify against you.
I am God, your God.
8*Not for your sacrifices do I rebuke you;*
your burnt offerings are continually before me.
9*I will not accept a bull from your house*
or goats from your folds.
10*For every beast of the forest is mine,*
the cattle on a thousand hills.
11*I know all the birds of the hills,*
and all that moves in the field is mine.
12*If I were hungry, I would not tell you,*
for the world and its fullness are mine.
13*Do I eat the flesh of bulls or drink the blood of goats?*
14*Offer to God a sacrifice of thanksgiving,*
and perform your vows to the Most High,
15*and call upon me in the day of trouble;*
I will deliver you, and you shall glorify me" (ESV).

OBSERVATION

What are these passages saying about...

God's people?

God's needs?

What God owns?

1 - DAY TWO

Homework

SCRIPTURE READING

Read Psalm 50:7-15

"Hear, O my people, and I will speak;
O Israel, I will testify against you.
I am God, your God.
8Not for your sacrifices do I rebuke you;
your burnt offerings are continually before me.
9I will not accept a bull from your house
or goats from your folds.
10For every beast of the forest is mine,
the cattle on a thousand hills.
11I know all the birds of the hills,
and all that moves in the field is mine.
12If I were hungry, I would not tell you,
for the world and its fullness are mine.
13Do I eat the flesh of bulls or drink the blood of goats?
14Offer to God a sacrifice of thanksgiving,
and perform your vows to the Most High,
15and call upon me in the day of trouble;
I will deliver you, and you shall glorify me" (ESV).

INTERPRETATION

Why would it be important to understand that God owns everything?

In what areas of your life is it hard to relinquish ownership to God? Why?

APPLICATION

The Personal Financial Statement

The Personal Financial Statement:

We now have a pretty good idea of what God owns – everything! So let's take stock and see what God owns as it relates to your situation. To do this, we'll be completing the Personal Financial Statement. This exercise is helpful for several reasons:

> **1. It gives a picture of your financial health.**
>
> **2. It allows you to see areas to celebrate and areas where improvements can be made.**
>
> **3. It shows what you could sell if you need cash.**

As you complete this exercise, keep in mind that it's not necessary to be absolutely precise; rather, estimate the value of each asset and the amount of each debt. ***You will not be asked to show the statement to anyone.***

You can find an example of this application at ***compasstools.org***

Date: ____________________

ASSETS

Cash on hand/Checking Account	____________________
Stocks and Bonds	____________________
Cash Value of life insurance	____________________
Home	____________________
Other Real Estate	____________________
Mortgages/Notes Receiveable	____________________
Business valuation	____________________
Automobiles/Vehicles	____________________
Furniture/Computer Equipment	____________________
Jewelry	____________________
Other Personal Property	____________________
IRA/Pension/Retirement Plan	____________________
Other Assets	____________________
Total Assets	____________________

DEBTS

Credit Card Debt	________
Automobile loans	________
Home Mortgage	________
Other real estate mortgage	________
Student loans	________
Business loans	________
Medical bills	________
Bank loans	________
Other past due bills	________
Other debts and loans	________
Total Debts	________
Net Worth (assets minus debts)	________

PRAYERS FOR TODAY

This prayer section is for personal use and isn't meant to be part of the group discussion.

For you...

For your family and friends...

For those in your group...

Additional Tools for the Journey!

To help you on your financial discipleship journey, we have provided practical resources from a variety of people in the financial world. Visit us at **compasstools.org** to check out these resources.

1 - DAY THREE

Homework

God's Provision

PRAYER

Pray for the Holy Spirit's guidance as you begin reading passages of Scripture. Ask for clarity and insight as you engage in God's word.

SCRIPTURE READING

Read Matthew 6:25-34.

"Therefore I tell you, do not be anxious about your life, what you will eat or
what you will drink, nor about your body, what you will put on. Is not life more
than food, and the body more than clothing? [26]Look at the birds of the air:
they neither sow nor reap nor gather into barns, and yet your heavenly Father
feeds them. Are you not of more value than they? [27]And which of you by being
anxious can add a single hour to his span of life? [28]And why are you anxious
about clothing? Consider the lilies of the field, how they grow: they neither toil
nor spin, [29]yet I tell you, even Solomon in all his glory was not arrayed like one
of these. [30]But if God so clothes the grass of the field, which today is alive and
tomorrow is thrown into the oven, will he not much more clothe you, O you of
little faith? [31]Therefore do not be anxious, saying, 'What shall we eat?' or 'What
shall we drink?' or 'What shall we wear?' [32]For the Gentiles seek after all these
things, and your heavenly Father knows that you need them all. [33]But seek first
the kingdom of God and his righteousness, and all these things will be added
to you.

[34]"Therefore do not be anxious about tomorrow, for tomorrow will be anxious
for itself. Sufficient for the day is its own trouble" (ESV).

OBSERVATION

What is this passage saying about...

Worrying?

Our Value?

Provision?

Homework

SCRIPTURE READING

Read Matthew 6:25-34.

“Therefore I tell you, do not be anxious about your life, what you will eat or what you will drink, nor about your body, what you will put on. Is not life more than food, and the body more than clothing? 26 Look at the birds of the air: they neither sow nor reap nor gather into barns, and yet your heavenly Father feeds them. Are you not of more value than they? 27 And which of you by being anxious can add a single hour to his span of life? 28 And why are you anxious about clothing? Consider the lilies of the field, how they grow: they neither toil nor spin, 29 yet I tell you, even Solomon in all his glory was not arrayed like one of these. 30 But if God so clothes the grass of the field, which today is alive and tomorrow is thrown into the oven, will he not much more clothe you, O you of little faith? 31 Therefore do not be anxious, saying, ‘What shall we eat?’ or ‘What shall we drink?’ or ‘What shall we wear?’ 32 For the Gentiles seek after all these things, and your heavenly Father knows that you need them all. 33 But seek first the kingdom of God and his righteousness, and all these things will be added to you.

34 “Therefore do not be anxious about tomorrow, for tomorrow will be anxious for itself. Sufficient for the day is its own trouble” (ESV).

INTERPRETATION

What could be some reasons why people worry?

What causes you to worry?

How have you experienced God's provision in your life?

APPLICATION

How can you apply the principles of this passage to your finances & possessions?

HOWARD'S HIGHLIGHTS

Provision

The Lord promises to provide for our needs. *"Seek first his kingdom and his righteousness, and all these things [food and clothing] will be given to you" (Matthew 6:33, NIV).*

The same Lord who fed manna to the children of Israel during their 40 years of wandering in the wilderness, and who satisfied the hunger of 5,000 with only five loaves and two fish, has promised to meet all of our needs. This is the same Lord who told Elijah, *". . . I have commanded the ravens to provide food for you . . . the ravens brought him bread and meat in the morning and bread and meat in the evening" (1 Kings 17:4-6).*

God is both predictable and unpredictable

God is totally predictable in His faithfulness to provide for our needs. What we can't predict is how He will provide. He uses different and often surprising means to care for us. He might meet our current need through an increase in income or an unexpected gift. On the other hand, He might choose to provide an opportunity to stretch limited resources through money-saving purchases. Then again, He might meet our needs through some circumstance that we can't even imagine right now. Regardless of how He chooses to provide for our needs, He is completely reliable.

Charles Allen tells a story that illustrates this principle. As World War II was drawing to a close, the Allied armies gathered up many orphans and placed them in camps where they were well fed. But despite excellent care, the orphans were afraid and slept poorly.

Finally, a doctor came up with a solution. When the children were put to bed, he gave each of them a piece of bread to hold. Any hungry children could get more to eat, but when they were finished, they would still have this piece of bread just to hold – not to eat. This practice produced wonderful results. The children went to bed knowing that they would have food to eat the next day, and that simple guarantee gave them restful sleep.

Similarly, the Lord has given us His guarantee – our "piece of bread." As we embrace His promises of provision, we can relax and be content. *"My God will meet all your needs according to the riches of his glory in Christ Jesus" (Philippians 4:19, NIV).*

PRAYERS FOR TODAY

This prayer section is for personal use and isn't meant to be part of the group discussion.

For you...

For your family and friends...

For those in your group...

1 - DAY FOUR

Homework

God's Control

PRAYER

Pray for the Holy Spirit's guidance as you begin reading passages of Scripture. Ask for clarity and insight as you engage in God's word.

SCRIPTURE READING

Read 1 Chronicles 29:10-13.

"Therefore David blessed the Lord in the presence of all the assembly. And
David said: 'Blessed are you, O Lord, the God of Israel our father, forever and
ever.[11]Yours, O Lord, is the greatness and the power and the glory and the
victory and the majesty, for all that is in the heavens and in the earth is yours.
Yours is the kingdom, O Lord, and you are exalted as head above all. [12]Both
riches and honor come from you, and you rule over all. In your hand are power
and might, and in your hand it is to make great and to give strength to all. [13]And
now we thank you, our God, and praise your glorious name'" (ESV).

OBSERVATION

What is this passage saying about...

The Lord?

Control?

INTERPRETATION

Why would it be important to know that the Lord is in control of our circumstances?

How have you experienced God's control of circumstances in your life?

1 - DAY FOUR

Homework

SCRIPTURE READING

Read 1 Chronicles 29:10-13.

"Therefore David blessed the Lord in the presence of all the assembly. And
David said: 'Blessed are you, O Lord, the God of Israel our father, forever and
ever.[11]Yours, O Lord, is the greatness and the power and the glory and the
victory and the majesty, for all that is in the heavens and in the earth is yours.
Yours is the kingdom, O Lord, and you are exalted as head above all. [12]Both
riches and honor come from you, and you rule over all. In your hand are power
and might, and in your hand it is to make great and to give strength to all. [13]And
now we thank you, our God, and praise your glorious name'" (ESV).

APPLICATION

How can you apply the principles of this passage to your finances & possessions?

HOWARD'S HIGHLIGHTS

Control

Besides being Creator and Owner, God is ultimately in control of every event. In Scripture we read:

". . . We adore you as being in control of everything" (1 Chronicles 29:11, TLB).

"Whatever the Lord pleases, He does, in heaven and on earth" (Psalm 135:6).

". . . I, [King] Nebuchadnezzar, . . . praised the Most High; I honored and glorified him who lives forever.. . . He does as he pleases with the powers of heaven and the peoples of the earth. No one can hold back his hand or say to him: 'What have you done?'" (Daniel 4:34-35, NIV).

The Lord is also in control of difficult events. *". . . I am the Lord, and there is no one else, the One forming light and creating darkness, causing well-being and creating disaster; I am the Lord who does all these" (Isaiah 45:6-7).*

It's important for us to realize that our heavenly Father uses even seemingly devastating circumstances for ultimate good in the lives of the godly. *"We know that God causes all things to work together for good to those who love God, to those who are called according to His purpose" (Romans 8:28).* The Lord allows difficult circumstances to enter our lives for at least three reasons: (1) to develop our character, (2) to accomplish His intentions, and (3) to lovingly discipline us when needed.

PRAYERS FOR TODAY

This prayer section is for personal use and isn't meant to be part of the group discussion.

For you...

For your family and friends...

For those in your group...

1 - DAY FIVE

Homework

Our Part

PRAYER

Pray for the Holy Spirit's guidance as you begin reading passages of Scripture. Ask for clarity and insight as you engage in God's word.

SCRIPTURE READING

Read 1 Corinthians 4:1-5.

"This is how one should regard us, as servants of Christ and stewards of the
mysteries of God. [2]Moreover, it is required of stewards that they be found
faithful. [3]But with me it is a very small thing that I should be judged by you or
by any human court. In fact, I do not even judge myself. [4]For I am not aware
of anything against myself, but I am not thereby acquitted. It is the Lord who
judges me. [5]Therefore do not pronounce judgment before the time, before
the Lord comes, who will bring to light the things now hidden in darkness
and will disclose the purposes of the heart. Then each one will receive his
commendation from God" (ESV).

Read Luke 16:10-13.

"One who is faithful in a very little is also faithful in much, and one who is
dishonest in a very little is also dishonest in much. [11]If then you have not been
faithful in the unrighteous wealth, who will entrust to you the true riches? [12]And
if you have not been faithful in that which is another's, who will give you that
which is your own? [13]No servant can serve two masters, for either he will hate
the one and love the other, or he will be devoted to the one and despise the
other. You cannot serve God and money" (ESV).

OBSERVATION

What do these passages say about...

Stewards?

Judgment?

Faithfulness?

1 - DAY FIVE

Homework

SCRIPTURE READING

Read 1 Corinthians 4:1-5.

"This is how one should regard us, as servants of Christ and stewards of the mysteries of God. [2]Moreover, it is required of stewards that they be found faithful. [3]But with me it is a very small thing that I should be judged by you or by any human court. In fact, I do not even judge myself. [4]For I am not aware of anything against myself, but I am not thereby acquitted. It is the Lord who judges me. [5]Therefore do not pronounce judgment before the time, before the Lord comes, who will bring to light the things now hidden in darkness and will disclose the purposes of the heart. Then each one will receive his commendation from God" (ESV).

Read Luke 16:10-13.

"One who is faithful in a very little is also faithful in much, and one who is dishonest in a very little is also dishonest in much. [11]If then you have not been faithful in the unrighteous wealth, who will entrust to you the true riches? [12]And if you have not been faithful in that which is another's, who will give you that which is your own? [13]No servant can serve two masters, for either he will hate the one and love the other, or he will be devoted to the one and despise the other. You cannot serve God and money" (ESV).

INTERPRETATION

What does it mean to be a steward?

What does a faithful steward look like as it relates to finances and possessions?

Who is somebody in your life that you would identify as a faithful steward? Why?

APPLICATION

The Deed

The Deed:

To help us fully grasp our role as a steward, we will be transferring all of "our" possessions to the Lord. To make this transfer, we will use a deed, because deeds are often used to transfer the ownership of property. ***This deed is not a legally binding document. It is solely for your use.***

By completing this deed, you establish a specific time when you acknowledge God's ownership. To complete the deed:

> *1. Insert today's date at the top of the deed and print your first names in the space after "From," because you are transferring your possessions.*
>
> *2. Please pray about the possessions you wish to acknowledge that God owns and write them in the large space on the deed.*
>
> *3. There are two blank lines for your signatures in the lower right-hand corner under the heading "Stewards." In the lower left-hand corner under the heading of "Witnesses," there are two blank lines where others in your group can sign. This will help to hold you accountable to recognize God as owner of your possessions.*

You can find an example of this application at ***compasstools.org***

This Deed, Made the

__________ Day of ______________ , 20 ______ ,

From: ______________________________________

To: The Lord

I (we) transfer to the Lord the ownership of the following possessions:

____________________	____________________
____________________	____________________
____________________	____________________
____________________	____________________
____________________	____________________
____________________	____________________
____________________	____________________
____________________	____________________

Signature of Witnesses	Signature of Stewards
____________________	____________________
____________________	____________________

PRAYERS FOR TODAY

This prayer section is for personal use and isn't meant to be part of the group discussion.

For you...

For your family and friends...

For those in your group...

Step One:

Watch the Video

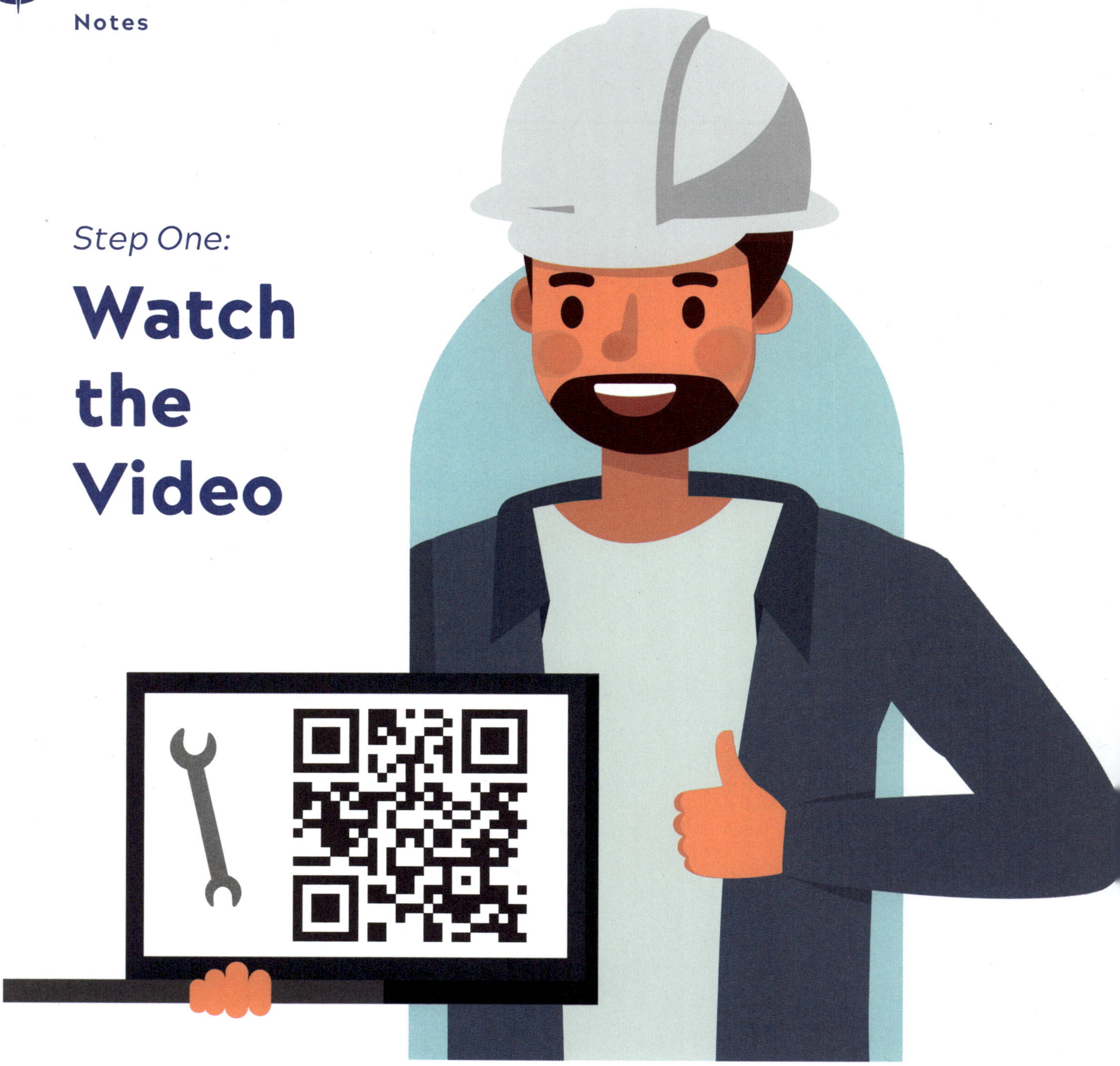

Open the camera on your phone to scan the QR code

OR

*Visit **compasstools.org** to view the video for this chapter*

Step Two:

Read the Notes

Not a fan of reading? You can listen to these notes at compasstools.org

> *This study will transform your life and finances as you learn and apply what the God of the universe says about handling money. Building your finances God's way is for everyone, regardless of where you are on your financial discipleship journey. So let's start with the most important part of the building process –* ***the foundation!***

How we handle money influences our fellowship with the Lord

We may think we can separate our spiritual life and our financial life into two different compartments. **Not so!**

Over and over, Jesus equates how we handle our money with the quality of our spiritual life. In Luke 16:11, He says, "Therefore if you have not been faithful in the use of unrighteous wealth, who will entrust the true wealth to you?" The true wealth in life grows out of a close relationship with the Lord.

It's a simple fact: If we handle money according to the principles of Scripture, we will enjoy closer fellowship with Christ. The parable of the talents demonstrates this, as the master congratulates the servant who managed his money faithfully:

> *"Well done, good and faithful Servant! You have been faithful with a few things; I will put you in charge of many things.* ***Come and share your master's happiness!"*** (Matthew 25:21, NIV, emphasis added).

As we handle money God's way, we have the opportunity of entering into the happiness of a more intimate relationship with the Lord.

Notes

Money and possessions compete with God for first place in our lives

Imagine for a moment that you have never read the Bible, and you are asked to fill in this blank space: "You cannot serve God and _________ ." What word would you choose? Why?

It surprises many to learn that money is a primary competitor with Christ for the lordship of our lives. In fact, Jesus Himself tells us we must choose to serve only one of these two masters.

> *"No one can serve two masters. Either you will hate the one and love the other, or you will be devoted to the one and despise the other. You cannot serve both God and money"* (Luke 16:13, NIV).

In the next verse, we are warned that many will reject this message.

> *"The Pharisees [religious leaders], who loved money, heard all this and were sneering at Jesus. He said to them, 'You are the ones who justify yourselves in the eyes of others, but God knows your hearts. What people value highly is detestable in God's sight'"* (Luke 16:14-15, NIV).

The Lord realizes that it is impossible for us to serve money – even in a small way – and still serve Him. When the Crusades were being fought during the twelfth century, the Crusaders purchased the services of mercenaries to fight on their behalf. Because it was a religious war, the Crusaders insisted that the mercenaries be baptized before fighting. As they were being baptized, the mercenaries would take their swords and hold them out of the water to symbolize that Jesus Christ was not in control of their swords. They wanted to retain the freedom to use their swords in any way they wished.

Though many people today may not be as blatant about it as were the mercenaries, they often handle their money in a similar fashion. Some Christians hold a wallet, purse, or stock portfolio "out of the water." In effect, these people are saying, "God, You may be the Lord of my entire life, except in the area of money – I am perfectly capable of handling that myself." Martin Luther recognized this struggle when he said, "There are three conversions: the conversion of the heart, of the mind and of the pocketbook."

Much of life revolves around the use of money

The Lord talked so much about money because he knew that much of our lives would revolve around its use. During your normal week, how much time do you spend earning money in your job, making decisions on how to spend money, thinking about where to invest money, or praying about your giving? Stress and confusion in this area of life can impact our marriage, our family life, our happiness, and even our health. Fortunately, God has adequately prepared us by giving us the Bible as His blueprint for living.

Division of responsibilities

When it comes to the responsibility of handling money, the Bible shows us a clear division. Simply put, God has a part, and we have a part. God has retained certain responsibilities and has delegated others to us. Most of the frustration we experience in handling money is because we don't realize which responsibilities are ours and which are His.

God's Part

This is the most important section of the entire study. Why? Because how we view God determines how we live. In the Bible, God calls Himself by multiple names. The name that best describes God's Part in the area of money is LORD.

For example, after losing his ten children and all his wealth – in a single day! – Job continued to worship God, saying,

> *". . . The LORD gave and the LORD has taken away. Blessed be the name of the LORD"* (Job 1:21).

Even in his grief, he understood God's role as Lord of his possessions. Moses walked away from the treasures of Egypt, choosing instead to suffer with God's people, because he accepted God's role as Lord of all. There are several facets to God's role.

Notes

Ownership

The Lord is the Creator of everything. *"For by Him [Jesus Christ] all things were created, both in the heavens and on earth, visible and invisible . . . all things have been created through Him and for Him . . . and in Him all things hold together"* (Colossians 1:16-17).

The Lord not only created everything, but He holds everything together. And by the way, He has never transferred the ownership of His creation to people. Whether you realize it or not, the Lord owns all your possessions.

> *"The earth is the Lord's, and* ***everything*** *in it" (Psalm 24:1, NIV, emphasis added). ". . . Everything in the heavens and earth is yours, O Lord . . ."* (1 Chronicles 29:11, TLB).

How much do you own? NOTHING! ZERO! Scripture even reveals specific items He owns.

> **God owns all the land.** *"The land, moreover, shall not be sold permanently, because the land is Mine; for you are only strangers and residents with Me"* (Leviticus 25:23).
>
> **God owns all the silver and gold.** *"'The silver is Mine and the gold is Mine,' declares the Lord of armies"* (Haggai 2:8).
>
> **God owns all the animals.** *"Every animal of the forest is Mine, the cattle on a thousand hills . . . everything that moves in the field is Mine. If I were hungry I would not tell you, for the world is Mine, and everything it contains"* (Psalm 50:10-12).

If we are to be genuine followers of Christ, we must transfer ownership of our possessions to the Lord. *"So then, none of you can be My disciple who does not give up all his own possessions"* (Luke 14:33). We must give up all claim to the ownership of all we have. Sometimes the Lord will test us by asking that we be willing to relinquish the very thing most precious to us.

The most vivid example of this in the Bible is when the Lord asked Abraham to *"Take now your son, your only son, whom you love, Isaac . . . and offer him there as a burnt offering"* (Genesis 22:2). When Abraham obeyed, demonstrating his willingness to give up his dear son, God responded, *"Do not lay a hand on the boy . . . Now I know that you fear God, because you have not withheld from me your son"* (Genesis 22:12, NIV).

When we acknowledge God's ownership, every spending decision becomes a spiritual decision. Instead of asking, "Lord, what do You want me to do with my money?" the question becomes, "Lord, what do You want me to do with Your money?" When we have this perspective and handle His money according to His wishes, all spending, saving, and investing decisions are equally as spiritual as giving decisions.

Recognizing God's Ownership

Nobody said it would be easy! Consistently recognizing God's ownership is difficult. It's way too easy to fall into the trap of making an intellectual assent to God's ownership without letting its truth filter down into the nitty-gritty of daily life – especially because our culture screams the opposite. Everything around us – the media, even the law – says that what you possess, you and you alone own. Genuinely acknowledging God's ownership requires nothing less than a total change of perception.

To help you us recognize God's ownership, meditate on this passage for the next thirty days when you first awake and just before going to sleep.

> *"Everything in the heavens and earth is yours, O Lord, and this is your kingdom. We adore you as being in control of everything. Riches and honor come from you alone, and you are the ruler of all mankind; your hand controls power and might, and it is at your discretion that men are made great and given strength"* (1 Chronicles 29:11-12, TLB).

IMPORTANT IN LEARNING CONTENTMENT

Recognizing the Lord's ownership is important in learning contentment. When you believe you own a particular possession, circumstances surrounding it will affect your attitude. When they are favorable, you will be happy; when unfavorable, you will be discontented.

Shortly after Jim came to grips with God's ownership, he purchased a car. He had driven the car only two days before someone rammed into it. Jim's first reaction was, "Lord, I don't know why You want a dent in Your car, but now You've got a big one." Jim was learning contentment!

Needs versus Wants

The Lord instructs us to be content when our basic needs are met. *"If we have food and clothing, we will be content"* (1 Timothy 6:8, NIV). It's important to understand the difference between a need and a want. Needs are the basic necessities of life – food, clothing, and shelter. Wants are anything in excess of needs. The Lord may allow us to have our wants, but He has not promised to provide all of them.

Getting to know God

God, as He is revealed in the Bible, differs greatly from the way most people imagine Him. Our tendency is to shrink Him down and fit Him into a mold with human abilities and limitations. We have a hard time recognizing God's Part because we fail to understand the greatness of God who "*. . . stretched out the heavens and laid the foundations of the earth*" (Isaiah 51:13). How do we capture the true perspective of God? Primarily by learning what the Bible tells us about Him. The following is but a sample:

HE IS THE LORD OF THE UNIVERSE

Carefully review some of His names and attributes:

Omniscient Creator	**Eternal King of kings**
Almighty Lord of lords	**Omnipresent Savior**

The Lord's power and ability are beyond our comprehension. Astronomers estimate that there are more than 100 billion galaxies in the universe, each containing billions of stars. The distance from one end of a galaxy to the other is often measured in millions of light years. Though our sun is a relatively small star, it could contain more than one million earths, and it has temperatures of 20 million degrees at its center. The enormity of the universe is mind boggling. "*Raise your eyes on high and see who has created these stars . . . He calls them all by name; because of the greatness of His might and the strength of His power, not one of them is missing*" (Isaiah 40:26).

HE IS LORD OF THE NATIONS

Examine the Lord's role and position relative to nations and people. Isaiah 40:21-24 tells us, "*Do you not know? Have you not heard? . . . It is He who sits above the circle of the earth, and its inhabitants are like grasshoppers . . . It is He who reduces rulers to nothing, who makes the judges of the earth meaningless. Scarcely have they been planted, scarcely have they been sown, scarcely has their stock taken root in the earth, but He merely blows on them, and they wither.*"

From Isaiah 40:15-17 we read, "*Behold, the nations are like a drop from a bucket, and are regarded as a speck of dust on the scales . . . All the nations are as nothing before Him, they are regarded by Him as less than nothing and meaningless.*"

HE IS LORD OF EACH INDIVIDUAL

God is not some aloof, disinterested, impersonal "force." On the contrary, He is intimately involved with each of us as individuals. Psalm 139:3-4 and Psalm 139:16 reveal, *"You are familiar with all my ways. Before a word is on my tongue you, Lord, know it completely. . .. All the days ordained for me were written in your book before one of them came to be"* (NIV). The Lord is so involved in our lives that He reassures us, *"Even the very hairs of your head are all numbered"* (Matthew 10:30, NIV). Our heavenly Father is the One who knows us the best and loves us the most.

God hung the stars in space, fashioned the earth's towering mountains and mighty oceans, and determined the destiny of nations. Jeremiah observed correctly: *". . . Nothing is too difficult for You"* (Jeremiah 32:17). Yet this is the same God who knows when a sparrow falls to the ground. He is the Lord of the vast universe and yet chooses to involve Himself in the smallest detail of your life.

Let's hold onto that thought for just a few seconds longer.

What in all the world, what in our life and current circumstances is "too difficult" for Him? N-O-T-H-I-N-G. The God who takes note of every hair follicle on every person throughout the whole world knows your situation, your needs, and even the deepest, unexpressed desires of your heart. Not just vaguely, but intimately.

Nothing in this study is more important than catching the vision of who God is and what His part is in our finances.

When I first studied God's Part, there was nothing that particularly surprised me. I knew all these truths – philosophically. My problem is that I don't always treat them as being true in a very practical way. Contemporary culture has had its influence on me, suggesting that God plays no serious part in financial matters.

Adding to the problem of our desire to be in control is that God has chosen to be invisible. Anything that is "out of sight" tends to become "out of mind." I get out of the habit of recognizing consistently that He is the Owner.

After learning God's Part, some quickly jump to the conclusion that little responsibility remains for us. But this is far from being true! As we study Our Part, we will discover that the Lord has entrusted us with great responsibility.

Our Part

Henry Parsons Crowell was born into a wealthy family, and as a young man received a large inheritance when his father died. He could have quit work that very day, adopting a life of leisure for the rest of his life. But that's not the option he chose. Instead, young Crowell decided to work hard, committing to give ten percent of his income to the Lord's work.

Crowell founded the Quaker Oats Company, and he proved to be a creative marketing genius. At that time, oats were sold in large barrels, often rotting before being consumed. Crowell introduced the smaller round packaging we are familiar with to this day, and he determined to use only the highest quality oats. His company literally changed the way Americans ate breakfast; in the process he became remarkably successful.

In 1898, Crowell's perspective on money and business was radically transformed by participating in a Bible study on money and possessions. Not only are we to honor Christ in our company, he thought to himself, but everything we have belongs to God – even the business.

Recognizing this changed everything! He felt as if he had been elevated from the role of just operating his business and handling his money, to the most important position possible – a person entrusted with managing God's business and resources. For more than 40 years, he gave away over half of his earnings.

Henry Parsons Crowell had embraced the two most significant truths for the follower of Christ in handling money – Ownership and Stewardship.

What is a steward?

The word that best describes Our Part is steward.

Today we would probably use the word "manager." In the Bible, the position of steward is one of great responsibility. He is the supreme authority under the master and has full responsibility for all the master's possessions entrusted to him.

Our responsibility is to be faithful. *"It is required of stewards that they be found faithful"* (1 Corinthians 4:2, ESV). Just as the purchaser of a complicated piece of machinery studies the manufacturer's manual to learn how to operate it, we need to examine the Creator's handbook – the Bible – to determine how He wants us to handle His possessions.

As we begin to study our responsibilities, it's important to remember that God loves and cares for us deeply. He is a God of mercy and grace. He has given us these principles because He wants the best for us. Most people discover areas in which they have not been faithful. Don't become discouraged. Simply seek to apply faithfully what you learn.

Several principles of faithfulness are important to understand.

BE FAITHFUL WITH IT ALL

As followers of Christ, we need to be faithful in handling all the money entrusted to us. Christians usually have been taught how to handle only ten percent of their income – the area of giving. While this is crucial, we rarely talk about our God-given responsibilities for the remaining 90 percent. Therefore, we know a lot more about the world's perspective on money than our Lord's perspective.

As a consequence of not being equipped to handle money biblically, many Christians develop wrong or distorted attitudes toward possessions, leading them to make some unwise financial decisions. Hosea 4:6 tells us, *"My people are destroyed for lack of knowledge."* Ignorance or disobedience of scriptural financial principles frequently causes suffocating materialism, fractured relationships, and even money problems.

Notes

BE FAITHFUL WITH WHAT WE ARE GIVEN

We are to be faithful regardless of how much God entrusts to us – whether it's a fortune or a handful of coins. This management parable illustrates this. *"It will be like a man going on a journey, who called his servants and entrusted his wealth to them. To one he gave five bags of gold, to another two bags, and to another one bag"* (Matthew 25:14-15, NIV).

When the owner returned, he held each one responsible for faithfully managing his possessions. The owner praised the faithful servants who received two bags and five bags: *"Well done, good and faithful servant! You have been faithful with a few things; I will put you in charge of many things. Come and share your master's happiness!"* (Matthew 25:21-23, NIV).

Interestingly, the servant who had been given two bags received the identical reward as the one who had been given five. The Lord rewards faithfulness, regardless of the amount over which we are responsible.

We are required to be faithful whether we are given much or little. As someone once said, "It's not what I would do if a million dollars were my lot; it's what I am doing with the ten dollars I've got."

BE FAITHFUL IN THE LITTLE THINGS

How will you know if your son will take good care of his first car? Observe how he cared for his bicycle! How do you know if a salesperson will do a competent job of serving a large client? Evaluate how she serves a small one. If we have the character to be faithful with small things, the Lord knows He can trust us with greater responsibilities. *"The one who is faithful in a very little thing is also faithful in much; and the one who is unrighteous in a very little thing is also unrighteous in much"* (Luke 16:10).

Almost every significant enterprise started out small. Apple founders, Steve Jobs and Steve Wozniak, tinker with a personal computer in their garage. Sam's Walton's first store was a small five-and-dime store in Bentonville, Arkansas, before he built the WalMart company.

Missionary pioneer Hudson Taylor said it this way, "Small things are small things, but faithfulness with a small thing is a big thing."

BE FAITHFUL WITH OTHER'S POSSESSIONS

Faithfulness with another's possessions will determine to some degree how much you are given. *"If you have not been faithful in the use of that which is **another's**, who will give you that which is your own?"* (Luke 16:12, emphasis added).

This principle is often overlooked. One of the most faithful men I know rented a vehicle from a friend and damaged it in an accident. He told the owner what happened and then delivered the vehicle to the owner's mechanic with these instructions: "Make it better than it was before the accident, and I will be responsible for the bill." What an example!

When someone allows you to use something, are you careful to return it promptly and in good shape? Are you careless with your employer's office supplies? Do you waste electricity when you're staying in a hotel room? Some people have not been entrusted with more because they have been unfaithful with the possessions of others.

If we waste possessions, the Lord may remove us as stewards

". . . There was a rich man who had a manager [steward], and this manager was reported to him as squandering his possessions. And he summoned him and said to him, 'What is this I hear about you? Give an accounting of your management, for you can no longer be manager'" (Luke 16:1-2).

Two principles emerge from this passage. First, when we waste our possessions it eventually becomes public knowledge and creates a poor testimony. Sooner or later, the word will get out. *"This manager was reported to him as squandering his possessions."* Second, the Lord may remove us as stewards if we squander what He has given us.

A local businessman earned a fortune in just three years and then went on a spending spree. Two years later he informed his staff that he had little left, and everyone would need to economize. Shortly thereafter, he left for an expensive vacation and had his personal office lavishly renovated. The Lord soon removed this man from the privilege of being steward over much, and today he is on the verge of bankruptcy.

If you waste the possessions entrusted to you, you may not be given more.

Benefits of Handling Money Faithfully

The faithful steward enjoys three benefits.

1.

More intimate fellowship with Jesus Christ

Remember what the master said to the servant who had been faithful with his finances: "Come and share your master's happiness" (Matthew 25:21, NIV). We can enter into closer fellowship with our Lord when we are faithful with the possessions He has given us.

Someone once told me that the Lord often allows a person to teach a subject because the teacher desperately needs it! This is certainly true for me. I have never met anyone who had more wrong-headed attitudes about money or who handled money more contrary to the Bible than I did. And yet . . . when I began to apply the principles set forth in these pages, I experienced a dramatic improvement in my fellowship with the Lord – exactly as He intended.

2.

The development of godly character

God uses money to refine character. As David McConaughy explained more than 100 years ago in his book, Money the Acid Test (written in 1918), "Money, most common of temporal things, involves uncommon and eternal consequences. Even though it may be done quite unconsciously, money molds people in the process of getting it, saving it, spending it, and giving it. Depending on how it's used, it proves to be a blessing or a curse. Either the person becomes master of the money, or the money becomes the master. Our Lord uses money to test our lives and as an instrument to mold us into the likeness of Himself."

All through the Bible there is a correlation between the development of people's character and how they handle money. Money is regarded as an index of a person's true character. You've no doubt heard the expression, "Money talks," and indeed it does. You can tell a lot about a person's character by examining his or her bank and credit card statements. Why? Because we spend our money on the things that are most important to us.

3.

Having our finances in order

As we apply God's principles to our finances, we will begin to get out of debt, spend more wisely, start saving for our future, and give even more to the work of Christ.

Step Three:

Answer the Discussion Questions

What in the notes (and video) did you find revealing or interesting?

What in the notes challenged you the most?

What did you find revealing or challenging about the application worksheets in this chapter? Did you have any questions about the worksheets?

Chapter 1

Compass Commentaries

DAY ONE The Bible is described in 2 Timothy as God's inspired writings that instruct, teach, correct, and convict us – all written for our benefit. We should embrace them as the single greatest source for wisdom. God conveys through Isaiah that our ways of thinking and acting are contrary to how He thinks and acts. That's why we often struggle to understand how and why God directs certain situations.

God always sees the big picture and knows what is best for us in the long run, what will draw us closer to Him. That's true of every aspect of our life, including financial matters. Daily Scripture reading should become a chosen habit for all of us who strive to grow closer to Christ. The process brings new insights, yielding greater wisdom than we had the day before for everyday living and solid financial decisions.

DAY TWO God created us, the world, and everything in it. He graciously allows us to use His creation for our benefit while we're here on earth. When we die, all of life's stuff stays behind. It's not ours to keep, nor was it ever intended to be. The one thing He asks of us – something He wants more than our sacrifice – is our hearts.

DAY THREE God created us in His image, and He knows our needs better than we do. He knows that we need food, water, and clothing. If God cares about the birds enough to supply them with food, does it make sense for us to waste even a moment in worry?

And look at the beautiful comparison between clothing and the magnificence of flowers! So many colors, designs, and fragrances our Father has lavished on each flower type, yet Jesus tells us that He values us far beyond them. He knows that we need food, drink, and clothing, and He will provide them. What does He want from us? To prioritize Him, to seek His kingdom and His righteousness ahead of everything else. And to trust Him enough to not worry!

DAY FOUR When we struggle with control, it's often because we don't like how someone else is affecting our life and circumstances. But we need to recognize that God ultimately controls everything. As we go through life, we will experience a lot less frustration if we recognize and embrace God as the Owner, the Creator, and the Controller of all that there is, ever was, and ever will be. And this includes our finances!

DAY FIVE It has been said that "faithfulness with a little thing is a big thing." When we hear that God is in control of everything, we might jump to the wrong conclusion that there's nothing we can do about anything. That's far from the truth.

God knows what we need, including responsibility. As He loves and provides for us, He righteously desires us to love Him and demonstrate our love through faithfulness. Our faithfulness then positions us to receive more responsibility from Him.

Because He gifts us with different skills, we may receive blessings that look different from those of other people. But we must always remember that our primary responsibility is to be faithful with what we have now – including our finances.

Additional Tools for the Journey!

To help you on your financial discipleship journey, we have provided practical resources from a variety of people in the financial world. Visit us at **compasstools.org** to check out these resources.

Chapter 2:

Counsel, Debt, & Saving

All tools, videos, resources and electronic applications for this chapter can be found at ***compasstools.org***

THIS CHAPTER'S MEMORY VERSE:

Proverbs 22:7

DAILY HOMEWORK:

Day One – Counsel

Day Two – Borrowing

Day Three – Getting Out of Debt, begin working on the Snowball Strategy

Day Four – Saving

Day Five – Dangers in Saving, begin working on the Life Insurance Worksheet

Day Six – Watch the Build Your Finances God's Way Video, Read the Notes, answer the discussion questions

BEFORE YOUR GROUP MEETING:

1. Memorize Proverbs 22:7, TLB. To prevent confusion when reciting the verse in a group setting, please memorize the version listed below.

> *"The rich rule over the poor, and the borrower is servant to the lender" (Proverbs 22:7, AMPC).*

2. Complete the Daily Homework.

Each day's homework is designed to take 20-30 minutes to complete.

2 - DAY ONE

Homework

Counsel

PRAYER

Pray for the Holy Spirit's guidance as you begin reading passages of Scripture. Ask for clarity and insight as you engage in God's word.

SCRIPTURE READING

Read Proverbs 1:1-10.

"The proverbs of Solomon, son of David, king of Israel: 2To know wisdom and instruction, to understand words of insight, 3to receive instruction in wise dealing, in righteousness, justice, and equity; 4to give prudence to the simple, knowledge and discretion to the youth – 5Let the wise hear and increase in learning, and the one who understands obtain guidance, 6to understand a proverb and a saying, the words of the wise and their riddles. 7The fear of the Lord is the beginning of knowledge; fools despise wisdom and instruction. 8Hear, my son, your father's instruction, and forsake not your mother's teaching, 9for they are a graceful garland for your head and pendants for your neck. 10My son, if sinners entice you, do not consent" (ESV).

Read Proverbs 15:20-23.

"A wise son makes a glad father, but a foolish man despises his mother. 21Folly is a joy to him who lacks sense, but a man of understanding walks straight ahead. 22Without counsel plans fail, but with many advisers they succeed. 23To make an apt answer is a joy to a man, and a word in season, how good it is!" (ESV).

Read 2 Timothy 3:16-17.

"All Scripture is breathed out by God and profitable for teaching, for reproof, for correction, and for training in righteousness, 17that the man of God may be complete, equipped for every good work" (ESV).

OBSERVATION

What do these passages say about…

God's word?

Wisdom?

Joy?

2 - DAY ONE

Homework

SCRIPTURE READING

Read Proverbs 1:1-10.

"The proverbs of Solomon, son of David, king of Israel: [2]To know wisdom and instruction, to understand words of insight, [3]to receive instruction in wise dealing, in righteousness, justice, and equity; [4]to give prudence to the simple, knowledge and discretion to the youth – [5]Let the wise hear and increase in learning, and the one who understands obtain guidance, [6]to understand a proverb and a saying, the words of the wise and their riddles. [7]The fear of the Lord is the beginning of knowledge; fools despise wisdom and instruction. [8]Hear, my son, your father's instruction, and forsake not your mother's teaching, [9]for they are a graceful garland for your head and pendants for your neck. [10]My son, if sinners entice you, do not consent" (ESV).

Read Proverbs 15:20-23.

"A wise son makes a glad father, but a foolish man despises his mother. [21]Folly is a joy to him who lacks sense, but a man of understanding walks straight ahead. [22]Without counsel plans fail, but with many advisers they succeed. [23]To make an apt answer is a joy to a man, and a word in season, how good it is!" (ESV).

Read 2 Timothy 3:16-17.

"All Scripture is breathed out by God and profitable for teaching, for reproof, for correction, and for training in righteousness, [17]that the man of God may be complete, equipped for every good work" (ESV).

INTERPRETATION

How can we ensure we are getting advice from the right sources?

How can we discern what the wrong sources of advice might be?

How have you experienced the wisdom of others in your life?

How has advice, both good and bad, impacted your finances?

APPLICATION

How can you apply the principles of these passages to your finances?

HOWARD'S HIGHLIGHTS

Why seek counsel?

Two attitudes keep us from seeking counsel. The first is pride. Our culture regards seeking advice as a sign of weakness. The second attitude is stubbornness, characterized by the statement, "Don't confuse me with the facts. My mind is already made up!" We often resist seeking counsel because we don't want to be told we can't afford what we already have decided to buy.

God encourages us to use a gift He has provided for our benefit – godly counselors. In Proverbs 19:20 we read, *"Listen to advice and accept discipline, and in the end you will be counted among the wise" (NIV)*. Proverbs 12:15 says, *"The way of a fool is right in his own eyes, but a person who listens to advice is wise."* And Proverbs 10:8 says, *"The wise man is glad to be instructed, but a self-sufficient fool falls flat on his face" (TLB)*.

We seek counsel to secure insights, suggestions, and alternatives that will aid in making a proper decision. It's not, however, the counselor's role to make the decision; we retain that responsibility.

Gather facts, but . . .

We need to assemble the facts that will influence our decisions, but we also need to seek God's direction as well. What we have to remember is that He will sometimes direct us in a way contrary to our assessment of the facts alone.

We can see this illustrated in the chapters of Numbers 13 and 14. Moses sent twelve spies into the Promised Land, and they all returned with an identical evaluation of the facts: it was a prosperous land inhabited by terrifying giants. Only two of the twelve spies, Joshua and Caleb, understood that the Lord wanted them to go in and possess the Promised Land anyway – in spite of the obstacles! Because the children of Israel relied only on the facts and did not act in faith on what the Lord wanted for them, they suffered 40 years of wandering in the wilderness until that entire generation died.

PRAYERS FOR TODAY

This prayer section is for personal use and isn't meant to be part of the group discussion.

For you...

For your family and friends...

For those in your group...

2 - DAY TWO

Homework

Borrowing

PRAYER

Pray for the Holy Spirit's guidance as you begin reading passages of Scripture. Ask for clarity and insight as you engage in God's word.

SCRIPTURE READING

Read Proverbs 22:7-10.

"The rich rules over the poor, and the borrower is the slave of the lender.
8Whoever sows injustice will reap calamity, and the rod of his fury will fail.
9Whoever has a bountiful eye will be blessed, for he shares his bread with the
poor. 10Drive out a scoffer, and strife will go out, and quarreling and abuse will
cease" (ESV).

Read Psalm 37:16-22.

"Better is the little that the righteous has than the abundance of many wicked. 17For the arms of
the wicked shall be broken, but the Lord upholds the righteous. 18The Lord knows the days of the
blameless, and their heritage will remain forever; 19they are not put to shame in evil times; in the
days of famine they have abundance. 20But the wicked will perish; the enemies of the Lord are
like the glory of the pastures; they vanish–like smoke they vanish away. 21The wicked borrows but
does not pay back, but the righteous is generous and gives; 22for those blessed by the Lord shall
inherit the land, but those cursed by him shall be cut off" (ESV).

Read Proverbs 6:1-5.

"My son, if you have put up security for your neighbor, have given your pledge for a stranger,
2if you are snared in the words of your mouth, caught in the words of your mouth, 3then do this,
my son, and save yourself, for you have come into the hand of your neighbor: go, hasten, and
plead urgently with your neighbor. 4Give your eyes no sleep and your eyelids no slumber; 5save
yourself like a gazelle from the hand of the hunter, like a bird from the hand of the fowler" (ESV).

OBSERVATION

What do these passages say about...

Borrowing?

The wicked?

Becoming surety (cosigning)?

2 - DAY TWO

Homework

SCRIPTURE READING

Read Proverbs 22:7-10.

*"The rich rules over the poor, and the borrower is the slave of the lender.
8Whoever sows injustice will reap calamity, and the rod of his fury will fail.
9Whoever has a bountiful eye will be blessed, for he shares his bread with the
poor. 10Drive out a scoffer, and strife will go out, and quarreling and abuse will
cease" (ESV).*

Read Psalm 37:16-22.

*"Better is the little that the righteous has than the abundance of many
wicked. 17For the arms of the wicked shall be broken, but the Lord upholds the
righteous. 18The Lord knows the days of the blameless, and their heritage will
remain forever; 19they are not put to shame in evil times; in the days of famine
they have abundance. 20But the wicked will perish; the enemies of the Lord are
like the glory of the pastures; they vanish–like smoke they vanish away. 21The
wicked borrows but does not pay back, but the righteous is generous and gives;
22for those blessed by the Lord shall inherit the land, but those cursed by him
shall be cut off" (ESV).*

Read Proverbs 6:1-5.

*"My son, if you have put up security for your neighbor, have given your pledge
for a stranger, 2if you are snared in the words of your mouth, caught in the
words of your mouth, 3then do this, my son, and save yourself, for you have
come into the hand of your neighbor: go, hasten, and plead urgently with your
neighbor. 4Give your eyes no sleep and your eyelids no slumber; 5save yourself
like a gazelle from the hand of the hunter, like a bird from the hand of the
fowler" (ESV).*

INTERPRETATION

What does a "slave to the lender" look like today?

How has debt had an impact on your life?

What would "putting up security" look like in our world today?

APPLICATION

How can you apply the principles of these passages to your finances and possessions?

HOWARD'S HIGHLIGHTS

Borrowing

The Bible is silent on when we can owe money. In our opinion it is permissible to owe money for a home mortgage or for your business or vocation. This "permissible debt," however, should meet three criteria.

- The item purchased should be an asset with the potential to appreciate or produce an income.
- The value of an item must exceed the amount owed against it.
- The debt should not be so high that repayment puts undue strain on the budget.

As we've seen during several financial crises, there are no guarantees that home values will always appreciate or that businesses will always be profitable. So, here's the rule of thumb if you take on permissible debt: borrow as little as possible and pay if off as quickly as possible!

Cosigning

Cosigning relates to debt. Anytime you cosign, you become legally responsible for the debt of another. It's just as if you went to the bank, borrowed the money, and gave it to your friend or relative who is asking you to cosign. In effect, you promise to pay back the entire amount if the borrower does not.

A Federal Trade Commission study found that 50 percent of those who cosigned for bank loans ended up making the payments. And 75 percent of those who cosigned for finance company loans ended up making the payments! Those are pretty good odds that if you cosign, you'll pay. The casualty rate is so high because the professional lender knows the loan is a bad risk. His stance: I won't touch this loan with a ten-foot pole unless I can get someone who is financially responsible to guarantee its repayment.

Fortunately, the Bible gives us clear direction about cosigning. Proverbs 17:18 says, *"It is poor judgment to countersign another's note, to become responsible for his debts" (NLT).* The phrase, *"poor judgment"* is literally translated, "destitute of mind"!

A parent often cosigns for a child's first automobile. We decided not to do this. We wanted to model for our children the importance of not cosigning, and to discourage them from using debt. Instead, we encouraged them to think ahead and save for the purchase of their first cars.

Already cosigned?

If you have already cosigned for a loan, the Scripture has counsel for you, too. Get out of it as fast as you can!

Proverbs 6:1-5 says, *"Son, if you endorse a note for someone you hardly know, guaranteeing his debt, you are in serious trouble. You may have trapped yourself by your agreement. Quick! Get out of it if you possibly can! Swallow your pride; don't let embarrassment stand in the way. Go and beg to have your name erased. Don't put it off . . . If you can get out of this trap you have saved yourself like a deer that escapes from a hunter, or a bird from the net" (TLB).*

Please use sound judgment and never cosign.

PRAYERS FOR TODAY

This prayer section is for personal use and isn't meant to be part of the group discussion.

For you...

For your family and friends...

For those in your group...

Getting Out of Debt

PRAYER

Pray for the Holy Spirit's guidance as you begin reading passages of Scripture. Ask for clarity and insight as you engage in God's word.

SCRIPTURE READING

Read 2 Kings 4:1-7.

"The wife of a man from the company of the prophets cried out to Elisha, 'Your servant my husband is dead, and you know that he revered the Lord. But now
his creditor is coming to take my two boys as his slaves.' [2]Elisha replied to her,
'How can I help you? Tell me, what do you have in your house?' 'Your servant has
nothing there at all,' she said, 'except a small jar of olive oil.' [3]Elisha said, 'Go
around and ask all your neighbors for empty jars. Don't ask for just a few. [4]Then
go inside and shut the door behind you and your sons. Pour oil into all the jars,
and as each is filled, put it to one side.' [5]She left him and shut the door behind
her and her sons. They brought the jars to her and she kept pouring. [6]When all
the jars were full, she said to her son, 'Bring me another one.' But he replied,
'There is not a jar left.' Then the oil stopped flowing. [7]She went and told the
man of God, and he said, 'Go, sell the oil and pay your debts. You and your sons can live on what is left'" (NIV).

OBSERVATION

What does this passage say about...

Eliminating debts?

The widow?

God's Provision?

2 - DAY THREE

Homework

SCRIPTURE READING

Read 2 Kings 4:1-7.

"The wife of a man from the company of the prophets cried out to Elisha, 'Your servant my husband is dead, and you know that he revered the Lord. But now his creditor is coming to take my two boys as his slaves.' [2]Elisha replied to her, 'How can I help you? Tell me, what do you have in your house?' 'Your servant has nothing there at all,' she said, 'except a small jar of olive oil.' [3]Elisha said, 'Go around and ask all your neighbors for empty jars. Don't ask for just a few. [4]Then go inside and shut the door behind you and your sons. Pour oil into all the jars, and as each is filled, put it to one side.' [5]She left him and shut the door behind her and her sons. They brought the jars to her and she kept pouring. [6]When all the jars were full, she said to her son, 'Bring me another one.' But he replied, 'There is not a jar left.' Then the oil stopped flowing. [7]She went and told the man of God, and he said, 'Go, sell the oil and pay your debts. You and your sons can live on what is left'" (NIV).

INTERPRETATION

Elisha asked the widow, "What do you have?" Why is this important?

What resources were used to help the widow collect oil?

Why did the oil stop flowing?

APPLICATION

List Your Debts & The Snowball Strategy

List Your Debts & The Snowball Strategy:

We've learned some great things about paying off debt in 2 Kings 4:1-7. So let's take a look and see how we can apply these principles to our situation.

The Listing Your Debts & Snowball Strategy worksheet will assist you in compiling your debts and prioritizing repayment. It also reveals the extent of your debt situation.

The columns are as follows:

> ***Creditor*** – *The one to whom the debt is owed.*
>
> ***Balance Due*** – *The amount of the current debt.*
>
> ***Monthly Payment*** – *The amount of the monthly payment. If payment is due more or less often than monthly, calculate the average amount paid each month.*
>
> ***Interest Rate*** – *The rate of interest charged for the debt.*
>
> ***Scheduled Pay-off Date*** – *The date by which the debt will be fully paid.*
>
> ***Snowball Priority*** – *Number the debts in the order you are going to pay them off.*

In addition to making the minimum payments on all your credit cards, focus on paying off the smallest-balance-card first. You'll be encouraged to see its balance go down, down, and finally disappear!

After the first debt is paid off, apply its payment toward the next-smallest one. After the second debt is paid off, apply what you were paying on the first and second toward the third-smallest. That's the snowball in action!

When you're on a roll like this, it starts getting exciting. Those "impossible" balances that have worried you and robbed you of your peace will begin diminishing before your very eyes.

You can find an example of this application at ***compasstools.org***

Go to compasstools.org to check out the electronic Snowball Debt Calculator.

It is pretty cool!

CREDITOR	Balance Due	Monthly Payment	Interest Rate	Scheduled Pay-Off Date	Snowball Priority
Credit Card Debt					
Auto Loans					
Medical Bills					
Home Mortgages					

CREDITOR	Balance Due	Monthly Payment	Interest Rate	Scheduled Pay-Off Date	Snowball Priority
Bank Loans					
Education					
Family/Friends					
Business/Investment					
Life Insurance					
Cosigned Loans					
TOTAL DEBT	______	______			

PRAYERS FOR TODAY

This prayer section is for personal use and isn't meant to be part of the group discussion.

For you...

For your family and friends...

For those in your group...

Additional Tools for the Journey!

To help you on your financial discipleship journey, we have provided practical resources from a variety of people in the financial world. Visit us at **compasstools.org** to check out these resources.

Saving

PRAYER

Pray for the Holy Spirit's guidance as you begin reading passages of Scripture. Ask for clarity and insight as you engage in God's word.

SCRIPTURE READING

Read Genesis 41:28-39.

"'It is as I told Pharaoh; God has shown to Pharaoh what he is about to do. [29]There will come seven years of great plenty throughout all the land of Egypt, [30]but after them there will arise seven years of famine, and all the plenty will be forgotten in the land of Egypt. The famine will consume the land, [31]and the plenty will be unknown in the land by reason of the famine that will follow, for it will be very severe. [32]And the doubling of Pharaoh's dream means that the thing is fixed by God, and God will shortly bring it about. [33]Now therefore let Pharaoh select a discerning and wise man, and set him over the land of Egypt. [34]Let Pharaoh proceed to appoint overseers over the land and take one-fifth of the produce of the land of Egypt during the seven plentiful years. [35]And let them gather all the food of these good years that are coming and store up grain under the authority of Pharaoh for food in the cities, and let them keep it. [36]That food shall be a reserve for the land against the seven years of famine that are to occur in the land of Egypt, so that the land may not perish through the famine.'

[37]This proposal pleased Pharaoh and all his servants. [38]And Pharaoh said to his servants, 'Can we find a man like this, in whom is the Spirit of God?' [39]Then Pharaoh said to Joseph, 'Since God has shown you all this, there is none so discerning and wise as you are'" (ESV).

OBSERVATION

What does this passage say about...

Changing circumstances?

Wisdom?

Saving?

2 - DAY FOUR

Homework

SCRIPTURE READING

Read Genesis 41:28-39.

*"'It is as I told Pharaoh; God has shown to Pharaoh what he is about to do.
29There will come seven years of great plenty throughout all the land of Egypt,
30but after them there will arise seven years of famine, and all the plenty will
be forgotten in the land of Egypt. The famine will consume the land, 31and the
plenty will be unknown in the land by reason of the famine that will follow, for
it will be very severe. 32And the doubling of Pharaoh's dream means that the
thing is fixed by God, and God will shortly bring it about. 33Now therefore let
Pharaoh select a discerning and wise man, and set him over the land of Egypt.
34Let Pharaoh proceed to appoint overseers over the land and take one-fifth
of the produce of the land of Egypt during the seven plentiful years. 35And let
them gather all the food of these good years that are coming and store up
grain under the authority of Pharaoh for food in the cities, and let them keep
it. 36That food shall be a reserve for the land against the seven years of famine
that are to occur in the land of Egypt, so that the land may not perish through
the famine.'*

*37This proposal pleased Pharaoh and all his servants. 38And Pharaoh said to his
servants, 'Can we find a man like this, in whom is the Spirit of God?' 39Then
Pharaoh said to Joseph, 'Since God has shown you all this, there is none so
discerning and wise as you are'" (ESV).*

INTERPRETATION

What should we do when we have an abundance?

What does it look like to prepare for troubling times in our world today?

How have you experienced savings, or a lack of savings, impacting your life?

APPLICATION

How can you apply the principles of these passages to your finances and possessions?

HOWARD'S HIGHLIGHTS

The Bible encourages us to save: *"The wise man saves for the future, but the foolish man spends whatever he gets"* (Proverbs 21:20, TLB). God commends the ant for saving. *"Four things on earth are small, yet they are extremely wise: ants are creatures of little strength, yet they store up their food in the summer"* (Proverbs 30:24-25, NIV). We need to think like ants! Even though they are small, they save. You may not be in a position to save a lot right now, but begin the habit.

Joseph saved during *"seven years of great plenty"* (Genesis 41:29) in order to survive during *"seven years of famine"* (Genesis 41:30). That's what saving is all about: not spending today so that you'll have something to spend in the future. Most people are poor savers because they don't see the value in practicing self-denial. Our culture screams that we "deserve" to get what we want, and when we want it!

The most effective way to save is to make it automatic. When you receive income, the first money you spend should be a gift to the Lord, and the second should go to savings. An automatic payroll deduction is a great way to save. Some people save their tax refunds or bonuses. Remember this: if you immediately save, you'll save more.

The Bible doesn't teach an amount to save. We recommend saving ten percent of your income. This may not be possible initially. But begin the habit of saving – even if it's only a dollar a month.

PRAYERS FOR TODAY

This prayer section is for personal use and isn't meant to be part of the group discussion.

For you...

For your family and friends...

For those in your group...

2 - DAY FIVE

Homework

Dangers in Saving

PRAYER

Pray for the Holy Spirit's guidance as you begin reading passages of Scripture. Ask for clarity and insight as you engage in God's word.

SCRIPTURE READING

Read 1 Timothy 6:6-10.

*"But godliness with contentment is great gain, 7for we brought nothing into
the world, and we cannot take anything out of the world. 8But if we have food
and clothing, with these we will be content. 9But those who desire to be rich
fall into temptation, into a snare, into many senseless and harmful desires that
plunge people into ruin and destruction. 10For the love of money is a root of all
kinds of evils. It is through this craving that some have wandered away from the
faith and pierced themselves with many pangs" (ESV).*

OBSERVATION

What does this passage say about...

Contentment?

Money?

Desires?

2 - DAY FIVE

Homework

SCRIPTURE READING

Read 1 Timothy 6:6-10.

"But godliness with contentment is great gain, [7]for we brought nothing into the world, and we cannot take anything out of the world. [8]But if we have food and clothing, with these we will be content. [9]But those who desire to be rich fall into temptation, into a snare, into many senseless and harmful desires that plunge people into ruin and destruction. [10]For the love of money is a root of all kinds of evils. It is through this craving that some have wandered away from the faith and pierced themselves with many pangs" (ESV).

INTERPRETATION

What does contentment look like for you?

What could be the danger in saving too much money?

How have you seen the "love of money" being destructive in our world today?

APPLICATION

The Life Insurance Worksheet

The Life Insurance Worksheet:

Life Insurance can be a great thing. The Life Insurance Worksheet is a tool to help you on your financial discipleship journey. It revolves around three things we've learned from this chapter: debt, saving, and counsel.

Why would I need life insurance?

> ***Debt*** *– If the breadwinner of the family passes away, it can leave all kinds of strains on the family – especially financially. Life Insurance can be used to pay off debt and leave your family in a more stable financial position.*
>
> ***Savings*** *– If the breadwinner of the family passes away, life insurance can also be used to help with savings goals such as paying for a child's education.*
>
> ***Counsel*** *– The Life Insurance Worksheet is a great exercise, but it is only intended to help you see what your life insurance needs might be – it is not intended to be precise. We encourage you to seek the counsel of an expert to determine your needs more accurately.*

You can find an example of this application at ***compasstools.org***

The Life Insurance Worksheet

Complete the Life Insurance Worksheet to approximate your life insurance needs...

1. Your **annual income needs** figure should represent your household's income needs.
2. Then, **subtract the deceased person's living expenses** that will no longer be needed if a breadwinner passes away, such as, income taxes reduced and less food consumed.
3. Also **subtract other income** survivors will receive from all sources, such as Social Security, investments, and the surviving spouse's earnings.
4. This calculation will give you the **net income** needed for the survivors to maintain their current standard of living.
5. To estimate the amount of insurance you will need for income, multiply the income required by 20. This assumes the survivors will earn a 5 percent return, after taxes, on the insurance proceeds.
6. Insurance coverage may also be needed to fund "lump sums," such as, paying off debt or funding a child's education. Determine these needs and add the to the total amount of the insurance.

1. Your annual income needs $____________
2. Subtract deceased person's needs $____________
3. Subtract other income $____________
4. = Net annual income needed $____________
5. Net annual income needed, multiplied by 20 (assume 5% after tax investment return on insurance proceeds) $____________
6. Lump Sum Needs

Debts $____________

Education $____________

Other $____________

Total lump sum needs $____________

Total life insurance needs $____________

PRAYERS FOR TODAY

This prayer section is for personal use and isn't meant to be part of the group discussion.

For you...

For your family and friends...

For those in your group...

See Their Story...

See how seeking and implementing God's word on advice saved this guy $70,000.

See how one swing of a golf club dramatically changed this couple's financial discipleship journey.

See how this one simple tool stopped the "blame game" in this marriage.

You can also watch these amazing stories at compasstools.org

Additional Tools for the Journey!

To help you on your financial discipleship journey, we have provided practical resources from a variety of people in the financial world. Visit us at **compasstools.org** to check out these resources.

Step One:

Watch the Video

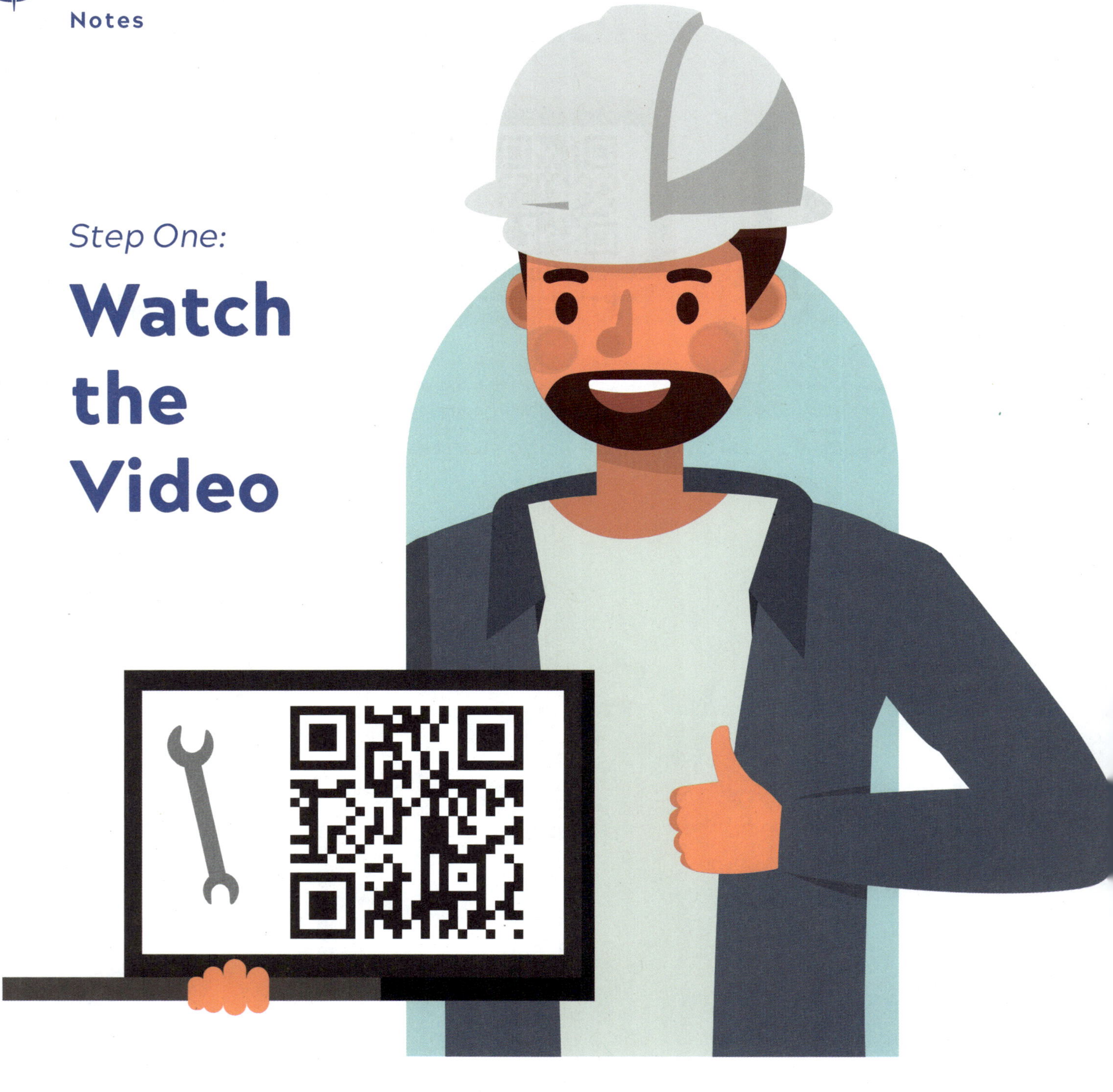

Open the camera on your phone to scan the QR code

OR

*Visit **compasstools.org** to view the video for this chapter*

Step Two:

Read the Notes

Not a fan of reading? You can listen to these notes at compasstools.org

Counsel

> *On your financial discipleship journey there will be one constant – a variety of people offering a variety of advice on how to handle your finances in a variety of ways. Some of this may be great advice, some of it may be absolutely terrible! So before we dig deep into topics such as debt, saving, giving, and investing, it's crucial that you are equipped with a filter to seek and receive advice that honors the Lord and empowers you on our financial discipleship journey.*

Notes

Sources of Counsel

What are the sources of counsel we need to seek? Before making a financial decision, particularly an important one, subject it to three sources of counsel.

THE BIBLE First, what does God's Word say about an issue? The psalmist wrote, *"Your laws are both my light and my counselors"* (Psalm 119:24, TLB). *"Your commands . . . make me wiser than my enemies. I have more insight than all my teachers, for I meditate on your statutes"* (Psalm 119:98-99, NIV). *"I understand more than those who are old, because I have complied with Your precepts"* (Psalm 119:100).

When we think of people who are skilled in financial decision making, we often think of experts, or those who are older and more experienced. Yet the Bible offers us more insight and wisdom than financial experts who don't know God's way of handling money. I would rather obey the truth of Scripture than risk suffering the consequences of following my own inclinations or the opinions of so-called experts.

The Bible makes this remarkable claim about itself: *"For the word of God is living and active, and sharper than any two-edged sword, and . . . able to judge the thoughts and intentions of the heart"* (Hebrews 4:12). The truths in the Bible are timeless. It is truly a living book that communicates God's direction to all generations.

You may have been surprised to learn that the Bible contains 2,350 verses dealing with how we should handle money. The fact is, the Scriptures are the very first filter through which we should run our financial decisions. If the Bible answers the question, we don't have to go any further, because it contains the Lord's written, revealed will.

> Bob and Barbara faced a difficult choice. Barbara's brother and his wife had just moved to Florida. Because they had previously experienced financial difficulties, the bank would not give them a home loan unless they had someone cosign it. They asked Bob and Barbara, and although Barbara pleaded for Bob to cosign, he was reluctant.
>
> A friend referred them to the verses that warn against cosigning. After reading the passages, Barbara said, "Who am I to argue with God? We shouldn't cosign." Bob was tremendously relieved.
>
> Two years later, Barbara's brother and his wife were divorced, and he declared bankruptcy. Can you imagine the strain on their marriage if Bob had cosigned? He might have said, "Barbara, you got me into this! I tried not to cosign but you forced me!" They probably would not have been able to survive financially.

If the Bible provides clear direction in a financial matter, we know what to do. If the Bible is not specific about an issue, we should subject our decision to the second source of counsel: godly people.

GODLY PEOPLE *"The godly man is a good counselor because he is just and fair and knows right from wrong"* (Psalm 37:30-31, TLB).

SPOUSE If you are married, the first person you need to consult is your spouse. Frankly, it has been a humbling experience for me to seek the counsel of my wife, Bev, in financial matters, because she has no formal financial training. Even so, she has saved us tons of money by her wise counsel.

Women tend to be gifted with a wonderfully sensitive intuition that is usually very accurate. Men tend to focus more objectively on the facts. The husband and wife need each other to achieve the proper balance for a correct decision.

If you are a husband, let me be blunt. Regardless of her business background or her financial aptitude, you must cultivate and seek your wife's counsel. I have committed never to proceed with a financial decision unless Bev agrees.

The husband and wife should agree, because they both will experience the consequences of the decision. Even if their choice proves to be disastrous, there are no grounds for an "I told you so" fracture in their relationship.

Seeking your spouse's counsel honors them and helps enormously in the development of a healthy self-esteem. When a husband or wife seeks the other's advice, he or she actually is communicating, "I love you. I respect you. I value your insight."

It also prepares your spouse for the future. Consistently asking for advice keeps your spouse informed of your financial condition. This is important in the event you predecease your spouse or are unable to work. My father suffered a heart attack that incapacitated him for two years. But because he had kept my mother informed about his business, she was able to step in and operate it until he recovered.

PARENTS Our parents are a source of counsel. *"My son, comply with the commandment of your father, and do not ignore the teaching of your mother; bind them continually on your heart; tie them around your neck. When you walk, they will guide you; when you sleep, they will watch over you; and when you awake, they will talk to you"* (Proverbs 6:20-22).

Our parents have the benefit of years of experience, and they know us well. In our opinion, we should seek their counsel even if they don't yet know Christ or have not been wise money managers themselves. Asking their advice is a way to honor our parents and to build a closer relationship with them. It's an expression of admiration.

One word of caution, however. Although the husband and wife should seek the counsel of their parents, the advice of the parents should be subordinate to the advice of the spouse – especially if a family conflict materializes. *"A man leaves his father and mother, and is united to his wife, and they become one flesh"* (Genesis 2:24, NIV).

EXPERIENCED PEOPLE We should also consult people experienced in the area in which we are attempting to make a decision. If you are considering a real estate investment, locate the most qualified real estate investor to counsel you.

Notes

A MULTITUDE OF COUNSELORS We read in Proverbs 15:22, *"Without consultation, plans are frustrated, but with many counselors they succeed."* And Proverbs 11:14 says, *"Where there is no guidance the people fall, but in an abundance of counselors there is victory."*

I meet regularly with a small group. The members of this group know each other well. Over the years, each person has experienced a difficult circumstance. We have learned that when someone suffers a painful situation, it can be difficult to make wise decisions. We have experienced the safety of having a group who love one another and can give objective counsel – even if it hurts. We are more receptive to constructive criticism when it comes from someone who cares for us.

Solomon describes the benefits of dependence upon one another: *"Two are better than one because they have a good return for their labor. For if either of them falls, the one will lift up his companion. But woe to the one who falls when there is not another to lift him up . . . And if one can overpower him who is alone, two can resist him. A cord of three strands is not quickly torn apart"* (Ecclesiastes 4:9-12).

When seeking a multitude of counselors, don't expect them all to offer the same recommendations. They may even disagree sharply, but a common thread usually develops. At other times, each counselor may supply a different insight you need to help you make the decision. We encourage you to include your pastor among your counselors, particularly when you face a major crossroads.

THE LORD During the process of analyzing the facts, searching the Bible, and obtaining the counsel of godly people, we need to seek direction from the Lord. In fact, this is the most important thing we can do. In Isaiah 9:6 we are told that one of the Lord's names is *"Wonderful Counselor."*

The Psalms also identify the Lord as our counselor. *"I [the Lord] will instruct you and teach you in the way which you should go; I will advise you with My eye upon you"* (Psalm 32:8). *"You [the Lord] guide me with your counsel"* (Psalm 73:24, NIV).

The Bible contains numerous examples of the unfortunate consequences of not seeking God's counsel. It also reveals the blessings of heeding His counsel. After the children of Israel began their campaign to capture the Promised Land, some of the natives (Gibeonites) attempted to enter into a peace treaty with Israel. The Gibeonites deceived the leaders of Israel into believing they were from a distant land. Joshua 9:14-15 reads, *"The men of Israel took some of their [Gibeonites'] provisions, and did not ask for the counsel of the Lord. And Joshua made peace with them and made a covenant with them, to let them live."*

The consequence of not seeking the Lord's counsel was that the Promised Land remained populated with ungodly people, and Israel became ensnared by their false gods. The leaders were influenced by the "facts" they could see – facts deliberately designed to deceive them into thinking that the Gibeonites lived far away. In many situations, only the Lord can reveal truth and proper direction.

Throughout Scripture we are encouraged to wait on the Lord. Whenever you feel hurried or pressured or confused concerning a decision, wait until you hear His still, small voice. The world screams "Hurry!" but our heavenly Father's advice is worth waiting for . . . a thousand times over.

Counsel to Avoid

THE WICKED We need to avoid the counsel of the wicked. *"Blessed is the person who does not walk in the counsel of the wicked"* (Psalm 1:1). A *"wicked"* person is one who lives without regard to God. A wicked person can be one who does not yet personally know the Lord or one who knows Jesus Christ as Savior but is not following Him in obedience.

In our opinion, when you are searching for facts or technical expertise, you may seek input from those who are knowledgeable in that area, whether they know Christ or not. Then, after considering their input, you are responsible to make the final decision.

FORTUNETELLERS, MEDIUMS AND SPIRITUALISTS The Bible clearly forbids seeking the advice of fortunetellers, mediums, or spiritualists: *"Do not turn to mediums or seek out spiritists, for you will be defiled by them. I am the Lord your God"* (Leviticus 19:31, NIV). Or consider this passage: *"Saul died because he was unfaithful to the Lord . . . and even consulted a medium for guidance, and did not inquire of the Lord. So the Lord put him to death"* (1 Chronicles 10:13-14, NIV). Saul died, in part, because he went to a medium. We should also avoid anything they use in forecasting the future, such as horoscopes and all other practices of the occult.

BIASED COUNSEL We need to be cautious of the counsel of the biased. When receiving financial advice, ask yourself: "What stake does this person have in the outcome of my decision? Does he or she stand to gain or lose from it?" If the advisor will profit, be cautious when evaluating this counsel and always seek a second, unbiased opinion.

A Word to the Counseled

When you are seeking advice, supply your counselor with all the important facts. Don't attempt to manipulate your advisor to give the answer you want by concealing information.

Whenever you face a major decision such as a job change or home purchase, it is very helpful to go to a quiet place where you can spend uninterrupted time praying, reading the Bible, and seeking the Lord's direction. We encourage you to consider fasting during this time.

As you seek counsel, don't be surprised if the answer comes out of your own mouth! Interacting with others allows you to verbalize thoughts and feelings that you may never have expressed clearly.

A Word to the Counselors

Counseling others can be frustrating if you misunderstand the proper role of the counselor. Simply stated, counselors should lovingly communicate their advice – and then leave the results to God. I have made the mistake of becoming involved emotionally in whether people would act on my recommendations. I discovered that some people aren't yet prepared to follow advice. It may have been the right word for them but in the wrong season of their lives. On other occasions, I later discovered that my counsel was flawed, and I was happy that they hadn't heeded my words!

When you don't know the answer to a question, be careful not to fabricate one. Simply respond: "I don't know." Often people come with problems that are outside of our experience. The best way to serve them is to refer them to someone who has expertise in their area of need.

Debt

The amount of debt in our nation has exploded – government debt, business debt, and personal debt. We are drowning in an ocean of red ink. To get a real sense of just how quickly debt is growing in our country, check out the US DEBT CLOCK and watch it for a few minutes. It's stunning!

It is estimated that more than one million individuals will file bankruptcy this year. And even more sobering, a Gallup Poll found that a majority of divorces are caused in part by financial tension in the home.

These sorts of financial tensions often result from believing advertisers. You've heard it ten thousand times: buy now and pay later with easy monthly payments. We all know that nothing about those monthly payments is easy. The ads fail to tell us the whole truth, leaving out one little word – Debt.

What is debt?

> The dictionary defines debt as "money that a person is obligated to pay to another." Debt includes bank loans, student loans, money borrowed from relatives, the home mortgage, past-due medical bills, and money owed to credit card companies. Bills that come due, such as the monthly electric bill, aren't considered debt if they're paid on time.

Notes

What debt really costs

We need to understand the real cost of debt. Assume you have $5,560 in credit card debt at an 18 percent interest rate. This would cost you $1,000 in interest annually. *Check out the chart below.*

	Year 10	Year 20	Year 30	Year 40
Amount of interest you paid	$10,000	$20,000	$30,000	$40,000
What you would accumulate on $1,000 invested annually earning 10%	$17,072	$63,286	$188,386	$527,039
How much the lender earns from your interest payment at 18%	$23,521	$146,628	$790,948	$4,163,213

You can see what lenders have known for a long time: the eye-popping impact of compounding interest working for them. If they earn 18 percent, they will accumulate more than $4 million on your $1,000 a year for 40 years! Is it any wonder credit card companies are eager for you to become one of their borrowers?

Now compare the $40,000 you paid in interest over 40 years with the $527,039 you would have accumulated if you earned 10 percent on $1,000 each year. The monthly income on $527,039 earning 10 percent – without ever touching the principal – is $4,392!

Debt has a much higher cost than many realize. Stop to consider this: When you assume debt of $5,560 and pay $1,000 a year in interest versus earning a 10 percent return on that $1000, it actually costs you $527,039 over 40 years. The next time you find yourself tempted to purchase something with debt, ask yourself if the long-term benefits of staying out of debt outweigh the short-term benefits of the purchase.

The other costs of debt

Debt often increases stress, which contributes to mental, physical, and emotional fatigue. It can stifle creativity and harm relationships. When a crisis occurs – think Corona Virus – that leads to a job loss or other challenge, debt can feel like a straitjacket and loss of freedom. Many people raise their lifestyle through debt, only to discover that its burden then controls their lifestyle.

What the Bible says about debt

While Scripture doesn't specifically call debt a sin, it strongly discourages it. Remember, God loves us and has given us these principles for our benefit. Read the first portion of Romans 13:8 from several different translations: *"Owe no man anything"* (KJV). *"Let no debt remain outstanding"* (NIV). *"Pay all your debts"* (TLB). *"Owe nothing to anyone"* (NASB). *"Keep out of debt and owe no man anything"* (AMPC). Any questions about God's view of debt?

Here's why the Lord wants you debt free.

DEBT IS CONSIDERED SLAVERY

Proverbs 22:7 reads: *". . . the borrower is slave to the lender"* (NIV). When we're in debt, we're in bondage to the lender. And the deeper we're in debt, the more like slaves we become. We don't have the freedom to decide where to spend our income, because it's already obligated to meet our debt payments.

In 1 Corinthians 7:23, Paul writes, *"You were bought with a price; do not become slaves of people."* Our Father made the ultimate sacrifice by giving His Son, the Lord Jesus Christ, to die for us. And He now wants His children free to serve Him rather than lenders.

Notes

DEBT WAS CONSIDERED A CURSE

In the Old Testament, being out of debt was one of the promised rewards for obedience.

"If you diligently obey the Lord your God, being careful to do all His commandments which I command you today, the Lord your God will put you high above all the nations of the earth. And all these blessings will come to you . . . You will lend to many nations, but ***you will not borrow"*** (Deuteronomy 28:1-2, Deuteronomy 28:12, emphasis added).

On the other hand, debt was listed among the curses for disobedience. *"If you do not obey the Lord your God, to be careful to follow all His commandments and His statutes which I am commanding you today, all these curses will come upon you and overtake you . . . The stranger who is among you will rise above you higher and higher, and you will go down lower and lower. He will lend to you, but you will not lend to him; he will be the head, and you will be the tail"* (Deuteronomy 28:15, Deuteronomy 28:43-44).

In God's view, then, being in debt moves you from a head position in life to the tail end!

DEBT PRESUMES UPON TOMORROW

When we get into debt, we're assuming that we will earn enough in the future to repay it. But can we really assume such a thing? We plan for our jobs to continue or our business to be profitable or our investments to increase in value. The Bible strongly cautions us against such presumption: *"You who say, 'Today or tomorrow, we will go to such and such a city, and spend a year there and engage in business and make a profit.' Yet* ***you do not know what your life will be like tomorrow. . . .*** *Instead, you ought to say, 'If the Lord wills, we will live and also do this or that'"* (James 4:13-15, emphasis added).

DEBT MAY DENY GOD AN OPPORTUNITY

Financial author Ron Blue tells of a young man who wanted to go to seminary to become a missionary. The young man had no money and thought the only way he could afford seminary was to secure a student loan. However, this would have left him with about $80,000 of debt by the time he graduated. He knew a missionary's salary would never be able to repay that much debt.

After a great deal of prayer, he decided to enroll without the aid of a loan, trusting the Lord to meet his needs. Several years later, he graduated without borrowing anything. Just as important, he had grown in his faith and in his appreciation for how God could provide his needs. This was the most valuable lesson learned in seminary as he prepared for life on the mission field.

How to Get Out of Debt

PRAY! In 2 Kings 4:1-7, we read about a widow threatened with losing her sons to an aggressive creditor. When she asked the prophet Elisha for help, he told her to borrow many empty jars from her neighbors. Then the Lord multiplied her only possession – a small amount of oil – until all the jars were filled to the brim. She sold the oil and paid her debts to free her children.

The same God who provided supernaturally for the widow is interested in freeing you from debt. And He is every bit as able of meeting your needs as He was the needs of that poor widow. The first step is to pray. Seek the Lord's help and guidance in your journey toward Debtless Day. He may act immediately or slowly over time. In either case, prayer is essential.

A trend is emerging. As people begin to eliminate debt, even little by little, the Lord blesses their faithfulness. Even if you can afford only a small monthly repayment of your debt, do it. The Lord is fully able to multiply your efforts.

INCREASE MONTHLY SURPLUS The larger your monthly surplus, the more money you can have available to pay down your debt. How do you increase that surplus? By increasing your income, reducing spending, and selling items you no longer need.

EARN ADDITIONAL INCOME Many people hold jobs that simply don't pay enough to allow them to pay off their debts quickly enough. A temporary part-time job – or some creative way to earn more money – can make a huge difference in how fast you can reach D-Day.

SPEND LESS BY BECOMING CONTENT WITH WHAT YOU HAVE Advertisers use powerful methods to get us to buy. Frequently the message is intended to foster discontentment with what we have. An example is the American company that opened a new plant in Central America because the labor was relatively inexpensive. Everything went well until the villagers received their first paycheck; afterward they didn't return to work. Several days later, the manager went down to the village chief to determine the cause of this problem. The chief responded, "Why should we work? We already have everything we need." The plant stood idle until someone came up with the idea of sending mail-order catalogs to every villager. There hasn't been an employment problem since!

Note these three realities of our consumer-driven economy.

- The more television you watch or surfing the web you do, the more you spend.
- The more you look at catalogs, magazines, and ads on social media, the more you spend.
- The more you shop, the more you spend.

There is an interesting passage in 1 Timothy 6:6: *"Godliness actually is a means of great gain when accompanied by contentment."* When we are content with what we have and wait to buy until we can do it using cash – that is great gain.

Notes

CONSIDER A RADICAL CHANGE IN LIFESTYLE A growing number of people have lowered their standard of living significantly to get out of debt more quickly. Some have downsized their homes, rented apartments, or moved in with family members. Many have sold cars with large monthly payments and purchased inexpensive ones for cash. In short, they have temporarily sacrificed their standard of living so they could pay off debt more quickly.

SELL WHAT YOU'RE NOT USING Evaluate your possessions to determine whether you should sell any of them to help you get out of debt more quickly. What about the clothes you no longer wear? The sports equipment gathering dust? Is there anything you can sell to help you get out of debt?

CREDIT CARDS When the credit card statements arrived, it signaled the beginning of a verbal war between Alex and Nancy Popovich. They carried seven cards between them, using cash advances from some to satisfy the minimum monthly payments on others.

The Popoviches aren't alone. The average household with an unpaid balance has about $7,000 in credit card debt. There has been an explosion in the number of credit cards for only one reason: the credit card companies make a ton of money charging high interest! The more you owe, the more interest they receive – and the more likely they can whack you with late fees and over-the-limit penalties.

Following are a few simple suggestions for paying off the plastic:

SNOWBALL THE PLASTIC

Snowball your way out of debt. And here's how. In addition to making the minimum payments on all your credit cards, focus on paying off the smallest-balance-card first. You'll be encouraged to see its balance go down, down, and finally disappear!

After the first credit card is paid off, apply its payment toward the next smallest one. After the second card is paid off, apply what you were paying on the first and second toward the third smallest. That's the snowball in action!

When you're on a roll like this, it starts getting exciting. Those "impossible" balances that have worried you and robbed you of your peace will begin diminishing before your very eyes. So . . . where do you start? Prioritize your debts, and every time you pay one of those cards off, use it as an occasion to celebrate and thank the Lord!

PERFORM PLASTIC SURGERY

When people use credit cards rather than cash, they spend about one-third more. Why? Because it just doesn't feel like "real money"; it's just plastic. As one shopper said to another, "I like credit cards more than money, because they go so much further!" If you don't pay the entire credit card balance at the end of each month, you may need to perform some plastic surgery – any good pair of scissors will do!

We started with nine credit cards. Today we carry two that we pay in full each month. To limit the temptations of additional cards, we opted out of receiving credit card offers by mail and telemarketing calls.

- Call toll-free 1-888-5-OPT-OUT (1-888-567-8688) or visit www.optoutprescreen.com. The phone number and website are operated by the major consumer reporting companies.
- Go to donotcall.gov or call 1-888-382-1222 from the phone you want to register. It's free. If you register your number at donotcall.gov, you'll get an email with a link you need to click on within 72 hours to complete your registration.

LOWER THE INTEREST RATE

There is a lot of competition among credit card companies for your business – and especially if you have a solid credit score. If your company is charging a high interest rate, phone and ask them to drop it. You may have to call several times, but 75 percent of the time, they'll lower the rate.

Another alternative is to transfer the balance to a card that charges less interest. Before switching to a lower-rate card, however, confirm that the new card has no transfer fee, no annual fee, and that the interest rate on transferred balances is not higher than the advertised rate. But remember, if you miss a payment or make a payment late, your interest rate will automatically skyrocket in most cases.

Notes

Consumer Debts

Seventy percent of all cars are financed, and many people never get out of car debt. It's one of the biggest obstacles for most people. Fortunately, there's a way to get out of car debt for good by following these three steps.

> Decide to keep your car at least three years longer than your car loan – and then pay off the loan.
>
> After your last payment, keep making the same payment, but pay it to yourself. Put it into an account that you will use to buy your next car.
>
> When you're ready to replace your car, the cash you have saved plus your car's trade-in value should be sufficient to buy a car without credit. It may not be a new car, but a low-mileage used car is a better value anyway.

UPSIDE DOWN AUTOS You've probably heard it said again and again: The moment you drive a car off the lot, it's worth less than you paid for it. It's so true. That new car smell may be pleasant, but it's also incredibly expensive. Rapid depreciation is why so many new car buyers find themselves upside down on their auto loans – owing more than the car is worth.

For this reason, we decided early in our marriage to buy only reliable used cars for cash – and drive them until the wheels fell off! My wife drove the same car for seventeen years. We used to call it "Puff" because of the smoking exhaust pipe whenever she accelerated.

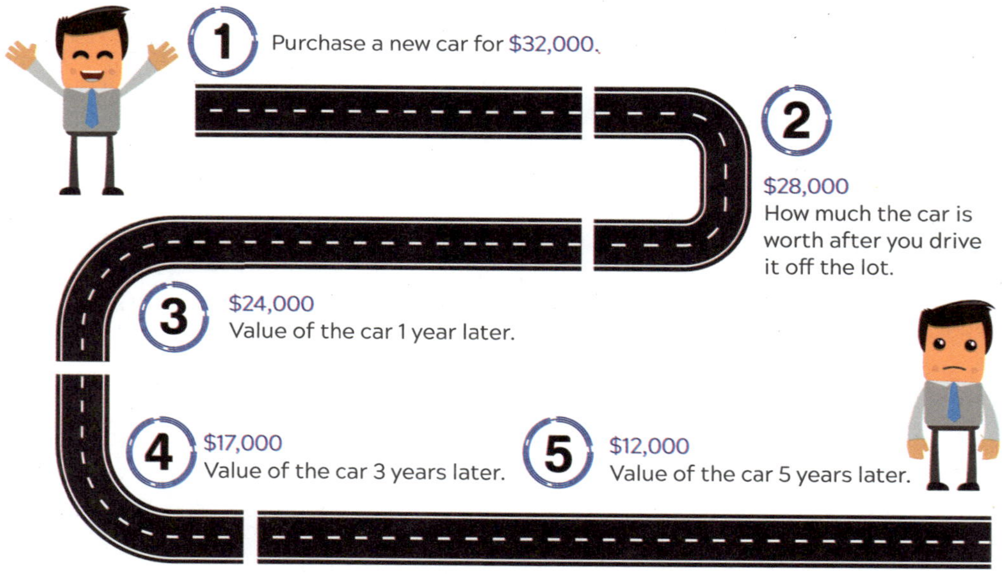

I once bought a truck that cost only a hundred dollars – and it looked it! A sympathetic neighbor borrowed it and brought it back, painted (it suddenly looked like a $200 truck!) While driving the truck one morning, I was enjoying a time of special worship and remembered Psalm 16:11: *". . . In Your presence is fullness of joy."*

You know what? In that moment it didn't matter whether I was driving my hundred-dollar clunker or the most expensive car on the market; I could experience fullness of joy because of my relationship with Jesus Christ. Advertisers have led us to believe that our deepest needs can be satisfied only by purchasing the newest and the best. Nothing could be further from the truth.

It's hard to overestimate the financial impact of driving debt-free cars. The average monthly new car payment is $550. If a 21-year-old drives debt-free cars and saves the $550 a month, earning an average return, he or she will accumulate about $2 million yielding almost $135,000 a year by age 65! Short-term spending sacrifices translate into enormous long-term benefits.

My advice: keep your cars as long as they are safe to drive, and consider buying low-mileage used cars to avoid new-car depreciation.

SNOWBALL CONSUMER DEBT After you have paid off your auto loans, focus on paying off your consumer debts in exactly the same way as you wiped out your plastic: snowball them. Make the minimum payments on all your consumer debts, but focus on accelerating the payment of your smallest consumer debt first. Then, after you pay off the first consumer debt, apply its payment toward the next smallest one. After the second one is paid off, apply what you were paying on the first and second to pay off the third, and so forth.

HOME MORTGAGE If you haven't yet purchased a home and want to, there are two rules of thumb for buying an affordable home: First, make a down payment of at least 20 percent. And forget adjustable-rate mortgages; get a fixed rate. If you don't yet have enough saved for 20 percent down, renting is usually much cheaper than owning. So, rent – and save like crazy.

Second, no more than 35 percent of your income should be required to cover all housing expenses. This includes mortgage payments, insurance, real estate taxes, utilities, and maintenance. If housing costs exceed 35 percent, you'll find yourself continually robbing money from other spending categories to balance your budget.

PAYING OFF THE HOME MORTGAGE When Bev and I learned God's financial principles, we became convinced that the Lord wanted us entirely out of debt – even our home. We understood this to be a really long-term goal because of the size of our mortgage. But we also realized that if we could pay it off, it would free up a big chunk of our income, enabling us to give more generously *and* save more aggressively.

Notes

We didn't start prepaying the mortgage until we wiped out all our credit card and consumer debt. Then we focused on the home by paying an extra amount each month to reduce the principal more quickly. The longer we did it, the more excited we became. Finally, we also started applying work bonuses and income tax refunds to our mortgage.

Prepaying your mortgage can save you tons of interest.

Some homeowners don't want to prepay the mortgage and decrease the interest payments, reasoning that interest is one of their biggest tax deductions. But this tax advantage is overrated. If you are in the 25 percent tax bracket, for each $1,000 you pay in home interest, you save only $250 in taxes – 25 percent of the $1,000 interest paid. So, while there is a tax benefit, it's not as much as many think. Paying $1,000 to save $250 is not that great a deal.

BUSINESS DEBT We also want to encourage you to pray about becoming debt free in your business if you have one. Many business owners are recognizing the competitive advantage and increased stability they enjoy when they eliminate business debt.

Here is our rule of thumb on business debt: use as *little* as possible and pay it off as quickly as possible.

CHURCH DEBT The Bible doesn't specifically address whether a church may borrow money to build or expand its facility. In our opinion, such debt is permissible if the church leadership clearly senses the Lord's leading to do so. If a church borrows, we recommend that it raise as much money as possible for the down payment and establish a plan to pay off the debt as rapidly as possible.

A growing number of churches have chosen to build without the use of any debt. For many of these churches, the members' faith has increased as they have observed the Lord providing the necessary funds. Many of these members have been encouraged to become debt free themselves.

Debt Repayment Responsibilities

PROMPT PAYMENT Many people delay paying creditors until payments are past due, even when they have the money. On this practice, however, the Bible is crystal clear. In Proverbs 3:27-28 we read: *"Do not withhold good from those to whom it is due, when it is in your power to do it. Do not say to your neighbor, 'Go, and come back, and tomorrow I will give it to you,' when you have it with you."*

Godly people should pay their debts and bills as promptly as they can. Some try to pay each bill the same day they receive it – to demonstrate to others that knowing Jesus Christ has made them financially responsible.

BANKRUPTCY A court can declare people bankrupt and unable to pay their debts. Depending on the type of bankruptcy, the court will either allow them to develop a plan to repay their creditors or it will distribute their property among the creditors as payment.

Should a godly person declare bankruptcy? Generally, no. Psalm 37:21 tells us, *"The wicked borrows and* ***does not pay back"*** (emphasis added).

However, in our opinion, bankruptcy is permissible under two circumstances:

> When a creditor or circumstances force a person into bankruptcy. Sometimes bankruptcy is the only viable option when the financial challenges become too extreme to reverse. That option needs to be exercised only after all others have been explored.
>
> When the emotional health of the borrower is at stake. If the debtor's emotional health is at risk because of inability to cope with the pressure of aggressive creditors, bankruptcy can be an option.

Declaring bankruptcy should never be a cavalier decision, because it remains on a credit report for ten years and often impairs one's ability to obtain future credit at reasonable interest rates. Potential employers and landlords are also likely to learn of a past bankruptcy. It can haunt people for years, and although it provides relief, it's not exactly the fresh start that some advertise.

After a person goes through bankruptcy, he should seek counsel from an attorney to determine if it's legally permissible to repay the debt, even though he is not obligated to do so. If it's allowable, every effort should be made to repay the debt. For a large debt, this may be a long-term goal that is largely dependent upon the Lord supernaturally providing the resources.

Notes

CREDIT REPORT AND SCORE Your credit score (FICO score) determines whether you can get credit. And your score may be high enough to get credit but not high enough to get a decent interest rate – whether you're looking for a mortgage, a car loan, or some other type of credit. Without good scores, your application to rent an apartment may be turned down. Your scores can affect your car insurance premiums and even your ability to get a job.

Both the wife and husband have their own separate credit scores. If only the husbands have credit in their names, wives don't have the opportunity to establish good credit on their own. This is a mistake! If a husband dies before his wife, she won't have a solid credit score – at the very time when she may need it most. We solved this problem by each securing a credit card in our name that we pay on time and in full every month. When we receive the credit card statements, we meet to review them so our communication remains intact.

A credit score is a number designed to help lenders and others measure your likelihood of making payments on time. FICO score ranges from 300-850, with the average score around 680. Higher scores are better. FICO scores above 700 indicate a good credit risk, while scores below 600 indicate a poor risk.

A low score can lead to much higher interest rates. For example, if you apply for a 30-year home mortgage and your credit score is too low, you could pay as much as three percent more. On a $200,000 mortgage, that three percent difference will cost you $400 per month. Over the life of the loan it adds up to $144,000!

CREDIT REPORT Everyone can get a copy of their credit report. It's a good idea to get a copy once a year from the three major credit reporting agencies: TransUnion, Equifax and Experian. You can order a free copy of your credit report by logging on to AnnualCreditReport.com. Carefully review it to make sure there are no mistakes or that you haven't been the victim of identity theft. The free copy of your credit report does not contain your credit score, but any of the three main credit agencies will sell it to you.

DON'T GIVE UP!

On October 29, 1941, Winston Churchill, Prime Minister of England, gave a school commencement address. World War II was devastating Europe, and England's very fate as a nation was in doubt. Churchill stood and said, "Never give up. Never give up. Never, never, never – in nothing, great or small, large or petty – never give up except to convictions of honor and good sense."

So, I want to encourage you to never give up in your effort to get out of debt. It may require hard work and sacrifice, but the freedom is worth the struggle. Remember, it is on God's heart for you to become debt free.

Saving

EMERGENCY FUND When beginning to save, first focus on saving $1,000 toward one month's living expenses for emergencies – unexpected, unbudgeted expenses that whack us all.

Why save for emergencies? Because emergencies happen! The refrigerator goes on the fritz, the car brakes have worn out, there's a health crisis in the family. If you have saved for the emergencies, you don't have to pile up more debt to pay for them.

After saving up to one month's living expenses, gradually increase your emergency savings to at least three month's living expenses. Keep these savings in an account that is safe and easily accessible.

MAJOR PURCHASES A car, a house down-payment, family vacations – these are some great things that may be a part of your life. And they all have one thing in common: they aren't cheap!

These types of major purchases don't pay for themselves, and we've already learned that we don't want to rely on credit to fund them. So how do we make major purchases like these become a reality? We need to plan. These steps can help:

1. Before making a major purchase, make sure you have your emergency fund fully funded to at least three months.
2. Identify what major purchases are the top priority and what the potential cost is.
3. Determine how much you are willing (and able) to spend upfront.

For example, let's say you are ready to buy a house and want to be a new homeowner in two to three years. You've looked at the housing market and are thinking about a home in the $200,000 range. Knowing that you should save for a 20 percent down payment, you realize you'll need around $40,000.

If you are going to reach $40,000 in two years, you'll need to begin saving over $1650 a month! Depending on your financial scenario, this may be realistic or it may be overwhelming. If it is overwhelming, you may need to manage your expectations by either looking at a less expensive home or waiting three to four years to buy. Changing your goal from 2 years to 4 years cuts the monthly amount you will need to save in half (just over $830 a month) and may make your goal of home ownership attainable.

Where should I put money for savings?

Keep these savings in an account that is safe and easily accessible. Below are several types of accounts to review:

SAVINGS ACCOUNT A savings account is an interest-bearing deposit account held at a bank or other financial institution. Though these accounts usually pay a small interest rate, their safety and reliability make them a great option for short-term needs.

HIGH-YIELD SAVINGS ACCOUNT A high-yield savings account offers protection of your principal, the safety of federal insurance, and a yield that's higher than a regular savings account. If you go this route, be sure to find an account that will maximize your earnings while letting you avoid any hidden fees such as early withdrawals.

MONEY MARKET ACCOUNT (BANK) A bank money market account is an interest-bearing account at a bank or credit union. Most money market accounts pay a higher interest rate than a regular savings account and often include check writing and debit-card privileges.

Step Three:

Answer the Discussion Questions

What in the notes (and video) did you find revealing or interesting?

What in the notes challenged you the most?

What did you find revealing or challenging about the application worksheets in this chapter? Did you have any questions about the worksheets?

Chapter 2

Compass Commentaries

DAY ONE We are never too old to learn, but we always need to assess from whom we are learning. These passages are rich in describing the value of receiving and embracing instruction, wisdom, insight, and discretion. They warn of the enticements of "sinful men" and the pitfalls they lead to. We should intentionally seek counsel from wise and godly people, including our parents. It improves the likelihood of our plans succeeding and the joy that will result. God's Word is an important source of wisdom and counsel, guiding us in our life and financial decisions.

DAY TWO Borrowing, including co-signing, is clearly discouraged in Scripture. Why do you think God takes that position? We quickly assume that He wants us to avoid the risks of getting out of control with debt. Certainly He does, but there is another important, though less obvious, reason. He wants us to recognize Him as our primary source and to trust Him to the extent of "waiting on the Lord."

It's easier to apply for a loan or swipe the credit card than it is to prayerfully submit ourselves to the Lord's will and accept His response. But when we get out in front of Him, we may be robbing Him of the opportunity to bless us and provide without having to borrow! Once we have borrowed or cosigned, we need to honor that commitment and pay it back no matter how long it takes. Not doing so dishonors the Lord and can tarnish our testimony.

DAY FOUR When times are good and everything is going our way, the last thing we are likely to think is "what if this changes?" But we should expect challenges in our life; Jesus told us explicitly that we will have trials. He also told us to trust God and not fear. God has given us the ability to think and plan and prepare for challenging times. He expects us to take the actions appropriate to Our Part. Some of those actions include setting aside resources from today that can be used when needed in the future.

DAY THREE Getting out of debt requires a plan and action; it doesn't happen by accident. The widowed woman in today's passage was desperate. She prayed, sought godly counsel, and followed the prophet's instruction explicitly, even though the instructions didn't seem logical. She demonstrated her faith through her obedience – taking action.

Only God can perform a miracle like this, but He often wants to see us actively participate with Him. Do you think the widow's problems would have been solved if she had just sat in her house all day waiting for her debts to be paid off? Probably not. As she did her part by obeying Elisha's instructions, God blessed her efforts and provided an amazing way for her to pay her debts and keep her family together. She had only a little bit, but God multiplied it for her benefit and His glory.

DAY FIVE While saving is a good thing, loving money and hoarding is not! The desire to get rich can become an impossible-to-satisfy obsession. Some people spend their whole lives accumulating wealth and belongings, never reaching contentment with what they have.

Money is simply a tool to accomplish God's purposes for our lives. The love of money redirects our focus away from the Creator and onto the created. Avoid the grief that results from loving money. Be content with what you have. Work diligently for God's honor and glory and not for the things of this world.

Chapter 3:

Generosity and Investing

*All tools, videos, resources and electronic applications for this chapter can be found at **compasstools.org***

THIS CHAPTER'S MEMORY VERSE:

Acts 20:35

DAILY HOMEWORK:

Day One – Our Attitude in Giving

Day Two – Giving Amount

Day Three – Giving and the Oppressed, begin working on the Generosity Grid

Day Four – Investing and Wealth

Day Five – Proverbs and Investing, begin working on the Compass Construction Plan

Day Six – Watch the Build Your Finances God's Way video, Read the Notes, answer the discussion questions

BEFORE YOUR GROUP MEETING:

1. Memorize Acts 20:35: To prevent confusion when reciting the verses in a group setting, please memorize the version listed below.

> *". . . Remember the words of the Lord Jesus, that He Himself said, 'It is more blessed to give than to receive'" (Acts 20:35).*

2. Complete the Daily Homework.

Each day's homework is designed to take 20-30 minutes to complete.

Our Attitude in Giving

PRAYER

Pray for the Holy Spirit's guidance as you begin reading passages of Scripture. Ask for clarity and insight as you engage in God's word.

SCRIPTURE READING

Read 1 Corinthians 13:1-3.

"If I speak in the tongues of men and of angels, but have not love, I am a noisy
gong or a clanging cymbal. [2]And if I have prophetic powers, and understand all
mysteries and all knowledge, and if I have all faith, so as to remove mountains,
but have not love, I am nothing. [3]If I give away all I have, and if I deliver up my
body to be burned, but have not love, I gain nothing" (ESV).

Read 2 Corinthians 9:6-11.

"The point is this: whoever sows sparingly will also reap sparingly, and whoever
sows bountifully will also reap bountifully. [7]Each one must give as he has
decided in his heart, not reluctantly or under compulsion, for God loves a
cheerful giver. [8]And God is able to make all grace abound to you, so that
having all sufficiency in all things at all times, you may abound in every good
work. [9]As it is written, 'He has distributed freely, he has given to the poor; his
righteousness endures forever.' [10]He who supplies seed to the sower and bread
for food will supply and multiply your seed for sowing and increase the harvest
of your righteousness. [11]You will be enriched in every way to be generous in
every way, which through us will produce thanksgiving to God" (ESV).

OBSERVATION

What do these passages say about...

Love?

Giving?

God?

SCRIPTURE READING

Read 1 Corinthians 13:1-3.

"If I speak in the tongues of men and of angels, but have not love, I am a noisy gong or a clanging cymbal. [2]And if I have prophetic powers, and understand all mysteries and all knowledge, and if I have all faith, so as to remove mountains, but have not love, I am nothing. [3]If I give away all I have, and if I deliver up my body to be burned, but have not love, I gain nothing" (ESV).

Read 2 Corinthians 9:6-11.

"The point is this: whoever sows sparingly will also reap sparingly, and whoever sows bountifully will also reap bountifully. [7]Each one must give as he has decided in his heart, not reluctantly or under compulsion, for God loves a cheerful giver. [8]And God is able to make all grace abound to you, so that having all sufficiency in all things at all times, you may abound in every good work. [9]As it is written, 'He has distributed freely, he has given to the poor; his righteousness endures forever.' [10]He who supplies seed to the sower and bread for food will supply and multiply your seed for sowing and increase the harvest of your righteousness. [11]You will be enriched in every way to be generous in every way, which through us will produce thanksgiving to God" (ESV).

INTERPRETATION

What do these passages mean to you?

How do our attitudes connect to our giving?

What does it look like to give with love?

How have you experienced cheerful giving in your life?

APPLICATION

How can you apply the principles of these passages to your finances?

HOWARD'S HIGHLIGHTS

Attitudes in Giving

God evaluates our actions on the basis of our attitudes. John 3:16 reveals His attitude toward giving: *"For **God so loved** the world, that **He gave** His only Son"* (emphasis added). Note the sequence. Because God loved, He gave. Because God is love, He is also a giver. He set the example of generosity motivated by love.

An attitude of love in giving is crucial: *"And if I give away all my possessions to charity . . . but do not have love, it does me no good"* (1 Corinthians 13:3). What could be more commendable than giving everything to charity? However, generosity without an attitude of love provides no benefit to the giver.

In God's economy, the attitude is more important than the amount. Jesus emphasized this in Matthew 23:23: *"Woe to you, teachers of the law and Pharisees, you hypocrites! You give a tenth of your spices – mint, dill and cumin. But you have neglected the more important matters of the law – justice, mercy and faithfulness. You should have practiced the latter without neglecting the former"* (NIV). The Pharisees had been careful to give the correct amount, but Christ rebuked them because of their attitude. He looks past the amount of the gift to the heart of the giver.

We can consistently give with love only when we recognize that we are giving to the Lord Himself. We see an example of this in Numbers 18:24: *"The tithe of the sons of Israel, which they offer as an offering **to the Lord**"* (emphasis added). If giving is merely to a church, a ministry, or a needy person, it's only charity. But giving to the Lord is always an act of worship, expressing love and gratitude to our Creator, Savior, and faithful Provider. Whenever we put something in the offering plate, we should remind ourselves that our gift goes to the Lord Himself.

In addition to giving with love, we are to give cheerfully. *"Each one must do just as he has decided in his heart, not reluctantly or under compulsion, for God loves a cheerful giver"* (2 Corinthians 9:7). The original Greek word for cheerful is "hilarios," which is translated into the English word "hilarious." What a picture that creates! We are to be joyful givers.

When was the last time you saw hilarity when the offering plate passed? The atmosphere more often reminds us of a patient in the dentist chair awaiting a painful extraction. So how do we develop this hilarity in our giving? Consider the early churches of Macedonia.

". . . We want you to know about the grace that God has given the Macedonian churches. In the midst of a very severe trial, their overflowing joy and their extreme poverty welled up in rich generosity" (2 Corinthians 8:1-2, NIV).

How did the Macedonians, who were in terrible circumstances, "severe trial," and "extreme poverty," still manage to give with "overflowing joy"? The answer is in verse 5: *"They gave themselves first of all to the Lord, and then by the will of God also to us."* The key to cheerful giving is to yield ourselves to Christ and ask Him to direct how much He wants us to give. That places us in a position to experience the advantages of giving with the proper attitude.

Stop and examine yourself. What is your attitude toward giving?

PRAYERS FOR TODAY

This prayer section is for personal use and isn't meant to be part of the group discussion.

For you...

For your family and friends...

For those in your group...

3 - DAY TWO

Homework

Giving Amount

PRAYER

Pray for the Holy Spirit's guidance as you begin reading passages of Scripture. Ask for clarity and insight as you engage in God's word.

SCRIPTURE READING

Read Malachi 3:6-12.

"For I the Lord do not change; therefore you, O children of Jacob, are not
consumed. [7]From the days of your fathers you have turned aside from my
statutes and have not kept them. Return to me, and I will return to you, says the Lord of hosts.
But you say, 'How shall we return?' [8]Will man rob God? Yet you are robbing me. But you say, 'How
have we robbed you?' In your tithes and contributions. [9]You are cursed with a curse, for you are
robbing me, the whole nation of you. [10]Bring the full tithe into the storehouse, that there may be
food in my house. And thereby put me to the test, says the Lord of hosts, if I will not open the
windows of heaven for you and pour down for you a blessing until there is no more need. [11]I will
rebuke the devourer for you, so that it will not destroy the fruits of your soil, and your vine in the
field shall not fail to bear, says the Lord of hosts. [12]Then all nations will call you blessed, for you
will be a land of delight, says the Lord of hosts" (ESV).

Read 1 Corinthians 16:1-4.

"Now concerning the collection for the saints: as I directed the churches of Galatia, so you also
are to do. [2]On the first day of every week, each of you is to put something aside and store it up,
as he may prosper, so that there will be no collecting when I come. [3]And when I arrive, I will send
those whom you accredit by letter to carry your gift to Jerusalem. [4]If it seems advisable that I
should go also, they will accompany me" (ESV).

OBSERVATION

What do these passages say about...

God?

Giving?

Blessing?

3 - DAY TWO

Homework

SCRIPTURE READING

Read Malachi 3:6-12.

"For I the Lord do not change; therefore you, O children of Jacob, are not consumed. [7]From the days of your fathers you have turned aside from my statutes and have not kept them. Return to me, and I will return to you, says the Lord of hosts. But you say, 'How shall we return?' [8]Will man rob God? Yet you are robbing me. But you say, 'How have we robbed you?' In your tithes and contributions. [9]You are cursed with a curse, for you are robbing me, the whole nation of you. [10]Bring the full tithe into the storehouse, that there may be food in my house. And thereby put me to the test, says the Lord of hosts, if I will not open the windows of heaven for you and pour down for you a blessing until there is no more need. [11]I will rebuke the devourer for you, so that it will not destroy the fruits of your soil, and your vine in the field shall not fail to bear, says the Lord of hosts. [12]Then all nations will call you blessed, for you will be a land of delight, says the Lord of hosts" (ESV).

Read 1 Corinthians 16:1-4.

"Now concerning the collection for the saints: as I directed the churches of Galatia, so you also are to do. [2]On the first day of every week, each of you is to put something aside and store it up, as he may prosper, so that there will be no collecting when I come. [3]And when I arrive, I will send those whom you accredit by letter to carry your gift to Jerusalem. [4]If it seems advisable that I should go also, they will accompany me" (ESV).

INTERPRETATION

Why would it be important to bring the *"full tithe"* to the storehouse?

What would be the difference between tithes and offerings?

What does it mean to give as one *"may prosper"*?

How have you seen or experienced God blessing those who faithfully give?

APPLICATION

How can you apply the principles of these passages to your finances and possessions?

HOWARD'S HIGHLIGHTS

Amount to Give

Let's survey what the Bible says about how much to give. Before the Old Testament Law, there were two instances of giving a known amount. In Genesis 14:20, Abraham gave 10 percent – a tithe – after the rescue of his nephew Lot. And in Genesis 28:22, Jacob promised to give the Lord a tenth of all his possessions if God brought him safely through his journey.

With the Law came the requirement of the tithe. The Lord condemns the children of Israel in Malachi 3:8-9 for not tithing properly: *"Will man rob God? Yet you are robbing me. But you say, 'How have we robbed you?' In your tithes and contributions. You are cursed with a curse, for you are robbing me, the whole nation of you"* (ESV).

In addition to the tithe, there were various offerings. The Lord also made special provisions for the poor. Every seven years all debts were forgiven; every 50 years the land was returned to the original land-owning families. Special harvesting rules allowed the poor to glean behind the harvesters.

God made another significant provision for the poor in Deuteronomy 15:7-8: *"If there is a poor person among you, one of your brothers, in any of your towns in your land which the Lord your God is giving you, you shall not harden your heart, nor close your hand from your poor brother; but you shall fully open your hand to him, and generously lend him enough for his need in whatever he lacks."* Even under the law, the extent of one's giving was not to be limited by a locked-in fixed percentage but was to be adjusted by surrounding needs.

The New Testament teaches that we are to give in proportion to the material blessing we receive. It also commends sacrificial giving.

What I like about the tithe is that it's systematic, and the amount of the gift is easy to compute. The danger of the tithe is that it can be treated as simply "another bill" to be paid. If we fall into that sort of attitude or rut, we won't be in a position to receive God's richest blessings.

Another potential danger of tithing is the assumption that once we have tithed, we have fulfilled all our obligations to give. For many Christians, the tithe should be the beginning of their giving, not the limit. And we should never, never close our hearts to the obvious needs we encounter in our path through life.

Approach to giving

During Paul's third missionary journey, one of his priorities was to take up a collection for the suffering believers in Jerusalem. We draw several practical applications from his instructions concerning this collection. *"On the first day of every week, each of you is to put aside and save as he may prosper, so that no collections need to be made when I come"* (1 Corinthians 16:2).

Giving should be periodic. *"On the first day of every week . . ."* The Lord understands that we need to give frequently. Giving only once a year is a mistake. We need to give regularly to be drawn consistently to Christ.

Giving should be personal. *"Each of you is to . . ."* It is the responsibility of every child of God, whether young or old, rich or poor, to give. The advantages of giving are intended for each person, and each one must participate to enjoy them to the full.

Giving should be out of a private deposit. *"Put aside and save . . ."* If you experience difficulty in monitoring the money you have decided to give, consider opening a separate account or setting aside a special "cookie jar" into which you deposit the money you intend to give. Then, as needs are brought to your attention, the money is ready to meet those needs.

Giving should be a priority. *"Honor the Lord from your wealth, and from* ***the first*** *of all your produce"* (Proverbs 3:9, emphasis added). As soon as we receive any income, we should set aside the amount we are going to give. This habit helps us to put Christ first in all we do – and defeats the temptation to spend what we have decided to give.

Giving should be premeditated. *"Each one must do just as he has decided in his heart"* (2 Corinthians 9:7). We should give prayerfully, exercising the same care in selecting where we give as we do when deciding where to invest.

PRAYERS FOR TODAY

This prayer section is for personal use and isn't meant to be part of the group discussion.

For you...

For your family and friends...

For those in your group...

3 - DAY THREE

Homework

Giving and the Oppressed

PRAYER

Pray for the Holy Spirit's guidance as you begin reading passages of Scripture. Ask for clarity and insight as you engage in God's word.

SCRIPTURE READING

Read Matthew 25:31-46.

"When the Son of Man comes in his glory, and all the angels with him, then
he will sit on his glorious throne. 32Before him will be gathered all the nations,
and he will separate people one from another as a shepherd separates the
sheep from the goats. 33And he will place the sheep on his right, but the goats on the left. 34Then
the King will say to those on his right, 'Come, you who are blessed by my Father, inherit the
kingdom prepared for you from the foundation of the world. 35For I was hungry and you gave
me food, I was thirsty and you gave me drink, I was a stranger and you welcomed me, 36I was
naked and you clothed me, I was sick and you visited me, I was in prison and you came to me.'
37Then the righteous will answer him, saying, 'Lord, when did we see you hungry and feed you,
or thirsty and give you drink? 38And when did we see you a stranger and welcome you, or naked
and clothe you? 39And when did we see you sick or in prison and visit you?' 40And the King will
answer them, 'Truly, I say to you, as you did it to one of the least of these my brothers, you did it
to me.' 41"Then he will say to those on his left, 'Depart from me, you cursed, into the eternal fire
prepared for the devil and his angels. 42For I was hungry and you gave me no food, I was thirsty
and you gave me no drink, 43I was a stranger and you did not welcome me, naked and you did
not clothe me, sick and in prison and you did not visit me.' 44Then they also will answer, saying,
'Lord, when did we see you hungry or thirsty or a stranger or naked or sick or in prison, and did
not minister to you?' 45Then he will answer them, saying, 'Truly, I say to you, as you did not do
it to one of the least of these, you did not do it to me.' 46And these will go away into eternal
punishment, but the righteous into eternal life" (ESV).

OBSERVATION

What does this passage say about...

God?

People?

The oppressed?

3 - DAY THREE

Homework

SCRIPTURE READING

Read Matthew 25:31-46.

*"When the Son of Man comes in his glory, and all the angels with him, then he
will sit on his glorious throne. 32 Before him will be gathered all the nations, and
he will separate people one from another as a shepherd separates the sheep
from the goats. 33 And he will place the sheep on his right, but the goats on the
left. 34 Then the King will say to those on his right, 'Come, you who are blessed
by my Father, inherit the kingdom prepared for you from the foundation of the
world. 35 For I was hungry and you gave me food, I was thirsty and you gave me
drink, I was a stranger and you welcomed me, 36 I was naked and you clothed
me, I was sick and you visited me, I was in prison and you came to me.' 37 Then
the righteous will answer him, saying, 'Lord, when did we see you hungry and
feed you, or thirsty and give you drink? 38 And when did we see you a stranger
and welcome you, or naked and clothe you? 39 And when did we see you sick or
in prison and visit you?' 40 And the King will answer them, 'Truly, I say to you, as
you did it to one of the least of these my brothers, you did it to me.' 41 "Then
he will say to those on his left, 'Depart from me, you cursed, into the eternal
fire prepared for the devil and his angels. 42 For I was hungry and you gave me
no food, I was thirsty and you gave me no drink, 43 I was a stranger and you did
not welcome me, naked and you did not clothe me, sick and in prison and you
did not visit me.' 44 Then they also will answer, saying, 'Lord, when did we see
you hungry or thirsty or a stranger or naked or sick or in prison, and did not
minister to you?' 45 Then he will answer them, saying, 'Truly, I say to you, as you
did not do it to one of the least of these, you did not do it to me.' 46 And these
will go away into eternal punishment, but the righteous into eternal life" (ESV).*

INTERPRETATION

What does this passage mean to you?

What can we learn from the "*sheep*"?

What can we learn from the "*goats*"?

How have you seen or experienced people helping the oppressed?

APPLICATION

The Generosity Grid

(see the following page for details)

3 - DAY THREE

The Generosity Grid:

Just as investors seek to grow investment portfolios on earth, so wise followers of Christ should view their giving as growing a giving portfolio in heaven. In Matthew 6:20, Jesus instructs us, *"Store up for yourselves treasures in heaven."* We believe that the Lord wants us to have an investor mentality when considering funding the work of God.

The Generosity Grid is intended to help you evaluate your giving. Few will have a perfectly balanced giving portfolio. For most, their giving is going to be more heavily weighted toward a ministry or need for which God has given them a particular passion.

The top of the grid represents the basic categories of recipients: your church, evangelism, discipleship, and the needy. The other axis represents geography. Christ said, *". . . You shall be My witnesses both in Jerusalem and in all Judea, and Samaria, and as far as the remotest part of the earth"* (Acts 1:8). Similarly, we have divided the geography into local (Jerusalem), national (Judea), and global (remotest parts of the earth).

Here's how it works:

1. *Fill in the appropriate amount for your income.*
2. *Prayerfully evaluate dollar amounts for giving to the different categories in the grid. We provide this grid as a reminder of the different areas of impact your giving can have and to challenge you to prayerfully determine where the Lord would have you give.*
3. *As you enter dollar amounts on the electronic version, the grid will calculate your percentage of giving based on your income.*

Income: ______________________________

% of giving	Church	Evangelism	Discipleship	Needy
Local				
National				
Global				

PRAYERS FOR TODAY

This prayer section is for personal use and isn't meant to be part of the group discussion.

For you...

For your family and friends...

For those in your group...

3 - DAY FOUR

Homework

**Compass – finances God's way does not recommend any investments. No one is authorized to use affiliation with Compass to promote the sale of any investments or financial services.*

Investing & Wealth

PRAYER

Pray for the Holy Spirit's guidance as you begin reading passages of Scripture. Ask for clarity and insight as you engage in God's word.

SCRIPTURE READING

Read Ecclesiastes 5:10-15.

*"He who loves money will not be satisfied with money, nor he who loves wealth
with his income; this also is vanity. 11When goods increase, they increase who
eat them, and what advantage has their owner but to see them with his eyes? 12Sweet is the
sleep of a laborer, whether he eats little or much, but the full stomach of the rich will not let him
sleep. 13There is a grievous evil that I have seen under the sun: riches were kept by their owner
to his hurt, 14and those riches were lost in a bad venture. And he is father of a son, but he has
nothing in his hand. 15As he came from his mother's womb he shall go again, naked as he came,
and shall take nothing for his toil that he may carry away in his hand" (ESV).*

Read Ecclesiastes 11:1-6.

*"Cast your bread upon the waters, for you will find it after many days. 2Give a portion to seven,
or even to eight, for you know not what disaster may happen on earth. 3If the clouds are full of
rain, they empty themselves on the earth, and if a tree falls to the south or to the north, in the
place where the tree falls, there it will lie. 4He who observes the wind will not sow, and he who
regards the clouds will not reap. 5As you do not know the way the spirit comes to the bones in
the womb of a woman with child, so you do not know the work of God who makes everything. 6In
the morning sow your seed, and at evening withhold not your hand, for you do not know which
will prosper, this or that, or whether both alike will be good" (ESV).*

OBSERVATION

What do these passages say about...

Riches and wealth?

Planning?

Risk?

3 - DAY FOUR

Homework

SCRIPTURE READING

Read Ecclesiastes 5:10-15.

*"He who loves money will not be satisfied with money, nor he who loves wealth
with his income; this also is vanity. [11]When goods increase, they increase who
eat them, and what advantage has their owner but to see them with his eyes?
[12]Sweet is the sleep of a laborer, whether he eats little or much, but the full
stomach of the rich will not let him sleep. [13]There is a grievous evil that I have
seen under the sun: riches were kept by their owner to his hurt, [14]and those
riches were lost in a bad venture. And he is father of a son, but he has nothing
in his hand. [15]As he came from his mother's womb he shall go again, naked as
he came, and shall take nothing for his toil that he may carry away in his hand"
(ESV).*

Read Ecclesiastes 11:1-6.

*"Cast your bread upon the waters, for you will find it after many days. [2]Give a
portion to seven, or even to eight, for you know not what disaster may happen
on earth. [3]If the clouds are full of rain, they empty themselves on the earth,
and if a tree falls to the south or to the north, in the place where the tree falls,
there it will lie. [4]He who observes the wind will not sow, and he who regards the
clouds will not reap. [5]As you do not know the way the spirit comes to the bones
in the womb of a woman with child, so you do not know the work of God who
makes everything. [6]In the morning sow your seed, and at evening withhold not
your hand, for you do not know which will prosper, this or that, or whether both
alike will be good" (ESV).*

INTERPRETATION

What do these passages mean to you?

What does giving a portion to *"seven, or even to eight"* look like for investing today?

How has investing impacted your finances?

APPLICATION

How can you apply the principles of these passages to your finances?

HOWARD'S HIGHLIGHTS

Investing warnings

Let's face it – most people want to get rich. I'll never forget how surprised I was the first time I realized the Bible's caution against it: *"Those who want to get rich fall into temptation and a trap and into many foolish and harmful desires that plunge men into ruin and destruction"* (1 Timothy 6:9, NIV). This verse declares that those who want to get rich give in to temptations and desires that ultimately lead to ruin. Wanting to get rich is incredibly dangerous, but why?

The next verse answers that question: *"For the love of money is a root of all kinds of evil. Some people, eager for money, have wandered away from the faith and pierced themselves with many griefs"* (1 Timothy 6:10, NIV). When we want to get rich, we actually love money. That has consequences I witnessed firsthand. Mike, a close friend, became consumed by a desire to get rich. He finally abandoned his wife and four young sons, and later denied Christ.

For much of my life I too wanted to become rich. Not just a little rich, but filthy rich! So dealing with this attitude in my own heart has been difficult. Here's what I discovered: When I wanted to get rich, my motivations were pride, greed, or an unhealthy urge to prepare for uncertain economic times. I loved money. However, after I learned God's perspective, my motive completely changed. I wanted to be a faithful steward, wisely investing the money God entrusted to me. I simply wanted to please Him. I loved God.

Is it wrong, then, to become rich? No, that's not what I'm saying here. Many heroes of the faith, such as Job, Abraham, and David, were rich. In fact, I rejoice when God enables a person who has been a faithful steward to prosper. Nothing is wrong with becoming wealthy if it is a by-product of being faithful.

Overcoming the temptation

How then, can a believer in Christ overcome the love of money and the desire to become rich? Let me put it in two words: split and submit.

Paul told Timothy to *"flee from [the desire to get rich], you man of God, and pursue righteousness, godliness, faith, love, perseverance and gentleness"* (1 Timothy 6:11). When you become aware of a desire to get rich, run from it!

You might begin by analyzing just what it is that triggers your desire. I discovered a habit of dreaming about wealth when I would take a long car trip. I broke the habit by listening to Christian radio and music to help me concentrate on the Lord instead.

The ultimate way of escape is submitting to the Lord. We can do this confidently because Jesus overcame a huge temptation to become rich. After fasting 40 days, He was tempted three times by the devil. Here's the final temptation: *"[the devil] led [Jesus] up and showed Him all the kingdoms of the world in a moment of time. And the devil said to Him, 'I will give You all this domain and its glory . . . if You worship before me'"* (Luke 4:5-7).

Jesus was offered all the kingdoms of the world in an instant. Because of His complete submission to God the Father, He was empowered by the same Holy Spirit who lives in us to resist that temptation.

I believe that our heavenly Father does not usually allow His children to prosper when they are motivated to get rich. Wanting to get rich – loving money – closely parallels greed. And *". . . greed . . . amounts to idolatry"* (Colossians 3:5). It is for our sake that the Father protects us from loving anything that would draw us away from Him.

PRAYERS FOR TODAY

This prayer section is for personal use and isn't meant to be part of the group discussion.

For you...

For your family and friends...

For those in your group...

3 - DAY FIVE

Homework

**Compass – finances God's way does not recommend any investments. No one is authorized to use affiliation with Compass to promote the sale of any investments or financial services.*

Proverbs & Investing

PRAYER

Pray for the Holy Spirit's guidance as you begin reading passages of Scripture. Ask for clarity and insight as you engage in God's word.

SCRIPTURE READING

Read the following Proverbs.

"The plans of the diligent lead surely to abundance, but everyone who is hasty comes only to poverty" (Proverbs 21:5, ESV).

"Know well the condition of your flocks, and give attention to your herds, for riches do not last forever; and does a crown endure to all generations?" (Proverbs 27:23-24, ESV).

"The prudent sees danger and hides himself, but the simple go on and suffer for it" (Proverbs 27:12, ESV).

"A faithful man will abound with blessings, but whoever hastens to be rich will not go unpunished" (Proverbs 28:20, ESV).

"Whoever oppresses the poor to increase his own wealth, or gives to the rich, will only come to poverty" (Proverbs 22:16, ESV).

"Wealth gained hastily will dwindle, but whoever gathers little by little will increase it" (Proverbs 13:11, ESV).

OBSERVATION

What do these verses say about...

Abundance and wealth?

Awareness?

Suffering and Poverty?

Homework

SCRIPTURE READING

Read the following Proverbs.

"The plans of the diligent lead surely to abundance, but everyone who is hasty comes only to poverty" (Proverbs 21:5, ESV).

"Know well the condition of your flocks, and give attention to your herds, for riches do not last forever; and does a crown endure to all generations?" (Proverbs 27:23-24, ESV).

"The prudent sees danger and hides himself, but the simple go on and suffer for it" (Proverbs 27:12, ESV).

"A faithful man will abound with blessings, but whoever hastens to be rich will not go unpunished" (Proverbs 28:20, ESV).

"Whoever oppresses the poor to increase his own wealth, or gives to the rich, will only come to poverty" (Proverbs 22:16, ESV).

"Wealth gained hastily will dwindle, but whoever gathers little by little will increase it" (Proverbs 13:11, ESV).

INTERPRETATION

What does it mean to know the condition of our flocks and herds?

What does it mean to be prudent?

What might *"wealth gained hastily"* look like today?

Which of these Proverbs resonated most with you? Why?

APPLICATION

Begin working on the Compass Construction Plan

THE COMPASS CONSTRUCTION PLAN

Over the last three chapters, you've learned and applied God's word on being a steward, debt, saving, giving, and investing.

Now it's time to develop a plan, and that's where the Compass Construction Plan comes in. The plan's four phases will help you set goals for each phase of your plan. Here's how it works.

The Compass Construction Plan

Starting Well

Taking this study indicates that you are starting well. Remember two things as you continue:

- Learning and applying God's way of handling money is a lifelong adventure. As you faithfully seek Him, God will faithfully lead you - in every phase.
- Financial discipleship is more than getting your finances in order: it's about helping others get their finances in order as well. So, don't hold it all in until the end: share with others what God is teaching you in every phase along the way.

The Four Phases

Review the Compass Construction Plan phase descriptions on the following pages.

- Check off the boxes you've already completed.
- The first uncompleted box determines your starting point. Once you've completed that phase, move on to the next phase of the plan.

Finishing Well

The finish line for your construction plan has only one question. And it isn't, "Did you pay off your house?" Or, "Did you become debt free?" Or, "Did you adequately fund your retirement?" These accomplishments are all great and worthy of celebrating, but here's the real question: "Have you been faithful with everything God has entrusted to you?"

Finishing Well is taking what God has given you and being faithful with it during every construction phase. Doing this brings you to the true finish line in which you will be able to hear Jesus say, "Well done, good and faithful servant . . . Enter into the joy of your master."

Each Phase, Step by Step:

PHASE 1

- **Start Giving** - And as we learned in this study, ten percent is a great place to start.
- **Create an Emergency Fund of $1000** - Emergencies are unexpected, unbudgeted expenses that whack us all. Why save for emergencies? Because emergencies happen! The refrigerator goes on the fritz, cars break down, health crises hit the family. If you have saved for emergencies, you don't have to pile up debt to pay for them.
- **Pay off Credit Card Debt** - Focus on paying off your credit cards first, because they usually have the highest interest rate. And don't forget to implement the Snowball Strategy!
- **Start Investing** - Remember, length of time is a critical factor when investing, so the sooner you start, the better. Don't be overly concerned with the amount at this stage. The goal is to start, even if it is a small amount. This could include contributing to retirement accounts like a 401k, a Roth IRA, or accounts for higher education.

PHASE 2

- **Reevaluate Giving** - You have just paid off your credit cards and should now have some extra money. Evaluate your giving and pray about increasing it, whether to current ministries or additional ones.
- **Build your Emergency Fund** - After saving $1000, gradually increase your emergency savings to at least three month's living expenses. Keep these savings in an account that is safe and easily accessible.
- **Pay off Consumer Debt** - Pay off auto loans and any other household debt (including student loans) by continuing to use the Snowball Strategy.
- **Reevaluate Investing** - With credit cards paid off, you should have a little extra money. Evaluate your investments and pray about whether you should increase any contributions.

PHASE 3

- **Reevaluate Giving** - You have just paid off your consumer debt and should now have some extra money. Evaluate your giving and pray about increasing it.
- **Save for Major Purchases** - These could include a car, children's education, a house down-payment, or family vacations. Major purchases don't pay for themselves, and you don't want to rely on credit to fund them. Prioritize major purchases, determine the cost, and start saving for whatever you've decided to tackle first.
- **Pre-Pay Home Mortgage** - Focus on paying off your house by adding an extra amount to your payment each month. This will reduce the principal, save a ton of interest, and help you pay off your home more quickly.
- **Reevaluate Investing** - Now free of consumer debt, you can again pray about increasing investment contributions.

PHASE 4

- **Reevaluate Giving** - Pray about increasing your giving to current or additional ministries. Also pray about what your giving will look like once you pay off your home.
- **Save for Major Purchases** - Continue saving for major purchases and prayerfully identify what purchases are top priorities for this phase.
- **Pay off Home Mortgage** - Continue pre-paying your home mortgage until it is paid off.
- **Reevaluate Investing** - Continue to evaluate your investing. Prayerfully consider what your contributions to investments will look like once your home is paid for. This is also a good time to ask the question, "How much is enough?" to determine an investment finish line.

ADDITIONAL DIRECTIONS FOR YOUR PLAN

1. The Compass Construction Plan is designed to guide you through whatever phase you are in. There may be times where you have to go back to a previous phase. For example, if you had an unexpected expense in Phase 3, you may have to temporarily go back to Phase 2 and rebuild your emergency account before continuing to focus on your Phase 3 goals. Don't be discouraged by these perceived setbacks; every building project has them. You can be patient, because God is faithful.

2. Celebrate. Before moving on to a new phase, don't forget to celebrate your faithfulness with God's provision. Celebrating these milestones is a great way to honor the Lord and encourage your family.

The Compass Construction Plan

Starting Well ▶

- ❑ Begin your journey of learning and applying God's way of handling money.
- ❑ Commit to multiply what you learn by sharing it with others during all phases of your journey.

Phase 1

- ❑ Start giving
- ❑ Create an emergency fund
- ❑ Pay off credit card debt
- ❑ Start investing

Phase 2

- ❑ Reevaluate giving
- ❑ Increase emergency fund
- ❑ Pay off consumer debt
- ❑ Reevaluate investing

Phase 3

- ❑ Reevaluate giving
- ❑ Save for major purchases
- ❑ Pre-pay home mortgage
- ❑ Reevaluate investing

Phase 4

- ❑ Reevaluate giving
- ❑ Save for major purchases
- ❑ Pay off home mortgage
- ❑ Reevaluate investing

Finishing Well ▶

Continue to learn, apply and multiply God's way of handling money so that you may one day hear, "Well done, good and faithful servant. Enter into the joy of your master."

PRAYERS FOR TODAY

This prayer section is for personal use and isn't meant to be part of the group discussion.

For you...

For your family and friends...

For those in your group...

See Their Story...

See how generosity completely changed this couple's life.

See how "steady plodding" dramatically impacted this couple's financial discipleship journey.

You can also watch these amazing stories at compasstools.org

Additional Tools for the Journey!

To help you on your financial discipleship journey, we have provided practical resources from a variety of people in the financial world. Visit us at **compasstools.org** to check out these resources.

Step One:

Watch the Video

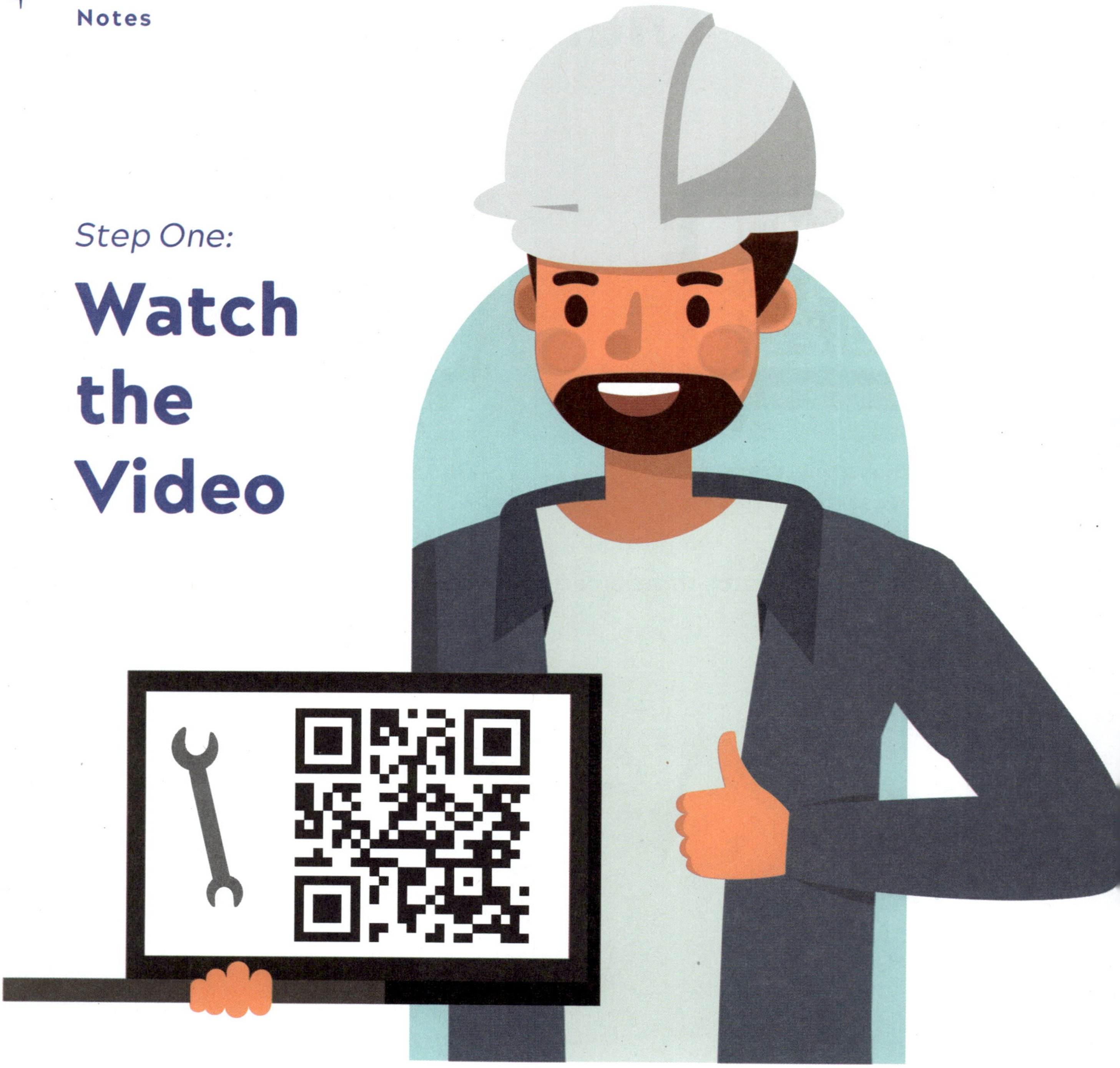

Open the camera on your phone to scan the QR code

OR

*Visit **compasstools.org** to view the video for this chapter*

Step Two:

Read the Notes

Not a fan of reading? You can listen to these notes at compasstools.org

Generosity

Few areas of the Christian life can be more misunderstood and frustrating than that of generosity. For several years after I met Christ, I did my best to avoid giving. On those occasions when I felt obligated to give in order to appear spiritual, I did so, but my heart wasn't in it.

My whole perspective changed after learning what the Bible actually teaches. Suddenly I wanted to be generous. But then I was frustrated by another problem: an unlimited number of needs versus my limited resources. How should I decide where to give? My church, the hungry poor, campus and prison ministries, missionary efforts, radio and television programs, and many other vital ministries needed financial support.

Intense competition for resources makes these decisions even more difficult. It seems as if my inbox and mailbox are full of appeals. I react to these requests with mixed emotions: compassion, gratitude, guilt, and even cynicism. I feel deep compassion and almost despair when confronted with those facing starvation of body or spirit. I am grateful for the people dedicated to meet those needs, and I feel guilty that perhaps we aren't giving enough. At other times, however, I feel cynical about being solicited – and perhaps manipulated – by people whose goals may be worthwhile but whose methods are questionable.

Notes

Advantages of Giving

Gifts obviously benefit the recipient. The church continues its ministry, the hungry are fed, the naked are clothed, and missionaries are sent. But in God's economy, gifts given with the proper attitude benefit the giver more than the receiver. ". . . Remember the words of the Lord Jesus, that He Himself said, *'It is more blessed to give than to receive'*" (Acts 20:35). As we examine Scripture, we find that the giver benefits in four significant areas.

AN INCREASE IN INTIMACY Above all else, giving directs our heart to Christ. Matthew 6:21 tells us, *"For where your treasure is, there your heart will be also."* This is why it's necessary to give each gift to the person of Jesus Christ: it draws our heart to Him.

Do you remember the faithful steward in the parable of the talents, and his eventual reward? *"Enter into the joy of your Master"* (Matthew 25:21). Giving is one of your responsibilities as a steward, and the more faithful you are in fulfilling your responsibilities, the more you can enter into the joy of knowing Christ more closely. Nothing in life compares with that.

AN INCREASE IN CHARACTER Our heavenly Father wants us – His children – to conform to the image of His Son. The character of Christ is that of an unselfish giver. Unfortunately, humans are selfish by nature. One essential way we become conformed to Christ is by regular giving. Someone once said, "Giving is not God's way of raising money; it is God's way of raising people into the likeness of His Son."

AN INCREASE IN HEAVEN Matthew 6:20 reads, *"Store up for yourselves treasures in heaven, where neither moth nor rust destroys, and where thieves do not break in or steal."* The Lord tells us that heaven has its own "First National Bank," where we can invest for eternity.

Paul wrote, *"Not that I seek the gift itself, but I seek the profit which increases to your account"* (Philippians 4:17). Each of us has an account in heaven that we will be able to enjoy for eternity. And although it's true that we "can't take it with us when we die," Scripture teaches that we can make deposits to our heavenly account before we die.

AN INCREASE ON EARTH Many people have a hard time believing that giving results in material blessings flowing back to the giver. Time and again, however, we encounter this very principle in the pages of Scripture.

Consider Proverbs 11:24-25: *"There is one who scatters, and yet increases all the more, and there is one who withholds what is justly due, and yet it results only in poverty. A generous person will be prosperous, and one who gives others plenty of water will himself be given plenty."*

Examine 2 Corinthians 9:6-11, *". . . the one who sows sparingly will also reap sparingly, and the one who sows generously will also reap generously. . . . God is able to make all grace overflow to you, so that, always having all sufficiency in everything, you may have an abundance for every good deed. . . . Now He who supplies seed to the sower and bread for food will supply and multiply your seed for sowing and increase the harvest of your righteousness; you will be enriched in everything for all liberality."*

These verses clearly teach that giving results in a material increase: *"will also reap generously . . . always having all sufficiency in everything . . . may have an abundance . . . will supply and multiply your seed . . . you will be enriched in everything."*

But note carefully why the Lord returns a material increase: *"Always having all sufficiency in everything, you may have an abundance for every good deed . . . will supply and multiply your seed for sowing . . . you will be enriched in everything for all liberality."* As shown in the diagram below, the Lord produces an increase so that we may give more and have our needs met at the same time.

Study the Circle of Giving. One reason the Lord reveals that we can anticipate a material increase is because He wants us to recognize that He is behind it. God has chosen to be invisible, but He wants us to experience His reality.

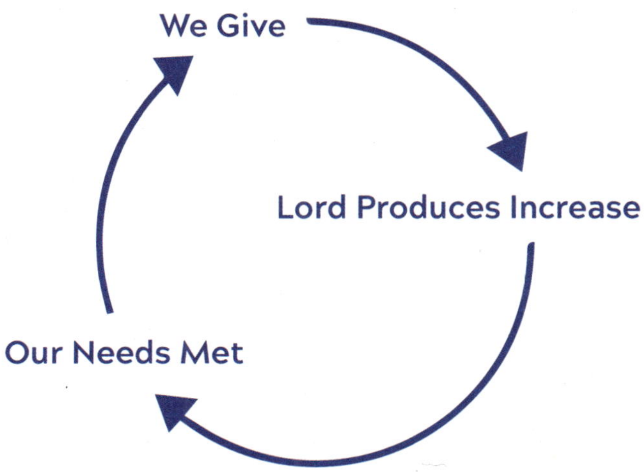

Circle of Generosity Diagram

When we give, we should do so with a sense of expectation – anticipating an increase from the Lord even though we have no idea how or when He may choose to provide it. Our experience has shown Him to be very creative! Remember, givers experience the advantages of giving only when they give cheerfully and with love – not when the motive is just to get.

Notes

Places For Giving

The Bible instructs us to give to three areas: the local church, ministries, and the poor and needy.

GIVING TO THE LOCAL CHURCH AND CHRISTIAN MINISTRIES Throughout its pages the Bible focuses on funding the ministry. The Old Testament priesthood received specific support: *"To the sons of Levi, behold, I have given all the tithe in Israel . . . in return for their service which they perform"* (Numbers 18:21). And New Testament teaching on ministerial support is just as strong. Unfortunately, some have wrongly taught poverty for Christian workers, influencing many to believe that everyone in Christian ministry should be poor. That position simply isn't scriptural. Listen to Paul's words to Timothy: *"Pastors who do their work well should be paid well and should be highly appreciated, especially those who work hard at both preaching and teaching"* (1 Timothy 5:17, TLB).

God never intended His servants to exist at the level of bare subsistence. Over the years, we have seen how many Christian workers have actually been distracted from their ministry and rendered less effective because of their inadequate support. As someone has said, "The poor and starving pastor should exist only among poor and starving people."

People ask us if we give only through our church. In our case, the answer is no. However, giving to the local church should be a priority as a tangible expression of our commitment to it. But we also give to others who directly impact us. *"The one who is taught the word is to share all good things with the one who teaches"* (Galatians 6:6).

GIVING TO THE POOR Matthew 25:34-45 teaches one of the most exciting and yet sobering truths in the Bible. Read this passage carefully.

"The King will say. . . 'For I was hungry and you gave Me something to eat; I was thirsty, and you gave Me something to drink.' . . . Then the righteous will answer Him, 'Lord, when did we see You hungry, and feed You, or thirsty, and give You something to drink?' . . . The King will answer and say to them . . . 'To the extent that you did it for one of the least of these brothers or sisters of Mine, you did it for Me.'

"Then He will also say to those on His left, 'Depart from Me, you accursed people, into the eternal fire. . . for I was hungry, and you gave Me nothing to eat; I was thirsty, and you gave Me nothing to drink . . . To the extent that you did not do it for one of the least of these, you did not do it for Me.'"

In a mysterious way we cannot fully understand, Jesus, the Creator of all things, personally identifies Himself with the poor. When we share with the needy, we are actually sharing with Jesus Himself. If that truth is staggering, then this is terrifying: when we do not give to the needy, we leave Christ Himself hungry and thirsty.

During Christ's earthly ministry, He consistently gave to the poor. When Jesus told Judas to go and carry out the betrayal during the Last Supper, *"none of those reclining at the table knew for what purpose He had said this to him. For some were assuming, since Judas kept the money box, that Jesus was saying to him, 'Buy the things we have need of for the feast'; or else, that he was to give something to the poor"* (John 13:28-29).

Giving to the needy was such a consistent part of Jesus' life that the disciples assumed He was sending Judas either to buy needed food or to give to the poor; no other alternative entered their minds.

After Paul met with the disciples to announce his ministry to the Gentiles, he said, *"They [the disciples] only asked us to remember the poor – the very thing I also was eager to do"* (Galatians 2:10). Think of all the issues the disciples could have discussed with Paul. But the only request they made was to remember the poor. Now that should tell us something!

Three areas of our Christian life are affected by whether we give to the poor.

PRAYER A lack of giving to the poor could be a source of unanswered prayer. *"Is this not the fast that I choose . . . to break your bread with the hungry and bring the homeless poor into the house? . . . Then you will call and the Lord will answer"* (Isaiah 58:6-9). *"One who shuts his ear to the outcry of the poor will also call out himself and not be answered"* (Proverbs 21:13).

PROVISION Our giving to the needy may determine our provision. *"One who gives to the poor will never lack anything, but one who shuts his eyes will have many curses"* (Proverbs 28:27).

KNOWING JESUS CHRIST INTIMATELY Those who refuse or neglect to share resources with the poor don't know the Lord as intimately as they could. "'He pled the cause of the afflicted and the poor, then it was well. Is that not what it means to know Me?' declares the Lord" (Jeremiah 22:16).

Giving to the poor has been discouraged, in part, because of government programs. But it's the church's job, not the government's, to meet the needs of the poor. The government often treats the needy impersonally, while the church has the potential to be sensitive to their dignity. We can also develop one-on-one relationships to meet their immediate physical needs – and then go on to focus on their longer-term physical and spiritual needs. Mother Theresa is one of the best examples in our time of serving the poor in a loving,

Notes

compassionate way.

If you don't already know some needy people, please consider asking the Lord to bring one into your life. You can do so by praying this prayer: "Father God, by Your grace create in me the desire to share with the needy. Bring a poor person into my life so that I might learn what it really means to give." This will be a significant step in maturing your relationship with Christ.

May we echo Job's statement: "I saved the poor who cried for help, and the orphan who had no helper . . . I made the widow's heart sing for joy . . . I was eyes to those who were blind and feet to those who could not walk. I was a father to the poor, and I investigated the case which I did not know" (Job 29:12-16).

SECULAR CHARITIES Numerous secular charities (schools, fraternal orders, organizations that fight diseases) compete vigorously for our donations. The Bible doesn't address (in so many words) whether we should give to these charities. Our family, however, has decided not to make these organizations part of our regular giving. Our reason is that even though many people support secular charities, only those who know the Lord support the ministries of Christ. We do, however, occasionally give to secular charities when the solicitor is a friend we want to encourage or influence for Christ, or we sense the Lord's specific prompting to give.

Investing

The Bible provides us with five basic guidelines for investing.

1. BE A STEADY PLODDER

The fundamental principle for becoming a successful investor is to spend less than you earn, and regularly invest the surplus. In other words, be a steady plodder. The Bible says, *"Steady plodding brings prosperity, hasty speculation brings poverty"* (Proverbs 21:5, TLB). The original words for "steady plodding" picture a person filling a large barrel one handful at a time. Little by little the barrel is filled.

Nothing replaces steady consistent, month-after-month investing. Just do it – regardless of the investment climate – because when you do, your investments will grow through compounding.

It has been said, "Compounding is the greatest mathematical discovery of all time." Compounding occurs when your investment's earnings are added to the principal, allowing both the earnings and the principal to grow.

2. AVOID RISKY INVESTMENTS

God warns us to avoid risky investments, yet each year thousands of people lose money in highly speculative investments and scams. Ecclesiastes 5:13-15 says, *"There is another serious problem I have seen everywhere – savings are put into risky investments that turn sour, and soon there is nothing left to pass on to one's son. The man who speculates is soon back to where he began – with nothing"* (TLB).

How many times have you heard of people losing their life's savings on some can't-miss, get-rich-quick scheme? Sadly, it seems that Christians are particularly vulnerable to scams because they trust others who appear to live by their same values. If you are offered an investment opportunity that seems too good to be true, it's probably too good to be true!

The strategy for avoiding scams or risky investments is to pray, seek wise counsel, and do your homework.

3. DIVERSIFY

Money can be lost on any investment. Stocks, bonds, real estate, gold – you name it – can perform well or poorly. Each investment has its own advantages and disadvantages.

Since the perfect investment doesn't exist, we need to diversify and not put all our eggs in one basket. *"Divide your portion to seven, or even to eight, for you do not know what misfortune may occur on the earth"* (Ecclesiastes 11:2).

Notes

4. COUNT THE COST

Every investment has costs: financial, time, effort, and sometimes even emotional stress. For example, a rental house will require time and effort to rent and maintain. If the tenant is irresponsible, you may have to try to collect rent from someone who doesn't want to pay – talk about emotions! Before you decide on any investment, consider all the costs.

5. LISTEN TO WISE AND EXPERIENCED COUNSEL

The decision to purchase or sell an investment is best made prayerfully. Despite what so-called financial experts and pundits so confidently express about what will happen to investments in the future, no one knows except the Lord. No one. Period!

God wants to be involved in every area of your finances, including investing. So humbly ask Him for wisdom as you consider an investment. Isaiah 48:17 says, *"I am the Lord your God, who teaches you to benefit, who leads you in the way you should go."* In Luke 8:18, Jesus warns us, *"So take care how you listen."* You could paraphrase those words like this: Be careful what you listen to. And be especially careful of receiving investment advice from those who do not have a biblical view of money.

Understanding Compounding

There are three variables in compounding: the amount you save, the percentage rate you earn, and the length of time you save.

THE AMOUNT The amount you save depends on your income and spending. We hope you will increase the amount available for saving as you learn God's way of handling money.

RATE OF RETURN The second variable is the rate you earn on an investment. The following table demonstrates how an investment of $1,000 a year grows at various rates.

Rate Earned	Year 5	Year 10	Year 20	Year 30	Year 40
4%	$5,633	$12,486	$30,969	$58,328	$98,827
6%	$5,975	$13,972	$38,993	$83,802	$164,048
8%	$6,336	$15,645	$49,423	$122,346	$279,781
10%	$6,716	$17,531	$63,002	$180,943	$486,852
12%	$7,115	$19,655	$80,699	$270,293	$859,142

As you can see, an increase in rate has a remarkable effect on the amount accumulated. A two percent increase almost doubles the total over 40 years. But since higher returns usually also carry higher risks, be careful not to shoot for unrealistic returns.

TIME Time is the third factor. Answer this: Who would accumulate more by age 65: Danielle who started saving $1,000 a year at age 21, saved for eight years, and then completely stopped; or Matt who saved $1,000 a year for 37 years starting at age 29? Both earned 10 percent. Is it Danielle who saved a total of $8,000 or Matt who saved $37,000? ***Check out the chart on the next page.***

Notes

Investments

	DANIELLE		MATT	
AGE	CONTRIBUTION	YEAR-END VALUE	CONTRIBUTION	YEAR-END VALUE
21	1,000	1,100	0	0
22	1,000	2,310	0	0
23	1,000	3,641	0	0
24	1,000	5,105	0	0
25	1,000	6,716	0	0
26	1,000	8,487	0	0
27	1,000	10,436	0	0
28	1,000	12,579	0	0
29	0	13,837	1,000	1,100
30	0	15,221	1,000	2,310
31	0	16,743	1,000	3,641
32	0	18,417	1,000	5,105
33	0	20,259	1,000	6,716
34	0	22,284	1,000	8,487
35	0	22,513	1,000	10,436
36	0	26,964	1,000	12,579
37	0	29,661	1,000	14,937
38	0	32,627	1,000	17,531
39	0	35,889	1,000	20,384
40	0	39,478	1,000	23,523
41	0	43,426	1,000	26,975
42	0	47,769	1,000	30,772
43	0	52,546	1,000	34,950
44	0	57,800	1,000	39,545
45	0	63,580	1,000	44,599
46	0	69,938	1,000	50,159
47	0	76,932	1,000	56,275
48	0	84,625	1,000	63,003
49	0	93,088	1,000	70,403
50	0	103,397	1,000	78,543
51	0	112,636	1,000	87,497
52	0	123,898	1,000	97,347
53	0	136,290	1,000	108,182
54	0	149,919	1,000	120,100
55	0	164,911	1,000	133,210
56	0	181,402	1,000	147,631
57	0	199,542	1,000	163,494
58	0	219,496	1,000	180,943
59	0	241,446	1,000	200,138
60	0	265,590	1,000	221,252
61	0	292,149	1,000	244,477
62	0	321,364	1,000	270,024
63	0	353,501	1,000	298,127
64	0	388,851	1,000	329,039
65	0	427,736	1,000	363,043

Incredibly, Danielle accumulated more because of the earlier start. Compounding is your friend, and the earlier you can start it working for you, the better. Start saving and investing today!

When Should I Start Investing?

Proverbs 21:5 tells us *"Steady plodding brings prosperity, hasty speculation brings poverty"* (Proverbs 21:5, TLB). *Other translations use the word "diligent" in place of "steady." Both of these terms have something in common in their definition – the word "constant."*

Investing is all about building up funds for the long term where they can take advantage of compound interest. You want to maximize the opportunity for growth over years or even decades before the funds will be required.

I believe, if possible, that you should begin investing as soon as you can, even if it is a small amount.

You may ask, what about my emergency fund or my debt or other expenses? Shouldn't they be the priority? I would say yes, they should be, but it doesn't need to be an all-or-nothing approach.

Investing right away can be helpful for several reasons:

It creates a consistent habit of investing.

It helps kickstart compounding. Time is your friend when it comes to compound interest, so starting early is incredibly beneficial!

It gives you an opportunity to learn gradually so that you have greater knowledge and tools to invest prayerfully as you have more to invest after accomplishing the early phases of building your finances.

However, if you are currently unable to invest even a small amount without feeling overwhelmed, I would encourage you to pause. Your best step for now might be to set a goal for when to start.

Notes

A Terrible Investment Strategy

A recent survey indicated that 20% of the 1000 Americans polled were counting on winning the lottery for their retirement. Lotteries and gambling of all types are sweeping our country. Internet gambling is exploding. Each year one in four Americans gambles at a casino. The average church member gives $20 a year to international missions, while the average person gambles $1,174 annually.

Sadly, more than 6 million Americans (including 1.1 million teens) are addicted to gambling, with consequences that break the hearts of their loved ones. Although the Bible doesn't specifically prohibit gambling, it's get-rich-quick motivation violates the steady-plodding principle.

In my opinion, we should never participate in gambling or lotteries – even for entertainment. We shouldn't expose ourselves to the risk of becoming compulsive gamblers, nor should we support an industry that enslaves so many.

God's Instructions to Successful Investors

God realizes that when our assets increase, they can become a potential barrier to a close relationship with Him. If you have a lot of resources, the Lord isn't disappointed or surprised; rather, He entrusted them to you for a purpose. In 1 Timothy 6:17-19, the Lord give us instructions to help those with resources to remain undistracted from loving and serving Him.

DON'T BE CONCEITED

"Instruct those who are rich in this present world not to be conceited" (1 Timothy 6:17). Wealth tends to produce pride. For several years we drove two vehicles. The first was the old pickup truck that cost $100 – and looked it! When I drove that truck to the bank drive-in window to cash a check, I was humble. I knew the cashier was going to carefully check my account to confirm that the driver of that beat-up truck had sufficient funds in his account. And when I received the money, I drove away with a song in my heart and praises on my lips.

Our other vehicle was a well-preserved, second-hand car that was expensive when it was new. When I drove that car to the bank, I appeared to be a different person. I was a person who deserved a certain amount of respect. I wasn't quite as patient when the cashier examined my account, and when I received the money I wasn't as grateful. Wealth often leads to pride.

PUT NO CONFIDENCE IN YOUR ASSETS

"Instruct those who are rich [successful investors] in this present world not . . . to set their hope on the uncertainty of riches, but on God, who richly supplies us with all things to enjoy" (1 Timothy 6:17).

The ability to accumulate assets without placing our confidence in them is a massive struggle. Someone once observed, "For every ninety-nine who can be poor and remain close to Christ, only one can become affluent and maintain close fellowship with Him." It must be human nature to cling to the Lord when it's obvious that He must provide our needs. Once people reach financial freedom, however, they often take the Lord for granted because they no longer think they have as much need of Him.

When you have resources, the tendency is to look first to your money to solve problems instead of praying and seeking the Lord first. We tend to trust in what we can see with our eyes, rather than in the invisible living God. King Solomon said it this way, *"The wealth of the rich is their fortified city; they imagine it a wall too high to scale"* (Proverbs 18:11, NIV). We need to remind ourselves that wealth – like health – is completely uncertain and can be lost in a heartbeat. The Lord alone can be fully trusted.

GIVE GENEROUSLY The antidote for pride and trusting in our assets is generosity. *"Instruct them to do good, to be rich in good works, to be generous and ready to share, storing up for themselves the treasure of a good foundation for the future, so that they may take hold of that which is truly life"* (1 Timothy 6:18-19). The Lord wants successful investors to be generous; He tells them of two benefits: (1) real eternal treasures that they will enjoy forever, and (2) the blessing of *"taking hold of that which is truly life."* By exercising generosity, they can live the fulfilling life God intends for them now.

We need to balance our saving and investing with generosity. Jesus told a parable of a farmer who harvested a bumper crop and said to himself, *"'I have no place to store my crops. . . . I will tear down my barns and build larger ones, and I will store all my grain and my goods there. . . .' But God said to him, 'You fool! . . . Such is the one who stores up treasure for himself, and is not rich in relation to God. . . . For where your treasure is, there your heart will be also'"* (Luke 12:16-21, 34).

The key word in this parable is the word *"all."* Jesus called the farmer foolish because he saved everything and didn't balance saving with giving. If we only pile up our investments, they will pull on our hearts like gravity. Our affection will be drawn away from God toward them because *"where your treasure is, there your heart will be also"* (Luke 12:34). However, if we give generously to God, we can invest and still love Him with all of our heart.

Notes

DANGERS OF PROSPERITY Scripture identifies a number of dangers associated with wealth. First, it's easy for those who are prosperous to turn from God. We might say to ourselves, "That would never happen to me." But Scripture makes it clear that an increase in possessions and wealth move us closer to spiritual danger. *"For when I [the Lord] bring them into the land flowing with milk and honey, which I swore to their fathers, and they eat and are satisfied and become prosperous, then they will turn to other gods and serve them, and spurn Me"* (Deuteronomy 31:20). We tend to cling to the Lord when it's obvious that He must provide our needs. Once people become prosperous, they often take the Lord for granted, thinking they no longer have as much need of Him. Paul warned Timothy, *"Instruct those who are rich in this present world not . . . to set their hope on the uncertainty of riches, but on God"* (1 Timothy 6:17).

Second, it's difficult for the rich to come to know Jesus Christ as their Savior. *"Jesus said to His disciples, 'Truly I say to you, it will be hard for a rich person to enter the kingdom of heaven'"* (Matthew 19:23). Again, this is because the rich generally feel less of a need for God. Riches also can destroy a spiritually fruitful life. *"The one sown with seed among the thorns, this is the one who hears the word, and the anxiety of the world and the deceitfulness of wealth choke the word, and it becomes unfruitful"* (Matthew 13:22). Riches are deceitful because they are tangible and can blind us from the reality of the unseen Lord. We imagine that our finances can do things for us that only Christ can really do.

Real financial security? We can find it in God alone. Apart from a relationship with Christ, it's nothing more than an illusion.

INVESTING IN CHILDREN

In 1904 the country of Wales experienced a remarkable revival. Thousands of people were introduced to Christ, and the results were dramatic. Bars closed because of lack of business. Policemen exchanged their weapons for white gloves, since crime disappeared. Wales was so evangelically minded that it sent missionaries all over the world.

One of those missionaries traveled to Argentina, where on the streets he led a young boy to Christ. The boy's name was Luis Palau. He has since become known as the "Billy Graham" of Latin America. Palau visited Wales to express his thankfulness for helping lead him to Christ. What he discovered was astonishing. Less than one-half of one percent of the Welsh attended church. Divorce was at an all-time high, and crime was increasing.

As a result of this experience, Palau produced a film titled God Has No Grandchildren. The thrust of the film is that each generation is responsible for passing on the truths of Scripture, including God's financial principles, to its children. Proverbs 22:6 reads, *"Train up a child in the way he should go, even when he grows older he will not abandon it."*

Parents should be MVP parents. MVP is an acronym that describes the three methods to teach children God's way of handling money: Modeling, Verbal communication, and Practical opportunities. All three are needed to train your children. Let's look at each.

MODELING Since children soak up parental attitudes toward money like a sponge soaks up water, parents must model handling money wisely. Paul recognized the importance of modeling when he said, *"Be imitators of me, just as I also am of Christ"* (1 Corinthians 11:1).

Luke 6:40 is a challenging passage. It reads, *". . . Everyone, when he has been fully trained, will be like his teacher."* Another way of saying this is that we can teach what we believe, but we only reproduce who we are. There is no substitute for parents being good models.

VERBAL COMMUNICATION Parents need to tell their children why they are handling money the way they are. The Lord charged the Israelites, *"These words, which I am commanding you today, shall be on your heart. You shall repeat them diligently to your sons and speak of them when you sit in your house, when you walk on the road, when you lie down, and when you get up"* (Deuteronomy 6:6-7). We must verbally instruct children in the ways of the Lord, but children need more than a good example and verbal instruction; they also need practical experience.

PRACTICAL EXPERIENCE There are money-management and money-making learning experiences that benefit children.

Notes

Learning Experiences in Money Management

Teaching money management must not just be delegated to teachers. Parents must also seize the opportunity because spending experiences are found outside the classroom. Consider five areas where this is possible.

INCOME As soon as children are ready for school, they should begin to receive an income to manage. Parents need to decide whether the child must earn an income or whether they wish to give an allowance in return for the child doing chores.

The amount of the income will vary according to factors such as the child's age, the ability to earn, and the financial circumstances of the family. The amount, however, isn't as important as the responsibility of handling money. At first, as with any new experience, the child will make many mistakes. When this happens, don't hesitate to let the "law of natural consequences" run its course. Yes, you will be tempted to help when the child spends all the income the first day on an unwise purchase. But don't bail the child out! Mistakes will be the best teacher.

Parents should establish boundaries and offer advice on how to spend money, but your child must have freedom of choice within these boundaries. Every Saturday I used to bicycle to the store with my son, Matthew, to buy him a pack of gum. Despite my advice, the entire pack would be consumed that day.

When he started to earn money, we decided that Matthew would have to buy his own gum. I will never forget the expression on his face as he came out of the store with his first purchase. "This gum cost me all my money!" he yelled. That pack of gum lasted all week.

BUDGETING When children start to receive an income, teach them to budget. Begin with a simple system consisting of three jars, labeled separately: GIVE, SAVE, and SPEND. The child distributes a portion of the income into each jar. Even a six-year-old can understand this method, because when the spend jar is empty, there's no more money to spend!

When children become teenagers, they should begin using a written budget – or train them to use one of the budgeting software or online programs that are available. During the training, teach shopping skills, the ability to distinguish needs from wants, and the importance of waiting on the Lord to provide. Warn him or her about the danger of impulse spending.

One valuable lesson you can teach children is to seek the Lord's provision through prayer. We often rob ourselves of this opportunity by buying things or charging purchases without praying for the Lord to supply them.

SAVING AND INVESTING The habit of saving should begin as soon as the child receives an income. As children mature, expose them to various types of investments: stocks, bonds, etc. Also, teach children the benefits of compounding interest. If they grasp this concept and become faithful savers, they will enjoy financial stability as adults. Parents should demonstrate this by saving for something that will directly benefit the children. Use a graph the children can fill in so they can visually chart the progress of saving.

Children should have both short-term and long-term saving goals. The younger the child, the more important the short-term goals are. To a four-year-old, a week seems like a lifetime to save for a purchase. They won't understand saving for their future education, but they will get excited about saving for a small toy.

DEBT Also teach how difficult it is to get out of debt. A father loaned his son and daughter money to buy bicycles. He drew up a credit agreement with a schedule for repayment of the loan including interest. After they went through the long process of paying off the loan, the family celebrated with a "mortgage burning" ceremony. The children appreciated those bikes more than any of their possessions. They also decided to avoid debt in the future.

GIVING The best time to establish the habit of giving is when you're young. It's helpful for children to give a portion of their gifts to a need they can see. For example, a child understands when the gift helps to buy food for a needy family he actually knows.

Richard Halverson, the late U. S. Senate chaplain, gave his son, Chris, this heritage as a child. Chris gave money to support Kim, an orphan who had lost his sight during the Korean War. Chris was taught to feel that Kim was like an adopted brother. One Christmas, Chris bought Kim a harmonica. Kim cherished this gift from Chris and learned to play it well. As the years went by Kim became an evangelist, and his presentation of the gospel included playing the harmonica.

When your child is a teenager, serving at the local homeless shelter or taking a mission trip to a developing country can be a powerful experience. Exposure to poverty can initiate a lifetime of giving to the needy. We also recommend a family time each week for dedicating that week's gifts to the Lord.

Notes

Learning Experiences in Making Money

Parents also have a responsibility to train children to develop work habits. If children learn how to work with the proper attitude, they will have taken a giant step toward becoming valuable in the job market. There are three areas to consider in this training:

LEARNING ROUTINE RESPONSIBILITIES One of the best ways for a child to become a faithful worker is to establish the habit of daily household chores. These are tasks that each member of the family is expected to perform.

EXPOSE CHILDREN TO YOUR WORK Many children have no idea how their father or mother earns an income. An important way to teach the value of work is to expose children to the parents' means of making a living.

One word of advice: Because most children are no longer with their parents at work, parents' work habits around the home will be a major influence. If a parent works hard away from home but complains about washing the dishes at home, what's being communicated to the children? Examine your attitudes when working around the house to ensure that your children see a good example.

WORKING FOR OTHERS Babysitting, bagging groceries, or waiting on tables will be an education. A job gives a child an opportunity to enter into an employee-employer relationship and to earn extra money. The objective of teaching children the value of work is to build character. A working child with the proper attitude will be a more satisfied individual. He or she will grow up with more respect for the value of money and the effort required to earn it.

Single Parents and Grandparents

Single parents are increasingly common, and we appreciate the added demands they face. But be encouraged. Some of the most responsible children I have ever met have been raised by a godly single mother or father.

If you are a grandparent, you have a wonderful opportunity to influence your grandchildren. Too often parents and grandparents have not reached agreement on how to train the next generation. This can lead to bruised relationships and ineffective training. It's important for grandparents to play a role in which they complement the objectives of the parents. We recommend that parents meet with grandparents and together design a strategy for training the grandchildren how to handle money.

Adult Children

My wife and I decided the wisest way to financially assist our children and their future spouses was to help them pay off their home mortgages. This would enable them to eliminate their largest monthly expense and focus on becoming more generous and more efficient in their saving and investing.

When my daughter and her husband bought their "fixer upper" first home, we matched whatever they prepaid on the home mortgage. They caught the vision for paying off their home and faithfully put whatever they could toward pre-paying on their mortgage. With their faithfulness and our matching gift, they were able to pay their home off in under five years.

We believe in helping our adult children to live in a mortgage-free home instead of giving them gifts that increase their lifestyle. We have also encouraged them to consider "paying it forward" to their children by duplicating this strategy.

Inheritance

Parents should try to leave an inheritance to their children. *"A good person leaves an inheritance to his grandchildren"* (Proverbs 13:22). But inheritances should not be disbursed until heirs have been trained to be wise stewards. *"An inheritance gained in a hurry at the beginning will not be blessed in the end"* (Proverbs 20:21).

Consider sprinkling distributions over several years as heirs mature enough to handle the responsibility of money. Select trustworthy people to help supervise the finances of young heirs until they are capable stewards. *"As long as the heir is a child, he does not differ at all from a slave, although he is owner of everything, but he is under guardians and managers until the date set by the father"* (Galatians 4:1-2).

Wills

It's important to prepare financially for your death. As Isaiah told Hezekiah, *". . . This is what the Lord says: 'Set your house in order, for you are going to die'"* (2 Kings 20:1). One of the greatest gifts you can leave your children and loved ones for that emotional time is an organized estate and a properly prepared will or revocable living trust.

Step Three:

Answer the Discussion Questions

What in the notes (and video) did you find revealing or interesting?

What in the notes challenged you the most?

What did you find revealing or challenging about the application worksheets in this chapter? Did you have any questions about the worksheets?

Chapter 3

Compass Commentaries

DAY ONE In the area of generosity and giving, one common theme permeates biblical instruction – love! Didn't Jesus Himself begin the well-known passage in John 3:16 with the words *"For God so loved the world, that He gave . . ."*? God's giving because of His love provides an example that we should follow. When I make an effort to be generous without first loving, it often reflects a heart of pride, the desire to be noticed and admired. But by loving before I give, my focus is on the recipient and not on myself as the giver.

Paul provides additional considerations regarding giving in his letters to the Corinthians: giving without love is worthless, we should give abundantly, willingly, with purpose, and without feeling pressured. Just as a farmer who plants one seed will receive a minimal harvest, so does the giver who gives grudgingly. God wants so much for us to see the benefits of giving that He joyfully replenishes what we give with even more – enabling us to give more yet.

DAY TWO God knows the importance of giving in freeing us from the love of materials goods. The people of Israel had turned away from the Lord and were no longer following His commands, so God called them on it, encouraging them to reengage in worship through their tithes and offerings. In addition, He challenged them to test Him. Nowhere else in all of the Bible does God say to test Him, but He does when it comes to giving. He wants everyone to understand that it is an act of worship and that through demonstrating our trust in Him by giving, He will bless us beyond expectation. Sometimes He does this financially; often He does it in a way that greatly exceeds mere finances. (Who would want money without joy and peace?) Giving should be done intentionally and purposefully, setting it aside for its intended purpose. This minimizes the chance that our good intentions will get redirected to something else. Once we have prayerfully made the decision to give, and in what amount, it should be placed in the "storehouse" of the church, a jar at home, or some other safe place where it can ultimately be given to the Lord for His work.

DAY THREE Today's passage gives us insight into the mind of Christ. He knows who are His own, those who really put their trust in Him rather than just pretending to. He divides humanity into two groups, judging their hearts and determining their destiny, whether to eternal death or eternal life with Him. One parable reveals that our hearts are exposed by how we use our time and money. Jesus tells us that when we give to Kingdom work, we are giving to Christ Himself. When we do acts of kindness to others, like ministering to the hungry, thirsty, sick, naked or imprisoned, we are expressing love directly to Jesus. Jesus identifies with these, the beneficiaries of our generosity. It is as if we give a cup of cold water to Christ Himself! A great inheritance awaits those who show love to others in the name of Christ.

DAY FOUR When our focus is on our money, wealth, or material goods, contentment seems to evade us: there is never enough to satisfy. Instead of a blessing, wealth can be a curse. Our investments create stress over losses and whether we made the right decisions.

The recognition that we cannot take anything with us when we die should be a wakeup call to shift our focus. Instead of using wealth to benefit ourselves and serve our own selfish purposes, we can use it for God's glory and build His Kingdom for all eternity.

One very basic but important principle to remember when we invest our resources is to diversify. So many have lost all of their savings and investments by placing them in one type of investment or specific market sector. When that sector is adversely impacted by situations beyond our ability to predict or control, it may crash and take our investment with it. Spreading assets over multiple kinds of investments can benefit from success in many areas; just as importantly, it reduces the risk of total loss when one fails. This is investing wisdom.

DAY FIVE Successful investing and money management require a variety of character traits. Be diligent and patient, not in a hurry to achieve financial growth. Keep track of your investments without obsessing over them. Be aware of market conditions that might impact your investments. Faithfulness is blessed by God; remember, it is His money anyway! Don't neglect opportunities to help those in need with your resources. Nothing good ever comes from acquiring something through dishonesty and deceit. Faithfully honoring God and living according to His principles will position you for His blessings.

Chapter 4:

Work & Honesty

*All tools, videos, resources and electronic applications for this chapter can be found at **compasstools.org***

THIS CHAPTER'S MEMORY VERSE:

Colossians 3:23-24 and Leviticus 19:11

DAILY HOMEWORK:

Day One – Work and God's Role

Day Two – Working Hard

Day Three – Proverbs and Work, begin working on the Estimated Spending Plan

Day Four – Honesty

Day Five – Honesty, Bribes, and Restitution, begin working on the Tracking Tool

Day Six – Watch the Build Your Finances God's Way video, Read the Notes, answer the discussion questions

BEFORE YOUR GROUP MEETING:

1. Memorize Colossians 3:23-24 and Leviticus 19:11. To prevent confusion when reciting the verses in a group setting, please memorize the versions listed below.

> *"Whatever you do, do your work heartily, as for the Lord and not for people . . . It is the Lord Christ whom you serve" (Colossians 3:23-24).*
>
> *"You shall not steal, nor deal falsely, nor lie to one another" (Leviticus 19:11).*

2. Complete the Daily Homework.

Each day's homework is designed to take 20-30 minutes to complete.

4 - DAY ONE

Homework

Work and God's Role

PRAYER

Pray for the Holy Spirit's guidance as you begin reading passages of Scripture. Ask for clarity and insight as you engage in God's word.

SCRIPTURE READING

Read Genesis 2:15-17.

"The Lord God took the man and put him in the garden of Eden to work it and keep it. [16]And the Lord God commanded the man, saying, 'You may surely eat of every tree of the garden, [17]but of the tree of the knowledge of good and evil you shall not eat, for in the day that you eat of it you shall surely die'" (ESV).

Read Genesis 3:17-19.

"And to Adam he said, 'Because you have listened to the voice of your wife and have eaten of the tree of which I commanded you, "You shall not eat of it," cursed is the ground because of you; in pain you shall eat of it all the days of your life; [18]thorns and thistles it shall bring forth for you; and you shall eat the plants of the field. [19]By the sweat of your face you shall eat bread, till you return to the ground, for out of it you were taken; for you are dust, and to dust you shall return" (ESV).

OBSERVATION

What do these passages say about...

God?

Us?

Work?

4 - DAY ONE

Homework

SCRIPTURE READING

Read Genesis 2:15-17.

"The Lord God took the man and put him in the garden of Eden to work it and keep it. [16]And the Lord God commanded the man, saying, 'You may surely eat of every tree of the garden, [17]but of the tree of the knowledge of good and evil you shall not eat, for in the day that you eat of it you shall surely die'" (ESV).

Read Genesis 3:17-19.

"And to Adam he said, 'Because you have listened to the voice of your wife and have eaten of the tree of which I commanded you, "You shall not eat of it," cursed is the ground because of you; in pain you shall eat of it all the days of your life; [18]thorns and thistles it shall bring forth for you; and you shall eat the plants of the field. [19]By the sweat of your face you shall eat bread, till you return to the ground, for out of it you were taken; for you are dust, and to dust you shall return" (ESV).

INTERPRETATION

What do these passages mean to you?

What consequences do we see from these passages?

How have you experienced God in your work?

APPLICATION

How can you apply the principles of these passages to your job and finances?

HOWARD'S HIGHLIGHTS

God's perspective on work

Despite what many believe, work was initiated for our benefit in the sinless environment of the garden of Eden. Work is not a result of the curse! *"The Lord God took the man and put him in the garden of Eden to cultivate it and tend it"* (Genesis 2:15). The very first thing the Lord did with Adam was to put him to work.

After the Fall, work became more difficult. *"Cursed is the ground because of you; with hard labor you shall eat from it all the days of your life. Both thorns and thistles it shall grow for you; yet you shall eat the plants of the field; by the sweat of your face you shall eat bread"* (Genesis 3:17-19).

Work is so important that in Exodus 34:21 God gives this command: *"You shall work six days."* The apostle Paul is just as direct: *"If anyone is not willing to work, then he is not to eat"* (2 Thessalonians 3:10). Examine the verse carefully. It says, *"If anyone is not willing to work."* It does not say, "If anyone cannot work." This principle does not apply to those who are physically or mentally unable to work; it is for those who are able but choose not to work.

A close friend of mine has a brother in his mid-forties whose parents have always supported him. He has never had to face the responsibilities and hardships involved in a job. Consequently, his character has not been properly developed, leaving him hopelessly immature in many areas of his life.

One of the primary purposes of work is to develop character. While the carpenter is building a house, the house is also building the carpenter. The carpenter's skill, diligence, manual dexterity, and judgment are refined. A job is not merely a task designed to earn money; it's also intended to produce godly character in the life of the worker.

God's part in work

Scripture reveals three responsibilities the Lord has in our work.

God gives job skills. Exodus 36:1 illustrates this truth: *". . . every skillful person in whom the Lord has put skill and understanding to know how to perform all the work . . . shall perform."* God has given each of us unique aptitudes. People have a wide variety of abilities, manual skills, and intellectual capacities. It's not a matter of one person being better than another, merely that each has received different abilities.

God gives success. The life of Joseph is a perfect example of God helping a person to succeed. *"The Lord was with Joseph, so he became a successful man.. . . His master saw that the Lord was with him and that the Lord made all that he did prosper"* (Genesis 39:2-3). Although we all have certain responsibilities, it is ultimately God who controls success.

God controls promotions. Psalm 75:6-7 says, *"For promotion and power come from nowhere on earth, but only from God"* (TLB). As much as it may surprise you, our bosses aren't the ones who control whether we will be promoted. Many people leave God out of work, believing that they alone are responsible for their abilities and success. One of the major reasons they experience stress and frustration in their jobs is because they don't understand God's role in work.

Consider this question for a few minutes: If God gives you your abilities and controls success and promotion, how should this perspective affect your work?

PRAYERS FOR TODAY

This prayer section is for personal use and isn't meant to be part of the group discussion.

For you...

For your family and friends...

For those in your group...

4 - DAY TWO

Homework

Working Hard

PRAYER

Pray for the Holy Spirit's guidance as you begin reading passages of Scripture. Ask for clarity and insight as you engage in God's word.

SCRIPTURE READING

Read 2 Thessalonians 3:6-13.

*"Now we command you, brothers, in the name of our Lord Jesus Christ, that
you keep away from any brother who is walking in idleness and not in accord
with the tradition that you received from us. 7For you yourselves know how you ought to imitate
us, because we were not idle when we were with you, 8nor did we eat anyone's bread without
paying for it, but with toil and labor we worked night and day, that we might not be a burden to
any of you. 9It was not because we do not have that right, but to give you in ourselves an example
to imitate. 10For even when we were with you, we would give you this command: If anyone is not
willing to work, let him not eat. 11For we hear that some among you walk in idleness, not busy at
work, but busybodies. 12Now such persons we command and encourage in the Lord Jesus Christ
to do their work quietly and to earn their own living. 13As for you, brothers, do not grow weary in
doing good" (ESV).*

Read Exodus 20:8-11.

*"Remember the Sabbath day, to keep it holy. 9Six days you shall labor, and do all your work,
10but the seventh day is a Sabbath to the Lord your God. On it you shall not do any work, you, or
your son, or your daughter, your male servant, or your female servant, or your livestock, or the
sojourner who is within your gates. 11For in six days the Lord made heaven and earth, the sea, and
all that is in them, and rested on the seventh day. Therefore the Lord blessed the Sabbath day
and made it holy" (ESV).*

OBSERVATION

What do these passages say about...

Work?

Rest?

4 - DAY TWO

Homework

SCRIPTURE READING

Read 2 Thessalonians 3:6-13.

*"Now we command you, brothers, in the name of our Lord Jesus Christ, that
you keep away from any brother who is walking in idleness and not in accord
with the tradition that you received from us. 7For you yourselves know how you
ought to imitate us, because we were not idle when we were with you, 8nor did
we eat anyone's bread without paying for it, but with toil and labor we worked
night and day, that we might not be a burden to any of you. 9It was not because
we do not have that right, but to give you in ourselves an example to imitate.
10For even when we were with you, we would give you this command: If anyone
is not willing to work, let him not eat. 11For we hear that some among you walk
in idleness, not busy at work, but busybodies. 12Now such persons we command
and encourage in the Lord Jesus Christ to do their work quietly and to earn
their own living. 13As for you, brothers, do not grow weary in doing good" (ESV).*

Read Exodus 20:8-11.

*"Remember the Sabbath day, to keep it holy. 9Six days you shall labor, and do
all your work, 10but the seventh day is a Sabbath to the Lord your God. On it you
shall not do any work, you, or your son, or your daughter, your male servant,
or your female servant, or your livestock, or the sojourner who is within your
gates. 11For in six days the Lord made heaven and earth, the sea, and all that
is in them, and rested on the seventh day. Therefore the Lord blessed the
Sabbath day and made it holy" (ESV).*

INTERPRETATION

What would *"idleness"* look like today?

How has overworking impacted you or your family?

What does (or would) a healthy balance of work and rest look like in your life?

APPLICATION

How can you apply the principles of these passages to your work and finances?

HOWARD'S HIGHLIGHTS

Our Part in Work

Did you know that in our work we actually serve the Lord rather than people? Paul writes: *"Whatever you do, do your work heartily, as for the Lord and not for people . . . It is the Lord Christ whom you serve"* (Colossians 3:23-24).

Recognizing that we work for the Lord has profound implications. If you could see Jesus Christ as your boss, would you try to be more faithful in your job? The most important question you need to answer every day as you begin your work is this: "For whom do I work?" The Bible makes it clear: The person who signs your paycheck is not your ultimate employer. No matter where you are or what you do, you work for Christ Himself.

Work Hard

"Whatever your hand finds to do, do it with all your might" (Ecclesiastes 9:10, NIV). *"The precious possession of a person is diligence"* (Proverbs 12:27). Scripture encourages hard work and diligence, while laziness is strongly condemned: *"One who is slack in his work is brother to one who destroys"* (Proverbs 18:9, NIV).

Paul's life was an example of hard work. *". . . with labor and hardship we kept working night and day so that we would not be a burden to any of you . . . in order to offer ourselves as a role model for you, so that you would follow our example"* (2 Thessalonians 3:8-9).

Your work should never be at such a level that people will equate laziness with God. Nothing less than hard work and the pursuit of doing the job well pleases Him. He doesn't require us to be workers who labor around the clock and never make mistakes, but He does expect us to pursue our responsibilities – whatever they may be – with diligence and integrity.

But don't overwork!

Hard work, however, must be balanced by the other priorities of life. If your job demands so much of your time and energy that you neglect your relationship with Christ or your loved ones, then you're working too much. This applies to those in secular careers as well as those in fulltime Christian service. If you find that your relationship with Christ, your wife or husband, or your children are suffering, sit down with your spouse and ask yourself a direct question or two. Is the job too demanding or do certain work habits need adjusting? If you tend to be a workaholic, be careful not to shortchange the other priorities of life.

Exodus 34:21 reads, *"You shall work six days, but on the seventh day you shall rest; even during plowing time and harvest you shall rest."* We believe this Old Testament principle of resting one day out of seven has application today. This has been difficult for me, particularly during "plowing time and harvest," when a project deadline approaches or I'm under financial pressure.

When you think about it, rest can really become an issue of faith. Is the Lord able to make our six days of work more productive than seven? Of course He is! Our Creator instituted weekly rest for our physical, mental, and spiritual health. It's a day a week we can focus much of our time on getting to know the Lord even better. Philippians 3:8, 10 emphasizes the importance of this: *"I consider everything a loss because of the surpassing worth of knowing Christ Jesus my Lord . . . I want to know Christ – yes, to know the power of his resurrection and participation in his sufferings, becoming like him in his death"* (NIV).

PRAYERS FOR TODAY

This prayer section is for personal use and isn't meant to be part of the group discussion.

For you...

For your family and friends...

For those in your group...

Proverbs and Work

PRAYER

Pray for the Holy Spirit's guidance as you begin reading passages of Scripture. Ask for clarity and insight as you engage in God's word.

SCRIPTURE READING

Read the following Proverbs.

"He who gathers in summer is a prudent son, but he who sleeps in harvest is a son who brings shame" (Proverbs 10:5, ESV).

"Whoever works his land will have plenty of bread, but he who follows worthless pursuits lacks sense" (Proverbs 12:11, ESV).

"From the fruit of his mouth a man is satisfied with good, and the work of a man's hand comes back to him" (Proverbs 12:14, ESV).

"Whoever works his land will have plenty of bread, but he who follows worthless pursuits will have plenty of poverty" (Proverbs 28:19, ESV).

"Prepare your work outside; get everything ready for yourself in the field, and after that build your house" (Proverbs 24:27, ESV).

"In all toil there is profit, but mere talk tends only to poverty" (Proverbs 14:23, ESV).

"Whoever is slack in his work is a brother to him who destroys" (Proverbs 18:9, ESV).

OBSERVATION

What do these verses say about...

Work?

People?

Consequences – good and bad?

SCRIPTURE READING

Read the following Proverbs.

"He who gathers in summer is a prudent son, but he who sleeps in harvest is a son who brings shame" (Proverbs 10:5, ESV).

"Whoever works his land will have plenty of bread, but he who follows worthless pursuits lacks sense" (Proverbs 12:11, ESV).

"From the fruit of his mouth a man is satisfied with good, and the work of a man's hand comes back to him" (Proverbs 12:14, ESV).

"Whoever works his land will have plenty of bread, but he who follows worthless pursuits will have plenty of poverty" (Proverbs 28:19, ESV).

"Prepare your work outside; get everything ready for yourself in the field, and after that build your house" (Proverbs 24:27, ESV).

"In all toil there is profit, but mere talk tends only to poverty" (Proverbs 14:23, ESV).

"Whoever is slack in his work is a brother to him who destroys" (Proverbs 18:9, ESV).

INTERPRETATION

What do these verses mean to you?

Which of the Proverbs resonated most with you? Why?

APPLICATION

The Estimated Spending Plan

(see the following page for details)

The Estimated Spending Plan:

Now that we know what God says about work, let's put what we learned into action by working on an Estimated Spending Plan! Here's how you start.

1. Estimate your income *– List all your income in the "Income" section of the Estimated Spending Plan. Some people don't receive steady, predictable income. This is especially common for the self-employed and commissioned salesperson. If your income is not consistent, estimate your yearly income and divide by 12 to determine your average monthly income.*

2. Estimate your expenses *– Complete and total each expense category on the Estimated Spending Plan. Business expense reimbursements should not be considered income. Avoid the temptation to spend expense money as if it were income. This can lead to increased debt when those bills come due.*

Not all spending is consistent each month. Spending that varies can include:

- *Irregular monthly expenses – such as food and utility bills. Simply estimate what you spend in an average month.*
- *Expenses that don't occur every month – such as auto maintenance, medical bills, clothing, and vacations. Estimate the annual amount spent for an item and divide by 12. For example, if you spend $600 a year for home repairs, set aside $50 a month to pay for repairs.*

3. Use the Compass Construction Plan – *Use the Compass Construction Plan (from Chapter 3) to help you build your Estimated Spending Plan.*

- *Start by reviewing your unchecked boxes from the Compass Construction Plan and identifying what phase you are starting from.*
- *Once you've identified the unchecked boxes in your phase, make the unchecked boxes a priority as you develop your Estimated Spending Plan. For example:*

Let's say you are in Phase 1 and you have an unchecked box for "Start Giving" and "Pay off Credit Cards".

If your goal for "Start Giving" is to give 10% this year, then incorporate that number into the "Giving" portion of the estimated spending plan.

If you already have a plan to "Pay off Credit Cards" with the snowball strategy, put the numbers from the List Your Debts & Snowball Strategy form (Chapter 2) in the "Debt" portion of the estimated spending plan.

4. The key word is estimate – *Do your best to identify all your income and expenses. We've provided a detailed list that can help you identify some that are easy to forget. Not all categories may be relevant for your situation, and if you don't see a line item for your specific income or expense, just put it in a place that makes the most sense to you.*

You can find an example of this application at **compasstools.org**

Income

Monthly Salary ____________
Interest ____________
Dividends ____________
Commissions, Bonus, Tips ____________
Retirement Income ____________
Net Business Income ____________
Cash Gifts ____________
Child Support/Alimony ____________
Total: ____________

1. Giving

Local Church ____________
Poor & Needy ____________
Ministries ____________
Total: ____________

2. Taxes

Federal ____________
Medicare/Social Security ____________
State & Local ____________
Total: ____________

3. Saving & Investing

Emergency Savings ____________
Auto Replacement ____________
Retirement Plans ____________
College Funds ____________
Stocks & Bonds ____________
IRA ____________
Total: ____________

4. Housing

Mortgage ______________
Pre-pay mortgage ______________
Property Tax ______________
Home/Flood Insurance ______________
Rent & Renter's Insurance ______________
Electricity ______________
Lawn & Garden Care ______________
Water/Sanitation ______________
Phone(s) ______________
Gas ______________
Maintenance/Pool ______________
TV & Internet ______________
Pest Control/Termite Bond ______________
HOA/Condo Dues ______________
Total: ______________

5. Food

Groceries ______________
Eating Out ______________
Total: ______________

6. Transportation

Auto Payments ______________
Gas & Oil ______________
Auto Insurance ______________
Licenses & Taxes ______________
Repairs & Maintenance ______________
Tolls/Parking/Transit ______________
AAA/Auto Club ______________
Total: ______________

7. Clothing

Adults ______________________
Children/Diapers ______________________
Laundry/Dry Cleaning ______________________
Total: ______________________

8. Medical & Health

Doctor ______________________
Dentist ______________________
Prescriptions ______________________
Eye Care/Glasses ______________________
Insurances ______________________
Disability Insurance ______________________
Long-Term Care Insurance ______________________
Deductibles ______________________
HSA/Flexible Spending ______________________
Total: ______________________

9. Education

Adult Education ______________________
Kids Tuition/Supplies ______________________
Tutoring/Activities ______________________
Total: ______________________

10. Entertainment/Vacation

Activities ______________________
Vacations/Travel ______________________
Books/Movies ______________________
Total: ______________________

11. Debts (see debt list) ______________________

12. Personal

Allowances ______________
Childcare/Babysitting ______________
Life Insurance ______________
Liability Insurance ______________
Cleaning Supplies ______________
Toiletries/Cosmetics ______________
Hair Care ______________
Vitamins/Supplements ______________
Gifts - Birthdays ______________
Gifts - Christmas ______________
Gifts - Weddings/Anniversaries ______________
Gifts - Graduation ______________
Postage ______________
Alimony/Child Support ______________
Pet Food/Supplies/Vet ______________
Vaccinations/Prescriptions ______________
Boarding/Pet Sitting ______________
Tax Preparation/Legal ______________
Sports/Hobbies ______________
Bank Charges/Fees ______________
Credit Card Charges/Fees ______________
Family Pictures ______________
Subscriptions/Dues ______________
Total: ______________

Total Income: ______________
Minus Total Expenses: ______________

Equals Surplus or Deficit: ______________

PRAYERS FOR TODAY

This prayer section is for personal use and isn't meant to be part of the group discussion.

For you...

For your family and friends...

For those in your group...

Additional Tools for the Journey!

To help you on your financial discipleship journey, we have provided practical resources from a variety of people in the financial world. Visit us at **compasstools.org** to check out these resources.

4 - DAY FOUR

Homework

Honesty

PRAYER

Pray for the Holy Spirit's guidance as you begin reading passages of Scripture. Ask for clarity and insight as you engage in God's word.

SCRIPTURE READING

Read Deuteronomy 25:13-16.

"You shall not have in your bag two kinds of weights, a large and a small. [14]You
shall not have in your house two kinds of measures, a large and a small. [15]A
full and fair weight you shall have, a full and fair measure you shall have, that your days may be
long in the land that the Lord your God is giving you. [16]For all who do such things, all who act
dishonestly, are an abomination to the Lord your God" (ESV).

Read Leviticus 19:9-18.

"When you reap the harvest of your land, you shall not reap your field right up to its edge, neither
shall you gather the gleanings after your harvest. [10]And you shall not strip your vineyard bare,
neither shall you gather the fallen grapes of your vineyard. You shall leave them for the poor and
for the sojourner: I am the Lord your God. [11]"You shall not steal; you shall not deal falsely; you
shall not lie to one another. [12]You shall not swear by my name falsely, and so profane the name of
your God: I am the Lord. [13]"You shall not oppress your neighbor or rob him. The wages of a hired
worker shall not remain with you all night until the morning. [14]You shall not curse the deaf or put
a stumbling block before the blind, but you shall fear your God: I am the Lord. [15]"You shall do no
injustice in court. You shall not be partial to the poor or defer to the great, but in righteousness
shall you judge your neighbor. [16]You shall not go around as a slanderer among your people, and
you shall not stand up against the life of your neighbor: I am the Lord. [17]"You shall not hate your
brother in your heart, but you shall reason frankly with your neighbor, lest you incur sin because
of him. [18]You shall not take vengeance or bear a grudge against the sons of your own people, but
you shall love your neighbor as yourself: I am the Lord" (ESV).

OBSERVATION

What do these passages say about...

Honesty?

God?

Neighbors?

4 - DAY FOUR

Homework

SCRIPTURE READING

Read Deuteronomy 25:13-16.

"You shall not have in your bag two kinds of weights, a large and a small. [14]You shall not have in your house two kinds of measures, a large and a small. [15]A full and fair weight you shall have, a full and fair measure you shall have, that your days may be long in the land that the Lord your God is giving you. [16]For all who do such things, all who act dishonestly, are an abomination to the Lord your God" (ESV).

Read Leviticus 19:9-18.

"When you reap the harvest of your land, you shall not reap your field right up to its edge, neither shall you gather the gleanings after your harvest. [10]And you shall not strip your vineyard bare, neither shall you gather the fallen grapes of your vineyard. You shall leave them for the poor and for the sojourner: I am the Lord your God. [11]"You shall not steal; you shall not deal falsely; you shall not lie to one another. [12]You shall not swear by my name falsely, and so profane the name of your God: I am the Lord. [13]"You shall not oppress your neighbor or rob him. The wages of a hired worker shall not remain with you all night until the morning. [14]You shall not curse the deaf or put a stumbling block before the blind, but you shall fear your God: I am the Lord. [15]"You shall do no injustice in court. You shall not be partial to the poor or defer to the great, but in righteousness shall you judge your neighbor. [16]You shall not go around as a slanderer among your people, and you shall not stand up against the life of your neighbor: I am the Lord. [17]"You shall not hate your brother in your heart, but you shall reason frankly with your neighbor, lest you incur sin because of him. [18]You shall not take vengeance or bear a grudge against the sons of your own people, but you shall love your neighbor as yourself: I am the Lord" (ESV).

INTERPRETATION

What would the term *"two kinds of weights"* look like today?

Why do you think God detests dishonesty so much?

How have you experienced any of the "do not" statements in your life?

APPLICATION

How can you apply the principles of these passages to your finances and possessions?

HOWARD'S HIGHLIGHTS

Total Honesty

God wants us to be completely honest for the following reasons.

We cannot practice dishonesty and love God. Two of the Ten Commandments address honesty. *"You shall not steal. . . You shall not give false testimony against your neighbor"* (Exodus 20:15-16). And Jesus told us, *"If you love Me, you will keep My commandments"* (John 14:15). In other words, we cannot disobey by practicing dishonesty and still claim to love God.

When being dishonest, we behave as if the living God doesn't even exist. It's a clear signal that we simply don't believe He is able to provide what we need, even though He has promised to do so (Matthew 6:33). We take the situation into our own hands and do it in our own dishonest way. We're also acting as if God is incapable of discovering our dishonesty and powerless to discipline us. If we really believe God will discipline us, we won't consider acting dishonestly.

At the heart of it all, honest behavior is really an issue of faith. An honest decision may look foolish in light of what we can see, but the godly person knows Jesus Christ is alive, even though invisible. Every honest decision – even a decision that may harm us in the short run – strengthens our faith and helps us grow into a closer relationship with Christ. When we choose to be dishonest, we are denying our Lord. It's impossible to love God with all our heart, soul, and mind if, at the same time, we act as if He doesn't exist. Scripture declares that the dishonest hate God. *". . . One who is devious in his ways despises Him"* (Proverbs 14:2).

Before learning God's view on honesty, I had no clue He felt so strongly about it. I was often dishonest in my financial dealings. Once I began breaking my dishonest habits, however, I realized that the Lord's primary interest in our honest behavior is so that we can experience a closer relationship with Him.

We cannot practice dishonesty and love our neighbor. The Lord requires honesty because dishonest behavior also violates the second commandment, *". . . You shall love your neighbor as yourself"* (Mark 12:31). Romans 13:9-10 reads, *"If you love your neighbor as much as you love yourself you will not want to harm or cheat him . . . or steal from him.. . . Love does no wrong to anyone"* (TLB).

When we act dishonestly, what we're really doing is stealing from another person. We may rationalize that it's a business or the government or an insurance company that is suffering the loss. Yet, if we look at the bottom line, it is the business owners or fellow taxpayers or policy holders from whom we are stealing. It's just as if we took the money from their wallets. In the final analysis, the victim is always a person.

Credibility for evangelism. Honesty enables us to demonstrate the reality of Jesus Christ to those who don't yet know Him. I will never forget the first time I told a neighbor how he could come to know Christ as his personal Savior. He angrily responded, "Well, I know a man who always goes to church and talks a lot about Jesus, but watch out if you ever get in a business deal with him! He'd cheat his own grandmother! If that's what it means to be a Christian, I don't want any part of it!"

Our actions speak louder than our words. "*. . . Prove yourselves to be blameless and innocent, children of God above reproach in the midst of a crooked and perverse generation, among whom you appear as lights in the world*" (Philippians 2:15).

We can influence people for Jesus Christ by handling money honestly. Robert had been trying to sell a car for months when someone finally made an acceptable offer. At the last moment, however, the buyer said, "I have one condition – you don't report this sale so I won't have to pay state sales tax."

Although he was tempted, Robert responded, "I'm sorry, I can't do that because Jesus Christ is my Lord." Robert later said, "You should have seen his reaction. He almost went into shock! Then his attitude completely changed. Not only did he buy the car, but he eagerly joined my wife and me at our dinner table. Rarely have I seen anyone as open to the truth about knowing Jesus Christ."

Confirms God's direction. Proverbs 4:24-26 reads, "*Rid yourself of a deceitful mouth and keep devious speech far from you. Let your eyes look directly ahead and let your gaze be fixed straight in front of you. Watch the path of your feet, and all your ways will be established.*"

What a great principle. As you are completely honest, "*all your ways will be established.*" Choosing to walk the narrow path of honesty eliminates the many possible avenues of dishonesty.

"If only I'd understood that," Raymond said. "Donna and I wanted that house so much. It was our dream home. But we had too much debt to qualify for the mortgage. The only way for us to buy it was to hide some of our debts from the lender.

"It was the worst decision of our lives. Almost immediately we were unable to meet the mortgage payment and pay our other debts, too. The pressure built and was more than Donna could stand. Our dream house ended up being a family nightmare. I not only lost the house but nearly lost my wife."

Had Raymond and Donna been honest, their lender would not have approved the loan, and they would have been unable to purchase that particular home. Had they prayed and waited, God might have brought something more affordable, thus avoiding the pressure that almost ended their marriage. Honesty helps confirm God's direction.

Even small acts of dishonesty are harmful. God requires us to be completely honest, because even the smallest act of dishonesty is sin and interrupts our fellowship with the Lord. The smallest white lie hardens our heart, making our conscience increasingly insensitive to sin. This single cancer cell of small dishonesty multiplies and spreads to greater dishonesty. *". . . Whoever is dishonest with very little will also be dishonest with much"* (Luke 16:10, NIV).

An event in Abraham's life challenges us to be honest in small matters. The king of Sodom offered Abraham all the goods he had recovered when he had rescued the people of Sodom. But he responded, *"I have sworn to the Lord God Most High, Possessor of heaven and earth, that I will not take a thread or a sandal strap or anything that is yours"* (Genesis 14:22-23).

Just as Abraham was unwilling to take so much as a thread, we challenge you to make a similar commitment. Covenant not to steal a stamp or a penny from your employer or anyone else. The people of God must be honest in even the smallest matters.

To love God, to guide our steps, and to be more effective ambassadors of His love to our family and neighbors. Is it any wonder that our Lord wants us to be completely honest?

PRAYERS FOR TODAY

This prayer section is for personal use and isn't meant to be part of the group discussion.

For you...

For your family and friends...

For those in your group...

4 - DAY FIVE

Homework

Honesty:
Bribes & Restitution

PRAYER

Pray for the Holy Spirit's guidance as you begin reading passages of Scripture. Ask for clarity and insight as you engage in God's word.

SCRIPTURE READING

Read Isaiah 33:13-16.

"Hear, you who are far off, what I have done; and you who are near, acknowledge
my might. 14The sinners in Zion are afraid; trembling has seized the godless:
'Who among us can dwell with the consuming fire? Who among us can dwell with everlasting
burnings?' 15He who walks righteously and speaks uprightly, who despises the gain of
oppressions, who shakes his hands, lest they hold a bribe, who stops his ears from hearing of
bloodshed and shuts his eyes from looking on evil, 16he will dwell on the heights; his place of
defense will be the fortresses of rocks; his bread will be given him; his water will be sure" (ESV).

Read Leviticus 6:1-7.

"The Lord spoke to Moses, saying, 2"If anyone sins and commits a breach of faith against the
Lord by deceiving his neighbor in a matter of deposit or security, or through robbery, or if he
has oppressed his neighbor 3or has found something lost and lied about it, swearing falsely – in
any of all the things that people do and sin thereby – 4if he has sinned and has realized his guilt
and will restore what he took by robbery or what he got by oppression or the deposit that was
committed to him or the lost thing that he found 5or anything about which he has sworn falsely,
he shall restore it in full and shall add a fifth to it, and give it to him to whom it belongs on the
day he realizes his guilt. 6And he shall bring to the priest as his compensation to the Lord a ram
without blemish out of the flock, or its equivalent, for a guilt offering. 7And the priest shall make
atonement for him before the Lord, and he shall be forgiven for any of the things that one may
do and thereby become guilty" (ESV).

OBSERVATION

What do these passage say about...

God?

Bribes?

Restitution?

4 - DAY FIVE

Homework

SCRIPTURE READING

Read Isaiah 33:13-16.

"Hear, you who are far off, what I have done; and you who are near, acknowledge my might. 14The sinners in Zion are afraid; trembling has seized the godless: 'Who among us can dwell with the consuming fire? Who among us can dwell with everlasting burnings?' 15He who walks righteously and speaks uprightly, who despises the gain of oppressions, who shakes his hands, lest they hold a bribe, who stops his ears from hearing of bloodshed and shuts his eyes from looking on evil, 16he will dwell on the heights; his place of defense will be the fortresses of rocks; his bread will be given him; his water will be sure" (ESV).

Read Leviticus 6:1-7.

"The Lord spoke to Moses, saying, 2"If anyone sins and commits a breach of faith against the Lord by deceiving his neighbor in a matter of deposit or security, or through robbery, or if he has oppressed his neighbor 3or has found something lost and lied about it, swearing falsely – in any of all the things that people do and sin thereby – 4if he has sinned and has realized his guilt and will restore what he took by robbery or what he got by oppression or the deposit that was committed to him or the lost thing that he found 5or anything about which he has sworn falsely, he shall restore it in full and shall add a fifth to it, and give it to him to whom it belongs on the day he realizes his guilt. 6And he shall bring to the priest as his compensation to the Lord a ram without blemish out of the flock, or its equivalent, for a guilt offering. 7And the priest shall make atonement for him before the Lord, and he shall be forgiven for any of the things that one may do and thereby become guilty" (ESV).

INTERPRETATION

What do these passages mean to you?

What do these verses tell us about those who are righteous?

How have you experienced bribery or restitution in your life?

APPLICATION

The Tracking Tool

(see the following page for details)

The Tracking Tool:

So this is where the fun begins! Now that you've created an Estimated Spending Plan, it's time to take the steps to make your plan a reality. That is where the Tracking Tool comes in. The Tracking Tool is designed to help you record your income and expenses over thirty days, gauge your progress as it relates to your plan, and to make changes or adjustments as you track.

Getting Started: Make sure you enter the totals from your Estimated Spending Plan into the Estimated Plan sections of the Tracking Tool. This number will be your target for your expenses from each category. Once you've done this, it's time to implement the four Cs of tracking!

Step One – CAPTURE

This chapter has revealed important truths about honesty that will be helpful as you track. In the process of tracking your income and expenses, you'll want to make sure that you are completely honest with yourself – and your spouse if you have one. Being honest and transparent is key to having a clear picture of where you are financially. Make sure to save any receipts and expenses over the next 30 days and enter them into the Tracking Tool each day. You can't get the data you need without tracking everything that comes in and everything that goes out.

Step Two – CATEGORIZE

Each transaction has a category (food, clothing, auto, transportation, etc.) The tracking tool is designed with one column for income and 12 columns for spending categories. If you aren't sure about where to put a transaction, review the estimated spending plan and choose a category that makes the most sense to you.

Step Three – COMPARE

Compare the suggested plan against the actual data you are tracking, both in and out. Are you reaching your goals? Are you staying on track? How much of your income should be spent on food, clothes, housing, and so forth? It's helpful to compare the percentage of income you're spending for these items against the recommended percentages that work for thousands of people. But remember, the recommendations are rules of thumb for average incomes, not exact prescriptions for every situation.

Although the Spending Percentage Guideline isn't meant to be rigid, it may give you an idea of where you could be overspending. If you have unusually high or low income, these numbers could change dramatically.

If you are spending more than the recommended amount for an item, it may be necessary to reduce your spending in that area to enjoy a balanced Spending Plan.

Step Four – CHANGE

Change is constant. Bills can go up and down each month, and you never know when you might have an unexpected expense. The bottom line is that if there is more going out than coming in, something needs to change. The Tracking Tool is designed to make you aware of those discrepancies and to adjust as you see them happening. This may mean looking for ways to delete an expense, lower an expense, or provide more income so that you can meet your category targets.

Spending Percentage Guideline

Item	Recommendation
Giving	10% or more
Saving/Investing	5-15%
Housing	30-40%
Food	5-15%
Transportation	10-15%
Clothing	2-7%
Medical/Health	5-10%
Education/Child Care	2-7%
Personal	5-10%
Entertainment/Vacation	5-10%
Debts	5-10%

Why do I need to do this?

A great question! There are a couple reasons.

First, it is your responsibility as a steward to know what you are doing with what God has entrusted to you. The Tracking Tool is a great way to get a visual representation of how you are doing in being a faithful steward of God's money.

Second, of the thousands of budgeting tools and programs in existence – envelope systems, banking tools, software programs, excel spreadsheets and mobile apps – do you know what they all have in common? Tracking! In some way, shape, or form they all incorporate tracking. It is the key to any budgeting tool, and we want to make sure you know how to track effectively. This will help you to be a faithful steward!

You can find an example of this application at ***compasstools.org***

Did you know you can also use the Financial Discipleship App to track your expenses? It takes the Tracking Tool Worksheet and makes it accessible from your smart device- calculating everything for you. Perfect for all you folks on the go! Available on the Apple App Store or on Google Play.

Download on the App Store

GET IT ON Google Play

The Tracking Tool

Month: ____________________

Year: ____________________

CATEGORY	INCOME	GIVING	TAXES	SAVE/INVEST	HOUSING	FOOD
DATE						
1						
2						
3						
4						
5						
6						
7						
8						
9						
10						
11						
12						
13						
14						
15						
15 DAY SUBTOTAL						
16						
17						
18						
19						
20						
21						
22						
23						
24						
25						
26						
27						
28						
29						
30						
(31)						
30 DAY SUBTOTAL						

ESTIMATED PLAN						

DIFFERENCE						

TRANSPORTATION	CLOTHING	MED./HEALTH	EDUCATION	PERSONAL	ENT./VAC.	DEBT

PRAYERS FOR TODAY

This prayer section is for personal use and isn't meant to be part of the group discussion.

For you...

For your family and friends...

For those in your group...

See Their Story...

See how this couple's attitude about money went from hostility to gratefulness, totally changing their financial discipleship journey.

See how God provided for this couple in amazing ways as they were faithful in following His calling.

You can also watch these amazing stories at compasstools.org

Additional Tools for the Journey!

To help you on your financial discipleship journey, we have provided practical resources from a variety of people in the financial world. Visit us at **compasstools.org** to check out these resources.

Step One:

Watch the Video

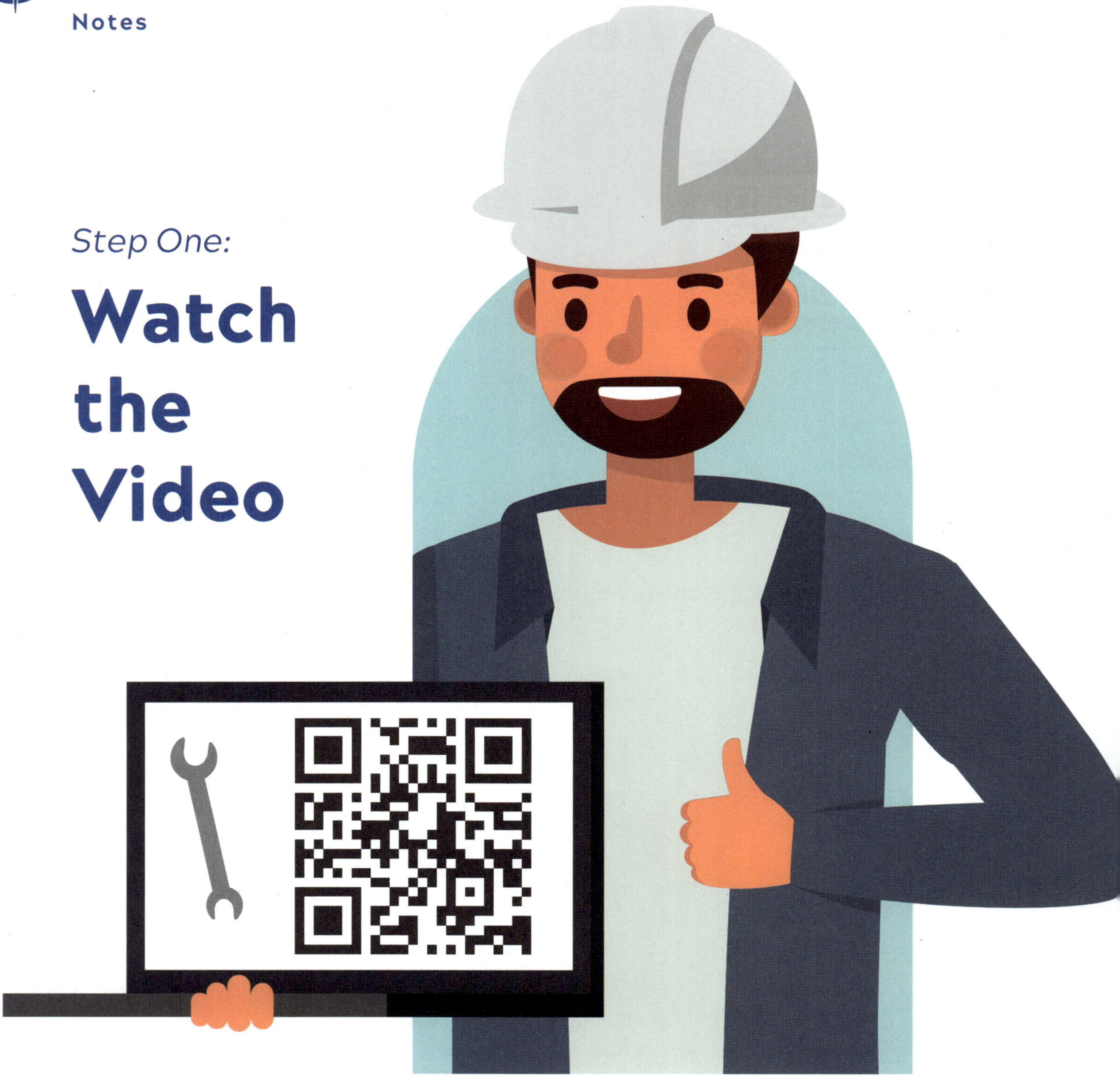

Open the camera on your phone to scan the QR code

OR

*Visit **compasstools.org** to view the video for this chapter*

Step Two:

Read the Notes

Not a fan of reading? You can listen to these notes at compasstools.org

Work

Over a lifetime, the average person spends about 100,000 hours working. Those hours usually include some degree of dissatisfaction. Perhaps no statistic demonstrates this more than job-change frequency. A survey found that the average man changes jobs every four and one-half years, and the average woman, every three years. Boredom, lack of fulfillment, inadequate wages, and countless other pressures contribute to this discontentment. Doctors, housewives, salespersons, blue-collar workers, managers, all – regardless of profession – have expressed similar frustrations. Understanding what God says about work will help you find satisfaction in your job. Implementing these principles will make you more valuable in the job market and possibly position you to increase your income.

All Honest Professions are Honorable

The Bible gives dignity to all types of work, not elevating any honest profession above another. David was a shepherd and a king. Luke was a doctor. Lydia was a retailer. Daniel was a government worker. Paul was a tentmaker. Mary was a homemaker. And, finally, the Lord Jesus Christ was a carpenter.

In God's economy, there is equal dignity in the labor of the janitor and the president of the company.

Notes

Employer's Responsibilities

Godly employers perform a balancing act. They are to love, serve, and encourage employees while leading them and holding them accountable for the completion of their assigned tasks. Let's examine several principles that should govern an employer's conduct.

SERVE YOUR EMPLOYEES The basis for biblical leadership is servanthood: "*. . . whoever wants to become prominent among you shall be your servant*" (Matthew 20:26). Employers should attempt to be creative as they serve their employees. For example, investing time and money to educate and upgrade their employees' job skills will help employees grow in value and earning power.

BE A GOOD COMMUNICATOR The Genesis account of building the tower of Babel supports the importance of good communication. At that time, everyone spoke the same language and adopted a common goal. The Lord makes this remarkable observation, "*If as one people speaking the same language they have begun to do this, then nothing they plan to do will be impossible for them*" (Genesis 11:6, NIV).

When people have good communication and pursue a common goal, then "*nothing they plan to do will be impossible for them*" – as long as it's within the will of God. Since building the tower was not what He wanted, He stopped construction. And how did God do it? He disrupted their ability to communicate, which was the foundation for successfully completing the tower. "*Come, let us go down and confuse their language so they will not understand each other*" (Genesis 11:7, NIV).

It is especially important to listen to employee complaints. A sensitive, listening ear is a tangible expression of care. When a complaint is legitimate, employers should take appropriate steps to solve the problem.

HOLD EMPLOYEES ACCOUNTABLE Employers are responsible for employees knowing what's expected on the job. Employers should regularly evaluate employee performance and communicate it to them. Employees who do not perform satisfactorily and who are unable or unwilling to change may require dismissal.

PAY EMPLOYEES A FAIR WAGE PROMPTLY The Bible warns employers to pay a fair wage. "*[The Lord will judge] those who oppress the wage earner in his wages*" (Malachi 3:5). It also commands them to pay wages promptly when due. "*You shall not oppress a hired [employee] . . . Give him his wages on his day before the sun sets . . . so that he does not cry out against you to the Lord, and it becomes a sin in you*" (Deuteronomy 24:14-15).

PRAY FOR GODLY EMPLOYEES The Lord may choose to bless an employer for having a godly employee. Joseph is an example. *"Joseph found favor in [Potiphar's] sight . . . It came about that from the time he made [Joseph] overseer in his house and over all that he owned, the Lord blessed the Egyptian's house on account of Joseph; so the Lord's blessing was upon all that he owned, in the house and in the field"* (Genesis 39:4-5).

This principle was my primary reason for employing Raymond, an especially godly construction worker. He was strong and did the work of two people, but far more important was his influence over the project. There was less profanity and pilferage, and he was an excellent model of hard work. This principle is not a command, but we believe wise employers will pray for the Lord to bring "Raymonds" to their company.

Employee's Responsibilities

We can identify five major responsibilities of godly employees by examining the story of Daniel in the lion's den. In the sixth chapter of Daniel, Darius, king of Babylon, appointed 120 people to administer the government, and three people – one of whom was Daniel – to supervise the administrators. Because of Daniel's outstanding service, the king decided to promote Daniel to govern the entire kingdom.

Daniel's jealous peers looked for a way to disqualify him but could find no basis for accusation. Knowing Daniel's devotion to God, they asked King Darius to enact a law requiring everyone to worship only the king or die in the lion's den. Daniel refused to stop worshipping God, and Darius reluctantly threw him to the lions. When God rescued Daniel by sending an angel to shut the lions' mouths, the thankful king ordered all of his subjects to honor the God of Daniel. Daniel modeled the five characteristics of godly employees.

HONESTY Daniel 6:4 tells us that Daniel's fellow employees could find no dishonesty in him, and there was no *"evidence of corruption"* in his work. To the chagrin of his enemies, Daniel was an example of total honesty.

FAITHFULNESS We discover the second characteristic of godly employees in Daniel 6:4 (NKJV): *"He was faithful."* Godly employees strive for this. We want our employers to say, "I've always been able to depend on Heather because she's so faithful."

Notes

PRAYER Godly employees are people of prayer. *"When Daniel learned that the document was signed [restricting worship to the king alone] . . . he continued kneeling on his knees three times a day, praying and offering praise before his God, just as he had been doing previously"* (Daniel 6:10). Daniel shouldered the responsibility of governing the most powerful country of his day. Few of us will ever face that kind of pressure or demands on our time. In spite of what must have been an extremely heavy schedule, however, Daniel knew and modeled the priority of prayer. If you aren't praying consistently, your work will suffer.

HONOR THOSE IN HIGHER POSITIONS *"Then Daniel spoke to the king, 'O king, live forever!'"* (Daniel 6:21). What a remarkable response from Daniel. The king had been tricked into sentencing Daniel to the lion's den. But Daniel's reaction was to honor the king – in spite of the terrible circumstance in which he found himself. Think how easy it would have been to disrespect the king and say something like, "You dummy! The God who sent His angel to shut the lions' mouths is now going to whack you!" Instead, he honored the king in front of everyone.

VERBALIZE YOUR FAITH King Darius would never have known about the Lord if Daniel hadn't communicated his faith at appropriate moments while at work. *". . . The king began speaking and said to Daniel, 'Daniel, servant of the living God, has your God, whom you continually serve, been able to rescue you from the lions?'"* (Daniel 6:20). Daniel's words and actions influenced King Darius, who observed his honesty, faithfulness, and hard work. Listen to the king's response: *"I issue a decree that in every part of my kingdom people must fear and reverence the God of Daniel. For he is the living God and he endures forever"* (Daniel 6:26, NIV).

Daniel influenced his employer, one of the most powerful people in the world, to believe in the only true God. You have that same opportunity in your God-given sphere of work.

Let me say this another way. A job well done earns you the right to tell others with whom you work about the reality of Christ. Viewing your work from God's perspective turns dissatisfaction to contentment with a job well done; drudgery becomes excitement over the prospect of introducing others to the Savior.

Other Work Issues

RETIREMENT The dictionary defines retirement as "withdrawal from an occupation, retreat from an active life." Our culture promotes the goal of retirement and ceasing all labor to pursue a life filled with leisure. Is this a biblical goal?

Numbers 8:24-26 – the only reference to retirement in the Bible – applied specifically to the Levites working in the tabernacle. While people are physically and mentally capable, there is no scriptural basis for retiring and becoming unproductive – the concept of putting an older but able person *"out to pasture."* Don't let age stop you from finishing the work God has called you to accomplish. He will provide you with the necessary strength and mental clarity. Remember Moses! He was 80 years old when he began his 40-year adventure of leading the children of Israel.

The Bible does imply, however, that the type or intensity of work may change as we grow older – shifting gears to a less demanding pace to become more of an *"elder seated at the gate."* During this season we can use the experience and wisdom gained over a lifetime. Even in the example of the Levites, they were instructed to continue to *"minister to their brothers in the tent of meeting by keeping guard."* In other words, they were told to continue to be productive. If we have sufficient income to meet our needs apart from our jobs, we may choose to leave work to invest more time in serving others as God directs.

AMBITION Scripture doesn't condemn ambition. Paul was certainly ambitious, writing: *"We also have as our ambition . . . to be pleasing to Him"* (2 Corinthians 5:9). The Bible does, however, condemn selfish ambition. The Lord *"will repay each person according to his deeds . . . those who are self-serving . . . wrath and indignation"* (Romans 2:6,8). *"But if you have . . . selfish ambition in your heart, do not be arrogant and so lie against the truth. This wisdom is not that which comes down from above, but is earthly, natural, demonic. For where jealousy and selfish ambition exist, there is disorder and every evil thing"* (James 3:14-16). *"But as for you, are you seeking great things for yourself? Do not seek them"* (Jeremiah 45:5).

Remember, the Bible is not the enemy of ambition, only of the wrong type of ambition. Our ambition should be to please Christ, work hard, and be faithful in our job to please Him.

YOUR CALLING God has given each of us a specific calling or purpose. *"We are His workmanship, created in Christ Jesus for good works, which God prepared beforehand so that we would walk in them"* (Ephesians 2:10). Study this passage carefully. *"We are His workmanship."* The Amplified Bible says, *"We are His handiwork."* God has given each of us special physical, emotional, and mental abilities. You may have heard the expression, "After the Lord made you, He threw away the mold." It's true! You are gifted uniquely. No one in all of history – past, present, or future – is like you.

Notes

The passage continues, "created in Christ Jesus for good works, which God prepared beforehand so that we would walk in them." The Lord created each of us for a particular task, endowing us with abilities and desires to accomplish it. Your calling may be fulltime Christian service or a secular job.

People often wonder whether God wants them to continue in their work after they commit their lives to Christ. Many feel they may not be serving Him in a significant way if they remain at their jobs. Nothing could be further from the truth. The key is for each person to identify God's call for his or her life. Stanley Tam addresses this in his book, God Owns My Business: "Although I believe in the application of good principles in business, I place far more confidence in the conviction that I have a call from God. I am convinced that His purpose for me is in the business world. My business is my pulpit."

To those who earn a living through secular pursuits, it is a great comfort to know that the "call" of holy vocation carries over into all walks of life. The key is for us to identify God's call for our life, recognizing that God strategically places His children everywhere!

Our primary calling at some stages of life may be obvious. But it's important for you to understand that God is at work around you as you seek to identify your calling. Consider this:

God prepares us.

God providentially allows us to experience circumstances to prepare us for our calling. God has been grooming you your entire life through your family, education, work, and your relationships. You may find this hard to believe, especially if these were not godly influences. Some of these experiences were positive and others were difficult. For example, the Lord might use a painful divorce to give someone the empathy and passion to serve others in similar situations.

God calls us.

God communicates to each of us in a personal, unique way because He wants our experience to be with Him as the living Lord rather than based on a technique. It is unusual for the Lord to speak to us as He did to Moses from something as spectacular as a burning bush. He will, however, usually give us a passion for our calling and confirm our direction through the Scriptures.

For six months I prayed, asking the Lord whether He wanted me to start a financial ministry or to continue in the real estate development business. Someone I deeply admired urged me to begin what has become Compass.

The next morning, I asked the Lord if this person's counsel was from Him. Immediately the Holy Spirit unmistakably impressed on my mind Esther 4:14, "*. . . And who knows whether you have not [been called] for such a time as this?*" This was the same passage He had originally given me when I was in the early stages of studying the biblical principles of finance. I knew with certainty that Christ was calling me to start a financial ministry.

God often provides few details.

Examine what Jesus said to the disciples when He called them, *"As Jesus was walking by the sea of Galilee, He saw two brothers, Simon, who was called Peter, and his brother Andrew, casting a net into the sea; for they were fishermen. And He said to them, 'Follow Me, and I will make you fishers of people"* (Matthew 4:18-19).

Think of those the Lord called: Abraham, David, Jeremiah, Paul, and others. How many details were they initially given? Not many! Without a close relationship with Christ, you will miss what He wants to do in and through you. He is more likely to ask you to follow Him one day at a time than He is to spell out all the details before you begin to obey Him.

Don't be surprised if it's out of your comfort zone!

Consider the people God used in the Bible. God called almost all of them to step outside their comfort zone. Way outside!

For example, the Lord asked Abraham to leave his home for an unknown location; Moses to lead two million people through the Red Sea; David to fight the nine-foot-tall giant Goliath; Daniel to spend a night in the lion's den; the engaged virgin Mary to give birth to the Savior.

I believe that the Lord delights in doing things through us that totally surprise us. There is no explanation for what is happening – except God's providence.

Your calling requires obedience.

In Henry Blackaby's outstanding *Experiencing God* small group study, he points out, "Through your relationship with Jesus Christ, God reveals His will and invites you to join Him where He is already at work. When you obey, God accomplishes through you something that only He can do."

Psalm 127:1 says it this way, *"Unless the Lord builds a house, they who build it labor in vain."* If we want our lives to count for eternity, we must be rooted in willingness to follow and obey Christ wherever He chooses to lead us. In fact, Jesus tells us that our obedience is evidence that we love Him. *"If you love me, keep my commands"* (John 14:15, NIV).

Notes

Partnerships

Scripture discourages business partnerships with those who do not know Christ. In 2 Corinthians 6:14-17 we read, *"Do not be mismatched with unbelievers; for what do righteousness and lawlessness share together, or what does light have in common with darkness? . . . or what does a believer share with an unbeliever? . . . 'Therefore, come out from their midst and be separate,' says the Lord."*

Many have suffered financially – and in every other way – for violating this principle. We should also be careful about entering into any partnership, even with another Christian. With my lifetime of contacts, I would consider only a few people as partners. These are people I know well. I've observed their commitment to the Lord, know their strengths and weaknesses, and have seen them handle money faithfully.

If, after prayerful consideration, you decide to form a partnership, first take the time to commit your understandings into writing. Develop this agreement with your future partner, and be sure to include a way to end the partnership. If you aren't able to agree in writing, don't become partners. Remember, don't rush into any partnership without prayer and plenty of godly counsel.

Procrastination

A procrastinator is someone who, because of laziness or fear, has a habit of putting things off until later. This habit often develops into a serious character flaw.

The book of Ruth introduces Boaz, one of my favorite examples in the Bible of a non-procrastinator. Ruth's mother-in-law, Naomi, made this revealing comment about Ruth's future husband, Boaz: *". . . Wait, my daughter, until you know how the matter turns out; for the man **will not rest until he has settled it today**"* (Ruth 3:18, emphasis added). Boaz had a reputation for acting promptly.

Here are some practical suggestions to help overcome procrastination:

> *List the things you need to do each day.*
>
> *Prayerfully review the list and prioritize it according to the tasks you need to accomplish first.*
>
> *Finish the first task on your list before starting the second. Often that first task is the most difficult or the one you fear the most.*
>
> *Ask the Lord to give you courage, remembering Philippians 4:13, "I can do all things through Him who strengthens me."*

Taxes

Our neighbor, Michael, had just gotten his first job and was really excited about his first paycheck – until he saw how much was taken out in taxes! Like a lot of people, he questioned why he would need to pay these taxes.

So what does the Bible say about paying taxes? That's the same question that was asked of Jesus. *"Is it permissible for us to pay taxes to Caesar, or not? . . . [Jesus] said to them, 'Show Me a [Roman coin]. Whose image and inscription does it have?' They said, 'Caesar's.' And He said to them, 'Then pay to Caesar the things that are Caesar's'"* (Luke 20:22-25).

Some people will tell you to avoid paying taxes at any cost. After all, they will reason, look how much the government squanders. But the Bible tells us to pay our taxes. *"Every person is to be subject to the governing authorities. For there is no authority except from God, and those which exist are established by God . . . because of this you also pay taxes, for rulers are servants of God, devoting themselves to this very thing. Pay to all what is due them: tax to whom tax is due"* (Romans 13:1,6-7). It's certainly permissible to reduce taxes by using legal tax deductions, but we should be careful not to make unwise decisions simply to avoid paying taxes.

From a practical standpoint, it is important to keep invoices, checks, statements, and receipts that are necessary for your income tax records or are the only evidence of a paid bill. Bev and I have benefited from a simple filing system dozens of times. It requires an average of less than one minute a day and can save you hours of searching. We suggest you keep the receipts for seven years before destroying them.

A Focus on the Home

Proverbs 31:10-31 tells us:

> *"An excellent wife who can find? She is far more precious than jewels. 11The heart of her husband trusts in her, and he will have no lack of gain. 12She does him good, and not harm, all the days of her life. 13She seeks wool and flax, and works with willing hands. 14She is like the ships of the merchant; she brings her food from afar. 15She rises while it is yet night and provides food for her household and portions for her maidens. 16She considers a field and buys it; with the fruit of her hands she plants a vineyard. 17She dresses herself with strength and makes her arms strong. 18She perceives that her merchandise is profitable. Her lamp does not go out at night. 19She puts her hands to the distaff, and her hands hold the spindle. 20She opens her hand to the poor and reaches out her hands to the needy. 21She is not afraid of snow for her household, for all her household are clothed in scarlet. 22She makes bed coverings for herself; her clothing is fine linen and purple. 23Her husband is known in the gates when he sits among the elders of the land. 24She makes linen garments and sells them; she delivers sashes to the merchant. 25Strength and dignity are her clothing, and she laughs at the time to come. 26She opens her mouth with wisdom, and the teaching of kindness is on her tongue. 27She looks well to the ways of her household and does not eat the bread of*

Notes

> *idleness. [28]Her children rise up and call her blessed; her husband also, and he praises her: [29]"Many women have done excellently, but you surpass them all." [30]Charm is deceitful, and beauty is vain, but a woman who fears the Lord is to be praised. [31]Give her of the fruit of her hands, and let her works praise her in the gates"* (ESV).

Let's look at the variety of tasks this wife accomplishes in her work; she acquires wool and flax, shops for food for her family, cares for the needs of others in the home, makes crafts, shows charity, shops for the needs of home, teaches in the home, and raises her children well. These were the normal tasks of a mother and wife working to keep an orderly home.

Looking closer, we also notice the wife working outside the home by making and selling goods in her own business, investing money in real estate, conserving wealth, remaining industrious and working hard in partnership with her husband for the good of the family.

While she is accomplishing a variety of tasks in different places, her focus and priority remains on her household.

Some women are gifted as homemakers, and there is no more important task than raising godly children. Other women may have skills they desire to express in work outside the home, and some must work to earn income.

When spouses feel called to stay at home and it feels like the family can't make it financially if they do, the *One or Two Income Calculator* at compasstools.org can be valuable. Examine how much income, after taxes and expenses, the second wage actually contributes.

Couples are often surprised to learn that the income earned by a second working spouse isn't as much as they had expected. Some have actually produced more net income (after reducing work-related expenses) when they decided to work in some creative way while staying at home. Of course, the financial benefits aren't the only factors to evaluate. Also consider the physical and emotional demands of working and how they may affect a family.

Honesty

HONESTY IN SOCIETY All of us have to make decisions about whether to handle money honestly. Do you tell the cashier when you receive too much change? Have you ever tried to sell something and been tempted not to tell the truth because you might lose the sale?

Deciding on a course of honesty and integrity is all the more difficult because so many around us act dishonestly. The verse that comes to mind is Judges 17:6, "*. . . everyone did what was right in his own eyes.*" People today formulate their own standards of honesty – and then change them when circumstances change.

HONESTY IN SCRIPTURE Hundreds of verses in the Bible communicate the Lord's desire for us to be completely honest in all our dealings. For instance, Proverbs 20:23 says, "*The Lord loathes all cheating and dishonesty*" (TLB). And Proverbs 12:22 states, "*Lying lips are an abomination to the Lord.*" And in Proverbs 6:16-17 we read, "*The Lord hates . . . a lying tongue.*"

Study the following comparison between what the Scriptures teach and what our society practices concerning honesty.

ISSUE	SCRIPTURE	SOCIETY
Standard of honesty:	Complete honesty	Changes with circumstance
God's concern about honesty:	He requires it	There is no God, or he looks the other way
The decision to be honest or dishonest is based upon:	Faith in the invisible, living God	Only facts can be seen
Question usually when deciding whether or not to be honest:	Will it please God?	Will I get away with it?

Notes

The God of Truth

Truthfulness is one of God's attributes. He is repeatedly identified as the God of truth. Jesus said, *"I am . . . the truth"* (John 14:6). Our loving heavenly Father commands us to reflect His honest and holy character: *". . . be holy yourselves also in all your behavior; because it is written: 'You shall be holy, for I am holy'"* (1 Peter 1:15-16).

In contrast to God's nature, John 8:44 describes the devil's character: *". . . He [the devil] was a murderer from the beginning, and does not stand in the truth because there is no truth in him. Whenever he tells a lie, he speaks from his own nature, because he is a liar and the father of lies."* The Lord wants us to conform to His honest character rather than to the dishonest nature of the devil.

Escaping the temptation of dishonesty

A friend was teaching these principles in a secular school when a young man raised his hand and said, "I think we'd all like to be honest, but I know in my heart that if the right opportunity comes along, I'm going to be dishonest."

Was that student just being cynical? No, apart from being yielded to the Holy Spirit, all of us will be dishonest. The Bible says, *"Walk by the Spirit, and you will not gratify the desires of the flesh. For the flesh desires what is contrary to the Spirit, and the Spirit what is contrary to the flesh"* (Galatians 5:16-17, NIV).

It's human nature is to act dishonestly. *"It is from within, out of a person's heart, that evil thoughts come . . . theft . . . deceit"* (Mark 7:21-22, NIV). The Holy Spirit who indwells our lives desires us to be honest. And we need His help! Just bear in mind that the totally honest life is supernatural. To experience that life, we need to submit ourselves entirely to Jesus Christ as Lord and allow Him to live His life through us. There is no other way.

I heartily recommend a short book by Andrew Murray titled Humility. It's an excellent study on yielding fully to Christ.

The following principles will help you develop the habit of honesty.

PRACTICE THE GOLDEN RULE *"Do not merely look out for your own personal interests, but also for the interests of others"* (Philippians 2:4). This verse is better translated, "look intently" after the interests of others.

The Lord used this passage to point out Warren's lack of concern for others just when he was about to purchase some land, taking advantage of a seller who knew nothing of its true value. Warren secretly congratulated himself, because he knew the purchase price he had offered was very low. Not once had he considered what would be fair to the seller.

Later, however, Warren reexamined the transaction in the light of "looking intently" after the seller's interests as well as his own. After an intense inner struggle (to the great surprise of the seller), he concluded that he should pay more for the property to reflect its true value. Practicing the Golden Rule is sometimes costly, but its reward is a clear conscience before God and other people.

AVOID PARTIALITY Study carefully James 2:1-9: *"My brothers and sisters, do not hold your faith in our glorious Lord Jesus Christ with an attitude of personal favoritism. For if a man comes into your assembly with a gold ring and is dressed in bright clothes, and a poor man in dirty clothes also comes in, and you pay special attention to the one who is wearing the bright clothes . . . have you not made distinctions among yourselves, and become judges with evil motives? . . . If, however, you are fulfilling the royal law, according to the Scripture, 'You shall love your neighbor as yourself,' you are doing well. But if you show partiality, you are committing sin and are convicted by the law as violators."*

Partiality doesn't have to be based on a person's wealth. It can also be based on a person's education, social position, or spiritual status. James 2:9 could not be more blunt: *"But if you show partiality,* ***you are committing sin*** *and are convicted by the law as violators"* (emphasis added). How do we break the habit of partiality? Romans 12:10 tells us, *"Be devoted to one another in brotherly love; give preference to one another in honor."* And Philippians 2:3 reads, *". . . With humility consider one another as more important than yourselves."*

We need to ask the Lord to ingrain in our thinking the habit of consciously elevating each person, regardless of his or her station in life, as more important than ourselves. One practical way to overcome partiality is to concentrate on the abilities of each person. Everyone can do some things better than I can. This realization helps me appreciate all people.

Notes

MAINTAIN A HEALTHY FEAR OF THE LORD When we talk of a healthy fear of the Lord, we're not implying that God is a big bully just waiting for the opportunity to punish us. Far from it. In fact, He is a loving Father who, out of infinite love, disciplines His children for their benefit. *"He disciplines us for our good, so that we may share His holiness"* (Hebrews 12:10).

God uses this healthy fear to motivate us toward honesty in all our dealings. Proverbs 16:6 says, *"By the fear of the Lord one keeps away from evil."* Hebrews 12:11 warns us: *"For the moment, all discipline seems not to be pleasant, but painful."* Discipline hurts! Given the choice, we should obey His Word rather than make a deliberate decision that will prompt our loving Father to discipline us.

We believe our heavenly Father will not allow us to keep anything we have acquired dishonestly. Proverbs 13:11 reads, *"Wealth obtained by fraud dwindles."*

STAY AWAY FROM DISHONEST PEOPLE Scripture teaches that we are deeply influenced by those around us, either for good or for evil. Paul wrote, *"Do not be deceived: 'Bad company corrupts good morals'"* (1 Corinthians 15:33). Solomon was even stronger: *"One who is a partner with a thief hates his own life"* (Proverbs 29:24).

If I observe a person who is dishonest in dealing with the government or in a small matter, I know this person will be dishonest in greater matters – and probably in dealing with me. I believe it is impossible for people to be selectively honest. Either they have made the commitment to be completely honest or their dishonesty will become more prevalent. It's much easier to remain absolutely honest if you are surrounded by others who hold to that same conviction..

GIVE GENEROUSLY We can help escape the temptation of acting dishonestly by giving generously to those in need. *"The one who steals must no longer steal; but rather he must labor, producing with his own hands what is good, so that he will have something to share with one who has need"* (Ephesians 4:28). Giving draws us closer to Christ and reduces our incentive to steal. After all, if we're going to give something away, there's no reason to steal it!

What to do when dishonest

Unfortunately, we sometimes slip and act dishonestly. Once we recognize it, we need to do the following:

RESTORE OUR FELLOWSHIP WITH GOD Anytime we sin, we break fellowship with God and need to restore it. First John 1:9 tells us how: *"If we confess our sins, He is faithful and righteous so that He will forgive us our sins and cleanse us from all unrighteousness."* We must agree with God that our dishonesty was sin and then thankfully accept His gracious forgiveness so we can again enjoy His fellowship. Remember, God loves us. He is kind and merciful, ready to forgive our dishonesty when we turn from it.

RESTORE OUR FELLOWSHIP WITH THE HARMED PERSON After our fellowship with God has been restored, we need to confess our dishonesty to the person we offended. *"Confess your sins to one another"* (James 5:16).

Ouch! This hurts. Only a handful of people have confessed wronging me. Interestingly, these people have become some of my closest friends. They so desired an honest relationship that they were willing to expose their sins.

Confessing has been very hard for me. My first experience came years ago when I went to someone I had wronged and confessed my sin – not that I hadn't had plenty of opportunities before! In the past, however, my pride had stood in the way. Afterward I sensed a great freedom in our relationship.

Failing to confess and restore fellowship may result in a lack of financial prosperity. *"One who conceals his wrongdoings will not prosper, but one who confesses and abandons them will find compassion"* (Proverbs 28:13).

RESTORE DISHONESTLY ACQUIRED PROPERTY If we have acquired anything dishonestly, we must return it to its rightful owner. *"Then it shall be, when he sins and becomes guilty, that he shall restore what he took by robbery . . . or anything about which he swore falsely; he shall make restitution for it in full and add to it a fifth more. He shall give it to the one to whom it belongs"* (Leviticus 6:4-5).

Restitution is a tangible expression of repentance and an effort to correct a wrong. Zacchaeus is a good example. He promised Jesus, *"If I have extorted anything from anyone, I am giving back four times as much"* (Luke 19:8).

If it's not possible for restitution to be made, then the property should be given to the Lord. Numbers 5:8 teaches, *"If the man has no redeemer to whom restitution may be made for the wrong, the restitution which is made for the wrong must go to the Lord."*

Notes

Honesty Required for Leadership

The Lord is especially concerned with the honesty of leaders, because they influence those who follow them. The owner of a trucking business began wearing cowboy boots to work. Within six months, all the men in his office were in boots. He suddenly changed to traditional business shoes, and six months later all the men were wearing business shoes.

In a similar way, a dishonest leader produces dishonest followers. *"If a ruler pays attention to falsehood, all his ministers become wicked"* (Proverbs 29:12). Leaders of a business, church, or home must set the example of honesty in their personal life before those under their authority can be expected to do the same.

Selection and Retention of Leaders

Dishonesty should disqualify a person from leadership. Listen to the counsel of Jethro, Moses' father-in-law: *"You shall select out of all the people able men who fear God, men of truth, those who hate dishonest gain; and you shall place these . . . as leaders of thousands, of hundreds, of fifties and of tens"* (Exodus 18:21). Two of the four criteria for leadership selection dealt with honesty: "men of truth, those who hate dishonest gain."

Not only are leaders selected in part by honest behavior, but a leader retains this position by acting honestly. *"A leader . . . who hates unjust gain will prolong his days"* (Proverbs 28:16). We have all witnessed leaders in business or government who have been removed because of personal corruption.

How can a leader maintain absolute honesty? By becoming accountable to others. It's necessary to establish guardrails that do not usurp the leader's authority but provide a structure to ensure accountability.

Bribes

A bribe is anything given to influence a person to do something illegal or wrong. The taking of bribes is clearly prohibited in the Bible: *"You shall not take a bribe, for a bribe blinds the clear-sighted and subverts the cause of the just"* (Exodus 23:8).

Bribes frequently come packaged as "gifts" or "referral fees." Evaluate any such offer to confirm that it is not a bribe in disguise. If you have any doubts or discomfort, politely refuse to receive any such benefit.

Blessings and Curses

Listed below are some of the blessings the Lord has promised for the honest–and some of the curses reserved for the dishonest. Read these slowly, asking God to use them to motivate you to a life of honesty.

Blessings for the Honest

BLESSING OF A MORE INTIMATE RELATIONSHIP WITH THE LORD *"For the devious are an abomination to the Lord; but He is intimate with the upright"* (Proverbs 3:32).

BLESSINGS ON THE FAMILY *"A righteous man who walks in his integrity – how blessed are his sons after him"* (Proverbs 20:7).

BLESSINGS OF LIFE *"Truthful lips will endure forever, but a lying tongue is only for a moment"* (Proverbs 12:19).

BLESSINGS OF PROSPERITY *"Great wealth is in the house of the righteous, but trouble is in the income of the wicked"* (Proverbs 15:6).

Curses Reserved for the Dishonest

CURSE OF ALIENATION FROM GOD *"For the devious are an abomination to the Lord"* (Proverbs 3:32)

CURSE ON THE FAMILY *"He who profits illicitly troubles his own house, but he who hates bribes will live"* (Proverbs 15:27).

CURSE OF DEATH *"The acquisition of treasures by a lying tongue is a fleeting vapor, the pursuit of death"* (Proverbs 21:6).

CURSE OF POVERTY *"Wealth obtained by fraud dwindles" (Proverbs 13:11).*

Step Three:

Answer the Discussion Questions

What in the notes (and video) did you find revealing or interesting?

What in the notes challenged you the most?

What did you find revealing or challenging about the application worksheets in this chapter? Did you have any questions about the worksheets?

Chapter 4

Compass Commentaries

DAY ONE God created the concept of work as something to be enjoyed and pleasurable to humankind. Along with it, He granted freedom to partake of everything in creation except the fruit of one particular tree. When Adam and Eve sinned, work became difficult and not as fulfilling as it had been designed to be. Painful and exhausting, it is now hard to produce desirable outcomes from the thorns and thistles that grow naturally. You recognize this as soon as you stop caring for a lawn, vineyard, orchard, or field of corn: in a short period of time, it gets overtaken by weeds, insects, and disease. Although sin brought a level of frustration to all of our work, God's concept for it remains intact, and He has a lot to say about how we do it.

DAY TWO Working hard is a desirable characteristic, allowing you to provide for your own needs without relying on someone else to bail you out. Knowing when to rest is also important. Laziness, however, is a different matter. Today, as in Bible times, some people are lazy and won't work. Paul noted that this sometimes led them to become busybodies, sticking their noses where they don't belong.

Everyone should work hard and do the best they can in every task. And as good as it is to work hard, it's also important to value and schedule rest. God modeled this in the creation of the world, resting one day out of seven. Knowing that our bodies and minds need rest, the Lord commanded us to take time away from work to spend time with Him, reflect on His blessings, and allow ourselves to be recharged for the work still to be done. Failure to maintain margin in our lives is unhealthy and unproductive, which is why it is contrary to God's design and commandments. Work hard but get rest!

DAY THREE Notice the many benefits derived from working diligently in today's verses from the Proverbs: prudence, abundant food, satisfaction with good things, reward, and profit. Compare these to the consequences of being lazy and distracted: shame, no sense, poverty, and destruction. Being productive begins with our attitude toward work. Willingness to work hard doesn't guarantee success in all of our ventures, but it does enable us to avoid the pitfalls of laziness.

DAY FOUR When we act honestly, we allow others to make the most of the opportunities afforded them. If we sell a pound of flour and weigh it correctly, the buyer can maximize the value of that flour for their own benefit or profit. If we cheat them by giving them less than they pay for, they lose the ability to make an honest profit.

Don't tell someone one thing and then do something else. People should be able to trust your word. God detests dishonesty and will punish us for it. He wants and expects us to be honest in everything, as He is always honest with us. He loves us and wants us to love others, but you cannot love God and love others by being dishonest.

DAY FIVE Bribes are used to influence someone to be biased in our favor, warping their judgment and perverting justice. Offering or accepting a bride is a form of dishonesty, and God hates dishonesty. When we are dishonest and sin against God and others, consequences follow; but God pronounces blessings on the honest.

Sometimes we may sin against someone who is not yet aware of it. But we know it, and we also know our need to confess it and do what we can to right the situation. This includes making full restitution and adding something to it – as a demonstration of our regret and an attempt to restore a relationship we have injured. Whether a civil judicial system assesses a penalty or not, our desire to reflect God's character should motivate us to do the right thing in God's sight. He is the one to whom we will ultimately give an account.

Chapter 5:

Crisis & Eternity

*All tools, videos, resources and electronic applications for this chapter can be found at **compasstools.org***

THIS CHAPTER'S MEMORY VERSE:

2 Corinthians 4:18

DAILY HOMEWORK:

Day One – Reacting to a Crisis

Day Two – Weathering a Storm

Day Three – Hope and Perseverance in a Crisis, begin working on the Crisis Budget

Day Four – Eternal Perspective

Day Five – Eternity and Judgment, begin working on the Organizing Your Estate Worksheet

Day Six – Watch the Build Your Finances God's Way video, Read the Notes, answer the discussion questions

BEFORE YOUR GROUP MEETING:

1. Memorize 2 Corinthians 4:18, (NIV). To prevent confusion when reciting the verse in a group setting, please memorize the version listed below.

> *"We fix our eyes not on what is seen, but on what is unseen, since what is seen is temporary, but what is unseen is eternal" (2 Corinthians 4:18, NIV).*

2. Complete the Daily Homework.

Each day's homework is designed to take 20-30 minutes to complete.

Reacting to a Crisis

PRAYER

Pray for the Holy Spirit's guidance as you begin reading passages of Scripture. Ask for clarity and insight as you engage in God's word.

SCRIPTURE READING

Read Mark 4:35-41.

*"On that day, when evening had come, he said to them, 'Let us go across to
the other side.' [36]And leaving the crowd, they took him with them in the boat,
just as he was. And other boats were with him. [37]And a great windstorm arose,
and the waves were breaking into the boat, so that the boat was already filling.
[38]But he was in the stern, asleep on the cushion. And they woke him and said
to him, 'Teacher, do you not care that we are perishing?' [39]And he awoke and
rebuked the wind and said to the sea, 'Peace! Be still!' And the wind ceased,
and there was a great calm. [40]He said to them, 'Why are you so afraid? Have you
still no faith?' [41]And they were filled with great fear and said to one another,
'Who then is this, that even the wind and the sea obey him?'" (ESV).*

OBSERVATION

What does this passage say about...

Storms?

The Disciples?

Jesus?

5 - DAY ONE

Homework

SCRIPTURE READING

Read Mark 4:35-41.

*"On that day, when evening had come, he said to them, 'Let us go across to
the other side.' [36]And leaving the crowd, they took him with them in the boat,
just as he was. And other boats were with him. [37]And a great windstorm arose,
and the waves were breaking into the boat, so that the boat was already filling.
[38]But he was in the stern, asleep on the cushion. And they woke him and said
to him, 'Teacher, do you not care that we are perishing?' [39]And he awoke and
rebuked the wind and said to the sea, 'Peace! Be still!' And the wind ceased,
and there was a great calm. [40]He said to them, 'Why are you so afraid? Have you
still no faith?' [41]And they were filled with great fear and said to one another,
'Who then is this, that even the wind and the sea obey him?'" (ESV).*

INTERPRETATION

What is your reaction when faced with a crisis?

What does it mean to have faith in a crisis situation?

How have you experienced the Lord helping you in a crisis?

APPLICATION

How can you apply the principles of this passage to your finances?

HOWARD'S HIGHLIGHTS

There was a knock at the door, and Bev and I glanced at each other. Would he be all we had dreamed?

We raced for the door, threw it open, and there he was. Tiny, gorgeous, and absolutely precious. Four-day-old Andrew, the baby we hoped to adopt, captured our hearts the moment we held him in our arms.

Several months later we began to suspect that Andrew might have some physical challenges. Tragically, his birth mother had been addicted to powerful narcotics during her pregnancy, and the doctors discovered he had been born with only a fraction of his brain.

It was a very difficult time for us – emotionally, physically, and financially. Andrew required multiple surgeries. Because he suffered constant pain, he required around-the-clock care, which led to Bev's exhaustion and almost a complete physical breakdown.

Some challenges build slowly and can be anticipated; others appear without warning. Some are resolved quickly; others are chronic. Some reflect the consequences of our actions; others are completely beyond our control. Some crises impact an entire nation; others are isolated to us as individuals.

A job loss, major illness, birth of a special-needs child, business reversal, death of a family member, a fractured relationship with someone close, or a financial crisis – these and a host of other serious crises can shake us to the core.

I call these challenges the "storms of life." While some of the storms amount to little more than a blustery rain shower, others feel like a category-five hurricane.

Please remember this one thing: No matter what the crisis, you don't face it alone. Put yourself in the sandals of a few of God's people in the Bible who faced terrifying category-five storms.

- Job – in a matter of just a few hours – lost his children, his financial resources, and ultimately his health.
- Joseph was sold into slavery and later slandered – just before he was thrown into prison.
- Moses and the children of Israel faced annihilation by Egypt's powerful army in a cul-de-sac at the Red Sea.
- Daniel was tossed into the lion's den.
- Paul was beaten, stoned, and left for dead on his missionary journeys. And chained to soldiers facing certain death the next day.
- Peter was incarcerated.

The list goes on and on.

Although storms are often emotional, scary, and painful, if we maintain God's perspective, we can survive and even grow through such dark days (and nights!).

PRAYERS FOR TODAY

This prayer section is for personal use and isn't meant to be part of the group discussion.

For you...

For your family and friends...

For those in your group...

Weathering a Storm

PRAYER

Pray for the Holy Spirit's guidance as you begin reading passages of Scripture. Ask for clarity and insight as you engage in God's word.

SCRIPTURE READING

Read Matthew 7:24-27.

"Everyone then who hears these words of mine and does them will be like a
wise man who built his house on the rock. [25]*And the rain fell, and the floods*
came, and the winds blew and beat on that house, but it did not fall, because it
had been founded on the rock. [26]*And everyone who hears these words of mine*
and does not do them will be like a foolish man who built his house on the sand.
[27]*And the rain fell, and the floods came, and the winds blew and beat against*
that house, and it fell, and great was the fall of it" (ESV).

OBSERVATION

What does this passage say about...

God's word?

Foundations?

The potential impact of storms?

SCRIPTURE READING

Read Matthew 7:24-27.

"Everyone then who hears these words of mine and does them will be like a wise man who built his house on the rock.
[25]And the rain fell, and the floods came, and the winds blew and beat on that house, but it did not fall, because it had been founded on the rock.
[26]And everyone who hears these words of mine and does not do them will be like a foolish man who built his house on the sand.
[27]And the rain fell, and the floods came, and the winds blew and beat against that house, and it fell, and great was the fall of it" (ESV).

INTERPRETATION

What would weathering a storm look like in preparing for a financial crisis?

What would weathering a storm look like in the context of a family crisis?

APPLICATION

How can you apply the principles of this passage to your finances and possessions?

HOWARD'S HIGHLIGHTS

The Eye of the Storm

There are several things we can do to survive – and even grow – when we find ourselves in the storm.

Get your finances in order. I've been close to many people facing gut-wrenching financial storms. And the first question they usually ask is, how can I solve the problem?

Jesus answers the question this way in Matthew 7:24-25: *"Everyone who hears these words of mine and puts them into practice is like a wise man who built his house on the rock. The rain came down, the streams rose, and the winds blew and beat against that house; yet it did not fall, because it had its foundation on the rock"* (NIV).

The key to solving your financial problems is learning and practicing God's way of handling money and operating a business if you have one. It truly is that simple. That's why this study is so important. When you finish it, you will know God's framework for handling money. But knowing is only half of what you need. The other half is applying what you have learned. It may take a long time and a lot of effort to navigate the storm, but you will know the basics of what you should do.

Part of what you've learned is to be a generous giver. When facing a financial crisis, the tendency is to hold on tightly to what we have at the expense of our generosity. A passage in the book of Acts, however, shows us a different way. In Acts 11:28-29 we read: *"Agabus [a prophet] . . . through the Spirit predicted that a severe famine would spread over the entire Roman world. (This happened during the reign of Claudius.) The disciples, as each one was able, decided to provide help for the brothers and sisters living in Judea"* (NIV).

Consider this. The Holy Spirit revealed through a prophet that a severe worldwide famine was coming soon, and their first reaction was to give! Don't allow a crisis to stop you from remaining generous. You may not be able to give as much as you did previously, but still give.

Never go through a storm alone. I want to emphasize the importance of not going it alone. It is almost impossible to make wise decisions in isolation in the midst of a crisis. Seek advice from people who have been through similar situations. You will draw strength not only from their emotional support, but also from their experience. There are people all around you who have weathered similar storms, and you can gain from their knowledge, learning of mistakes to avoid and resources to help. Ask your church and friends to pray; it's their most powerful contribution.

Live one day at a time. Roberto Menendez started and built a successful construction business. He was extremely generous and enjoyed a wonderful reputation. And then came the crushing financial crisis of 2008 – crippling his business and pushing him to the brink of bankruptcy.

Roberto confided, "In a crisis, the tendency is to look ahead and become overwhelmed with all the problems. We are to plan ahead, but for our mental and emotional health we must follow what Jesus Christ told us: *"Do not worry about tomorrow, for tomorrow will worry about itself. Each day has enough trouble of its own"* (Matthew 6:34, NIV).

Live focused on today! And if the crisis becomes overwhelming, focus on one moment at a time in close fellowship with Christ. This is not "escape from reality"; it is a practical way to stay close to the only One who can help us through the challenge.

Be patient, waiting for God's timing. Expectations can be damaging during a crisis. When we assume that the Lord will solve our problems in a certain way or by a certain time, we set ourselves up for disappointment and frustration.

Someone described patience as accepting a difficult situation without giving God a deadline for removing it. Remember, God's primary purpose in allowing a crisis in the first place is to conform you to Jesus Christ. He is at work in your life, and He knows exactly how long it will take to produce the results He wants. Ecclesiastes 3:1 says, *"There is an appointed time for everything. And there is a time for every matter under heaven."*

The late Larry Burkett used to say with a smile, "God is seldom early, but He's never late." Be patient. Be careful not to set deadlines for the Lord to act.

Glance at the problem, gaze at Christ. We are to work diligently to solve problems, while keeping full awareness that we need the moment-by-moment help and counsel of the Lord who loves us. Think of it this way: we are to glance at the problem and gaze at Christ.

To help you gaze on the Lord, meditate on Scripture, maintaining a silent conversation with the Lord through your day. Listening to quality Christian music also promotes awareness of God's presence.

One of my favorite passages when facing difficulties is Philippians 4:6-7. Every phrase is loaded with meaning. *"Do not be anxious about anything, but in every situation, by prayer and petition, with thanksgiving, present your requests to God. And the peace of God, which transcends all understanding, will guard your hearts and your minds in Christ Jesus"* (NIV).

Forgive others. God realizes how critical it is for us to forgive those who have caused or contributed to our crisis, regardless of their motivation. One of the most impressive characteristics of Jesus Christ was His willingness to forgive. Imagine hanging on a cross in unspeakable agony and at the same time praying for those who had crucified you: *"Father, forgive them; for they do not know what they are doing"* (Luke 23:34).

In order to grow more like Christ and experience the benefits He intends for us during a crisis, we must forgive. And more than forgive, we are to be kind, compassionate, and seek to be a blessing. *"Be kind and compassionate to one another, forgiving each other, just as in Christ God forgave you"* (Ephesians 4:32, NIV). *"Not returning evil for evil or insult for insult, but giving a blessing instead; for you were called for the very purpose that you would inherit a blessing"* (1 Peter 3:9).

Unforgiveness can be a daily battle, particularly if the crisis has been horribly hurtful. But it harms the person who refuses to forgive. Someone described it as swallowing poison and hoping the other person will die. When we refuse to forgive, the bitterness in our heart can turn toxic, consuming our thoughts and eating away our emotional health. Forgiveness and seeking to bless the other person, however, leads to freedom.

It is imperative to pray regularly for the Lord to give us the desire to forgive, and then to give us His love for the people who may have harmed us. Jesus tells us also to pray for them, *"Love your enemies and pray for those who persecute you, so that you may prove yourselves to be sons of your Father who is in heaven"* (Matthew 5:44-45). It's hard to remain bitter toward someone for whom you are praying regularly.

PRAYERS FOR TODAY

This prayer section is for personal use and isn't meant to be part of the group discussion.

For you...

For your family and friends...

For those in your group...

Homework

Hope & Perseverance in a Crisis

PRAYER

Pray for the Holy Spirit's guidance as you begin reading passages of Scripture. Ask for clarity and insight as you engage in God's word.

SCRIPTURE READING

Read Lamentations 3:16-27.

"He has made my teeth grind on gravel, and made me cower in ashes; [17]my soul is bereft of peace; I have forgotten what happiness is; [18]so I say, 'My endurance has perished; so has my hope from the Lord.' [19]Remember my affliction and my wanderings, the wormwood and the gall! [20]My soul continually remembers it and is bowed down within me. [21]But this I call to mind, and therefore I have hope: [22]The steadfast love of the Lord never ceases; his mercies never come to an end; [23]they are new every morning; great is your faithfulness. [24]'The Lord is my portion,' says my soul, 'therefore I will hope in him.' [25]The Lord is good to those who wait for him, to the soul who seeks him. [26]It is good that one should wait quietly for the salvation of the Lord. [27]It is good for a man that he bear the yoke in his youth" (ESV).

Read James 1:2-12.

"Count it all joy, my brothers, when you meet trials of various kinds, [3]for you know that the testing of your faith produces steadfastness. [4]And let steadfastness have its full effect, that you may be perfect and complete, lacking in nothing. [5]If any of you lacks wisdom, let him ask God, who gives generously to all without reproach, and it will be given him. [6]But let him ask in faith, with no doubting, for the one who doubts is like a wave of the sea that is driven and tossed by the wind. [7]For that person must not suppose that he will receive anything from the Lord; [8]he is a double-minded man, unstable in all his ways. [9]Let the lowly brother boast in his exaltation, [10]and the rich in his humiliation, because like a flower of the grass he will pass away. [11]For the sun rises with its scorching heat and withers the grass; its flower falls, and its beauty perishes. So also will the rich man fade away in the midst of his pursuits. [12]Blessed is the man who remains steadfast under trial, for when he has stood the test he will receive the crown of life, which God has promised to those who love him" (ESV).

OBSERVATION

What do these passages say about...

Facing challenges?

God's part in adversity?

Our part in adversity?

SCRIPTURE READING

Read Lamentations 3:16-27.

"He has made my teeth grind on gravel, and made me cower in ashes; [17]my soul is bereft of peace; I have forgotten what happiness is; [18]so I say, 'My endurance has perished; so has my hope from the Lord.' [19]Remember my affliction and my wanderings, the wormwood and the gall! [20]My soul continually remembers it and is bowed down within me. [21]But this I call to mind, and therefore I have hope: [22]The steadfast love of the Lord never ceases; his mercies never come to an end; [23]they are new every morning; great is your faithfulness. [24]'The Lord is my portion,' says my soul, 'therefore I will hope in him.' [25]The Lord is good to those who wait for him, to the soul who seeks him. [26]It is good that one should wait quietly for the salvation of the Lord. [27]It is good for a man that he bear the yoke in his youth" (ESV).

Read James 1:2-12.

"Count it all joy, my brothers, when you meet trials of various kinds, [3]for you know that the testing of your faith produces steadfastness. [4]And let steadfastness have its full effect, that you may be perfect and complete, lacking in nothing. [5]If any of you lacks wisdom, let him ask God, who gives generously to all without reproach, and it will be given him. [6]But let him ask in faith, with no doubting, for the one who doubts is like a wave of the sea that is driven and tossed by the wind. [7]For that person must not suppose that he will receive anything from the Lord; [8]he is a double-minded man, unstable in all his ways. [9]Let the lowly brother boast in his exaltation, [10]and the rich in his humiliation, because like a flower of the grass he will pass away. [11]For the sun rises with its scorching heat and withers the grass; its flower falls, and its beauty perishes. So also will the rich man fade away in the midst of his pursuits. [12]Blessed is the man who remains steadfast under trial, for when he has stood the test he will receive the crown of life, which God has promised to those who love him" (ESV).

INTERPRETATION

How does God give a perspective on better things to come?

Why would James ask us to be joyful when facing trials?

How have you experienced hope and perseverance in challenging times?

APPLICATION

The Crisis Budget

The Crisis Budget:

As we learned in this chapter, crises can happen. The best time to prepare for a crisis is before one happens because you are not under the strain and emotional stress that crises bring.

The Crisis Budget will help you determine your essential needs, what expenses could be temporarily eliminated, and what expenses could be adjusted if your income were to change because of a crisis.

You can find an example of this application at ***compasstools.org***

Let's get started on your Crisis Budget!

Review your Estimated Spending Plan and...

1. Identify categories (expenses) that you would consider **NON-ESSENTIAL.** These are expenses that could be temporarily eliminated if a crisis should occur.
2. Identify categories (expenses) that could be **ADJUSTED.** These could include things like using less water, adjusting your thermostat, saving gas by car pooling to work, etc.
3. Make a commitment to not take on any new **DEBT** in a crisis. Trust in God's provision and lean on Him. Don't use debt as a crutch in a crisis.
4. Begin working on the Crisis Budget on the next sheet. Once you've completed it, keep it in an accessible place so that if a crisis does occur, you'll know where to find it.

EXPENSE	ELIMINATE OR ADJUST	AMOUNT REDUCED

TOTAL AMOUNT REDUCED: ____________

PRAYERS FOR TODAY

This prayer section is for personal use and isn't meant to be part of the group discussion.

For you...

For your family and friends...

For those in your group...

Additional Tools for the Journey!

To help you on your financial discipleship journey, we have provided practical resources from a variety of people in the financial world. Visit us at **compasstools.org** to check out these resources.

Eternal Perspective

PRAYER

Pray for the Holy Spirit's guidance as you begin reading passages of Scripture. Ask for clarity and insight as you engage in God's word.

SCRIPTURE READING

Read Psalm 39:4-6.

"O Lord, make me know my end and what is the measure of my days;
let me know how fleeting I am! 5Behold, you have made my days a few
handbreadths, and my lifetime is as nothing before you. Surely all mankind
stands as a mere breath! Selah 6Surely a man goes about as a shadow! Surely
for nothing they are in turmoil; man heaps up wealth and does not know who will gather!" (ESV)

Read 2 Corinthians 4:16-18.

"So we do not lose heart. Though our outer self is wasting away, our inner self
is being renewed day by day. 17For this light momentary affliction is preparing
for us an eternal weight of glory beyond all comparison, 18as we look not to the
things that are seen but to the things that are unseen. For the things that are seen are transient, but the things that are unseen are eternal" (ESV).

OBSERVATION

What do these passages say about...

Life?

Eternity?

Homework

SCRIPTURE READING

Read Psalm 39:4-6.

"O Lord, make me know my end and what is the measure of my days;
let me know how fleeting I am! 5Behold, you have made my days a few
handbreadths, and my lifetime is as nothing before you. Surely all mankind
stands as a mere breath! Selah 6Surely a man goes about as a shadow! Surely
for nothing they are in turmoil; man heaps up wealth and does not know who
will gather!" (ESV)

Read 2 Corinthians 4:16-18.

"So we do not lose heart. Though our outer self is wasting away, our inner self
is being renewed day by day. 17For this light momentary affliction is preparing
for us an eternal weight of glory beyond all comparison, 18as we look not to the
things that are seen but to the things that are unseen. For the things that are
seen are transient, but the things that are unseen are eternal" (ESV).

INTERPRETATION

What would be a reason for "numbering" our days?

How does an eternal perspective impact the way you spend your time and money?

Who do you know that lives with an eternal perspective?
How do their lives look different from others?

APPLICATION

How can you apply the principles of these passages to your finances and possessions?

HOWARD'S HIGHLIGHTS

The long and short of it

The Bible frequently reminds us that life on earth is brief: *". . . [God] is mindful that we are nothing but dust"* (Psalm 103:14). Our earthly bodies are called "tents" (2 Peter 1:13, NIV), temporary dwelling places of our eternal souls. David recognized this and sought to gain God's perspective on the brevity of life. He asked of the Lord, *"Show me, Lord, my life's end and the number of my days; let me know how fleeting my life is.. . . Everyone is but a breath . . . everyone goes around like a mere phantom; in vain they rush about, heaping up wealth without knowing whose it will finally be"* (Psalm 39:4-6).

Billy Graham observed shortly before his 90th birthday, "The greatest surprise of my life, is the brevity of life."

Moses realized that true wisdom requires an awareness and understanding of the brevity of our lives. With that in mind, he asked the Lord to help him number the days he had on earth. *"As for the days of our life, they contain seventy years, or if due to strength, eighty years . . . for it quickly passes and we disappear.. . . So teach us to number our days, that we may present to You a heart of wisdom"* (Psalm 90:10,12).

I encourage you to actually number the estimated days you have left on earth. If I live as long as my father, I have about 1,900 days left. This has helped me focus on investing my life and resources in eternally important matters. In light of the brevity of life, Matthew Henry said, "It ought to be the business of every day to prepare for our last day."

Eternity is long.

Eternity, on the other hand, never ends. It is forever. Imagine a cable running through the room where you are now. To your right, the cable runs billions of light years, all the way to the end of the universe; to your left, it runs to the other end of the universe. Now imagine that the cable to your left represents eternity past, and the cable to your right, eternity future. Imagine taking out a marker and making a tiny line on the cable in front of you. That tiny mark represents your brief life on earth.

Most people, however, lacking such an eternal perspective, live their lives as if the mark was everything. They make mark choices, live in mark houses, drive mark cars, wear mark clothes, raise mark children, and dream mark dreams. Devotional writer A. W. Tozer referred to eternity as "the long tomorrow." This is the backdrop against which all the questions of life and the use of our resources must be answered.

PRAYERS FOR TODAY

This prayer section is for personal use and isn't meant to be part of the group discussion.

For you...

For your family and friends...

For those in your group...

Eternity & Judgment

PRAYER

Pray for the Holy Spirit's guidance as you begin reading passages of Scripture. Ask for clarity and insight as you engage in God's word.

SCRIPTURE READING

Read 1 Corinthians 3:10-15.

"According to the grace of God given to me, like a skilled master builder I laid a foundation, and someone else is building upon it. Let each one take care how he builds upon it. 11For no one can lay a foundation other than that which is laid, which is Jesus Christ. 12Now if anyone builds on the foundation with gold, silver, precious stones, wood, hay, straw – 13each one's work will become manifest, for the Day will disclose it, because it will be revealed by fire, and the fire will test what sort of work each one has done. 14If the work that anyone has built on the foundation survives, he will receive a reward. 15If anyone's work is burned up, he will suffer loss, though he himself will be saved, but only as through fire" (ESV).

Read Hebrews 4:12-13.

"For the word of God is living and active, sharper than any two-edged sword, piercing to the division of soul and of spirit, of joints and of marrow, and discerning the thoughts and intentions of the heart. 13And no creature is hidden from his sight, but all are naked and exposed to the eyes of him to whom we must give account" (ESV).

OBSERVATION

What do these passage say about...

Building?

Judgment?

Homework

SCRIPTURE READING

Read 1 Corinthians 3:10-15.

"According to the grace of God given to me, like a skilled master builder I laid a foundation, and someone else is building upon it. Let each one take care how he builds upon it. [11]For no one can lay a foundation other than that which is laid, which is Jesus Christ. [12]Now if anyone builds on the foundation with gold, silver, precious stones, wood, hay, straw – [13]each one's work will become manifest, for the Day will disclose it, because it will be revealed by fire, and the fire will test what sort of work each one has done. [14]If the work that anyone has built on the foundation survives, he will receive a reward. [15]If anyone's work is burned up, he will suffer loss, though he himself will be saved, but only as through fire" (ESV).

Read Hebrews 4:12-13.

"For the word of God is living and active, sharper than any two-edged sword, piercing to the division of soul and of spirit, of joints and of marrow, and discerning the thoughts and intentions of the heart. [13]And no creature is hidden from his sight, but all are naked and exposed to the eyes of him to whom we must give account" (ESV).

INTERPRETATION

What do these passages mean to you?

How does the reality of judgments and rewards impact you today?

APPLICATION

The Organizing Your Estate Worksheet

The Organizing Your Estate Worksheet:

As we learn about eternity, we realize that our time on earth is temporary and we should focus on eternal things rather than the things of this world. So if heaven is our home, why would we need to think about what we leave behind?

1 Timothy 5:8 tells us, *"Anyone who does not provide for their relatives, and especially for their own household, has denied the faith and is worse than an unbeliever"* (NIV).

God's plan is that we care for our family. There are very few practical ways to care for our families when we are gone from this earth, but organizing your estate is one of them.

Begin working on the Organizing Your Estate worksheet, and review the information with your spouse or heirs. After the review, give a completed copy to your attorney or accountant and a trusted family member or friend who will be involved in settling your estate. The Organizing Your Estate Worksheet is designed to be brief and is not intended to completely organize your estate.

You can find an example of this application at ***compasstools.org***

MEETING WITH AN ATTORNEY

You will save time and money if you are prepared when meeting with an attorney to draft your will. In addition to the Organizing Your Estate Worksheet, answering these questions will help prepare you:

1. Who will be my personal representative, and who will be the successor personal representative of my estate?
2. Who will be the guardian and successor guardian of our children?
3. Who are my heirs, and what will each of them receive?
4. How much do I want to give from my estate to the Lord's work?

It will also save time if you bring with you the Personal Financial Statement that was completed in Chapter 1.

WILL AND/OR TRUST

The Will (Trust) is located:

____

The person designated to carry out its provisions is:

____

If that person cannot or will not serve, the alternate is:

____

Attorney: ______________________ Phone: __________

Accountant: ____________________ Phone: __________

INCOME BENEFITS

1. Company Benefits

My (our) heirs will receive the following company benefits:

____

Contact: ______________________ Phone: __________

2. Social Security Benefits

To receive Social Security benefits, go to the ______________ Social Secuity office.

Do this promptly because a delay may void benefits. When you go, take:

(1) my Social Secuity card; (2) my death certificate; (3) your birth certificate; (4) our marriage certificate; (5) birth certificates for each child.

3. Veterans' Benefits

You are/are not eligible for veterans' benefits: ______________

To receive these benefits, you should do the following:

4. Life Insurance Coverage

Insurance company: ______________ Policy #: __________________

Face Value: ______ Person insured: ________ Beneficiary: ________

Insurance company: ______________ Policy #: __________________

Face Value: ______ Person insured: ________ Beneficiary: ________

FAMILY INFORMATION

Family member's name:

_______________ Address: _______________
Social Security #: _______________

_______________ Address: _______________
Social Security #: _______________

_______________ Address: _______________
Social Security #: _______________

_______________ Address: _______________
Social Security #: _______________

_______________ Address: _______________
Social Security #: _______________

MILITARY SERVICE HISTORY

Branch of Service: ____________ Service Number: ____________

Length of Service: ____________ From: ________ Until: ________

Rank: ________________________

Location and description of important military documents:

FUNERAL INSTRUCTIONS

Funeral Home: ____

Address: _____________________________ Phone: ____________

My (our) place of burial is located at: _________________________

I (we) request burial in the following manner: ___________________

I (we) request that memorial gifts be given to the following church/organization:

Name: ____

Address: ____

Name: ____

Address: ____

PRAYERS FOR TODAY

This prayer section is for personal use and isn't meant to be part of the group discussion.

For you...

For your family and friends...

For those in your group...

See Their Story...

See this woman's courageous journey of navigating through a devastating crisis.

You can also watch these amazing stories at compasstools.org

Additional Tools for the Journey!

To help you on your financial discipleship journey, we have provided practical resources from a variety of people in the financial world. Visit us at **compasstools.org** to check out these resources.

Step One:

Watch the Video

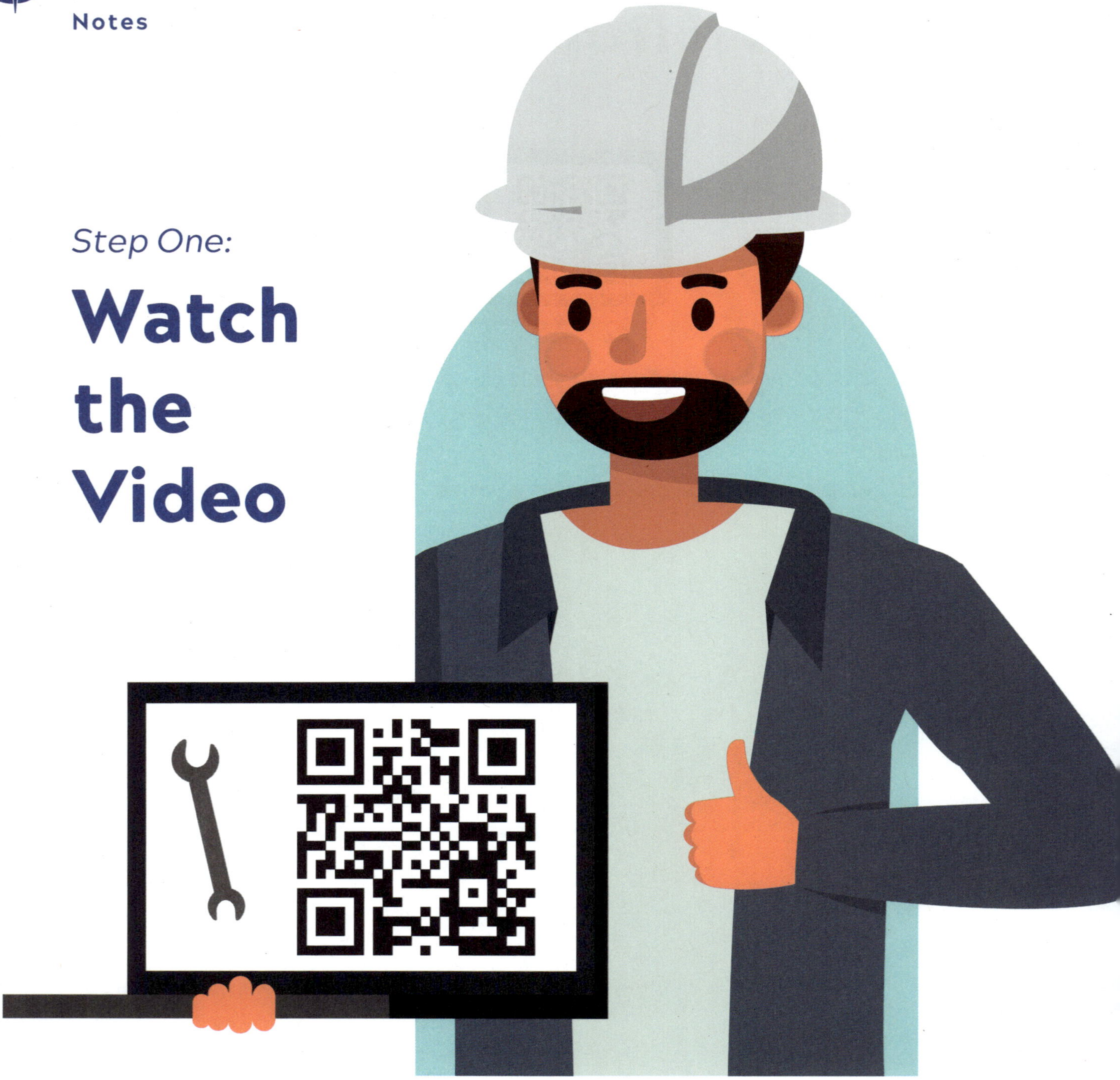

Open the camera on your phone to scan the QR code

OR

*Visit **compasstools.org** to view the video for this chapter*

Step Two:

Read the Notes

Not a fan of reading? You can listen to these notes at compasstools.org

Crisis

God's Role

When facing a crisis, nothing is more important than knowing who God is – His love, care, control, and power. Only the Bible reveals the true extent of God's involvement in our challenges. If we have an inadequate or warped view of God and His purposes, we won't fully embrace and learn from our challenges. What's more, we will forfeit the peace, contentment, and even joy that God makes available to us in the midst of the storm.

Notes

God loves you.

First John 4:8 sums up God's nature: *". . . God is love."* God loves you and remains intimately involved with you as an individual throughout your whole life. Consider Psalm 139:17-18 from two different translations.

- *"How precious to me are your thoughts, God! How vast is the sum of them! Were I to count them, they would outnumber the grains of sand"* (NIV).
- *"How precious it is, Lord, to realize that you are thinking about me constantly! I can't even count how many times a day your thoughts turn toward me"* (TLB).

In other words, as mind-boggling as this concept might be – the Creator of the universe never stops thinking about you!

In any crisis, it's critical to be reminded of God's unfailing love and faithfulness. Why? Because it's so very easy to become discouraged and even lose hope in such times. It's easy to forget God's love and care for you, especially when adversity first strikes – or goes on and on for what feels like an eternity.

I've discovered that even in a crisis, the Lord will do kind, loving things that offer clear evidence of His care and concern for us. Consider Joseph. While a slave, *"[Joseph's] master saw that the Lord was with him"* (Genesis 39:3), so his master put him in charge of all he owned. Later in prison, *"the Lord was with Joseph and extended kindness to him, and gave him favor in the sight of the warden of the prison"* (Genesis 39:21).

God is in Control.

God is ultimately in control of every event. This is but a sampling of passages that affirm His control:

- *"Our God is in the heavens; He does whatever He pleases"* (Psalm 115:3).
- *". . . We adore you as being in control of everything"* (1 Chronicles 29:11, TLB).
- *"Whatever the Lord pleases, He does, in heaven and on earth . . ."* (Psalm 135:6).
- *". . . My [the Lord's] purpose will stand, and I will do all that I please"* (Isaiah 46:10, NIV).
- *"For nothing will be impossible with God"* (Luke 1:37).

The Lord is in control even of difficult events. *". . . I am the Lord, and there is no one else, the One forming light and creating darkness, causing well-being and creating disaster; I am the Lord who does all these things"* (Isaiah 45:6-7).

God has a purpose for adversity.

The Cecropia moth emerges from its cocoon only after a long, exhausting struggle to free itself. A young boy, wishing to help the moth, carefully slit the exterior of the cocoon. Soon it came out, but its wings were shriveled and couldn't function. What the young boy didn't realize was that the moth's struggle to liberate itself from the cocoon was essential to the development its wings and its ability to fly.

Much like the cocoon of the moth, adversity has a part to play in our lives. God uses those difficult, sometimes heartbreaking times to mature us in Christ. James 1:2-4 says it this way: *"Consider it pure joy, my brothers and sisters, whenever you face trials of many kinds, because you know that the testing of your faith produces perseverance. Let perseverance finish its work so that you may be mature and complete, not lacking anything"* (NIV).

God designs challenging circumstances for our ultimate benefit. Romans 8:28-29 tells us, *"We know that in all things God works for the good of those who love him, who have been called according to his purpose. For those God foreknew he also predestined to be conformed to the image of his Son. . ."* (NIV). The primary good that God works in our lives is to make us more like Christ.

We see this same thought expressed in Hebrews 12:6-11, *"For whom the Lord loves He disciplines . . . He disciplines us for our good, so that we may share in his holiness. For the moment, all discipline seems not to be pleasant, but painful; yet to those who have been trained by it, afterward it yields the peaceful fruit of righteousness."* God makes no mistakes. He knows exactly what He wants us to become, and He also knows exactly what is necessary to produce that result in our lives.

Bev and I have endured – and benefited – from many storms: from the birth and death of a precious special-needs child, to an unwanted career change, to Bev's double mastectomy to rid her of breast cancer that later spread to her bones and liver. Through the crucible of our pain and tears, many of the Bible's truths grew from wispy theory into rock-solid reality. Although we would never want to repeat these experiences, we are incredibly grateful for how the Lord has used them in our lives.

Author Ron Dunn observed: "If God subtracted one pain, one heartache, one disappointment from my life, I would be less than the person I am now, less the person God wants me to be, and my ministry would be less than He intends."

Notes

Please don't miss this point. You and I need to recognize difficulties as opportunities to grow into the people God wants us to be. In adversity we learn things we just couldn't learn any other way.

You can be comforted knowing that your loving heavenly Father is in absolute control of every situation you will ever face. He intends to use each circumstance for a good purpose. First Thessalonians 5:18 says it well, *"Give thanks in all circumstances, for this is God's will for you in Christ Jesus"* (NIV).

Sometimes, even when we fully obey the Lord, we will experience a major crisis because the Lord intends to use it to fulfill His purposes. Luke 8:22-25 records such an example. *"Jesus said to his disciples, 'Let us go over to the other side of the lake.' . . . So they got into the boat and set out. As they sailed, he fell asleep. A squall came down on the lake, so that the boat was being swamped, and they were in great danger. The disciples went and woke him, saying, 'Master, Master, we're going to drown!' He got up and rebuked the wind and the raging waters; the storm subsided, and all was calm. 'Where is your faith?' he asked his disciples"* (NIV).

Consider this: The disciples did exactly what Jesus asked of them. Several of the disciples were seasoned fisherman who surely spent thousands of hours fishing on the lake in all kinds of weather. When the unexpected squall swept the lake, they panicked because they knew all too well that their lives were at risk.

After Jesus calmed the storm, He challenged the disciples about their lack of faith. In fact, His whole agenda had been to increase their faith by placing them in a life-threatening situation that only He could solve. And He solved it by simply commanding the storm to be calm.

Trust God.

We should view challenges and crises through the lens of God's love, faithfulness, and control. The Bible makes it clear that God offers security only in Himself – not in money, not in a career, and not in other people. External things offer the illusion of security, but the Lord alone can be fully trusted. *"The Lord is good, a refuge in times of trouble. He cares for those who trust in him"* (Nahum 1:7, NIV). *"When I am afraid, I will put my trust in you. In God, whose word I praise, in God I have put my trust; I shall not be afraid.. . ."* (Psalm 56:3-4).

Common Challenges

Let's examine two of the most common financial challenges people face.

JOB LOSS Losing your job ranks among life's most stressful events – not just for you but for your spouse as well if you are married. Meet together as soon as possible after the job loss and discuss ways to minimize the emotional and financial toll on both of you. And encourage each other, because often a job loss is a blessing in disguise. God may bring you a better career opportunity, and it can build your faith as you experience Him providing your needs even without a job.

Next, formulate a game plan for the job search – from drafting a resume to networking with friends. When you lose a job, your fulltime job should be finding a new job.

In addition to cutting back on spending for discretionary items, there are two financial goals to keep in mind. First, make every effort to avoid using debt for living expenses. Many people mask the real situation by using debt to fund current spending. Make good, hard decisions not to spend one penny you don't have to. Every borrowed penny must be repaid with interest, and although spending it is easy, repayment is always hard work.

Second, do what you can to maintain health insurance. You may be able to assume your health insurance coverage through a plan from your former employer. If not, get advice from others on cost-efficient coverage.

Notes

ILLNESS OR ACCIDENT If you suffer a major illness or accident, it's a double whammy. Medical expenses pile on as income plunges. If the condition is severe enough to prevent future employment, you will need to make permanent adjustments. And if either health insurance or disability coverage is inadequate, it can be financially catastrophic.

If married, be prepared for the possibility that one of you may need to make important decisions without the benefit of input from the other. A long time ago, Bev and I had decided that if one of us got seriously ill, the other would make the financial and health-related decisions. We each knew the location of all important records and how to use them.

Don't be embarrassed to make your needs known to your family, friends, and church. Extend to them the opportunity to help meet your needs. Giving to those in need is a big part of what it means to follow Christ. Galatians 6:2 reminds us, *"Carry each other's burdens, and in this way you will fulfill the law of Christ"* (NIV).

Conflict Resolution

Thousands of lawsuits are filed each day in the United States. Unfortunately, many pit Christian against Christian. Suing seems to be a national pastime: A woman sued a man whom she said kicked her at a nightclub. She sought $200,000 as compensation for her injury and the time she lost on the dance floor. These types of lawsuits can create a financial and emotional crisis in our lives.

The court system uses an adversarial process, which frequently creates animosities between the parties involved. Instead of trying to heal, the system provides a legal solution – but leaves the problems of toxic unforgiveness and anger untouched.

The Bible stresses that the goal should be reconciliation. *"Therefore, if you are presenting your offering at the altar, and there you remember that your brother has something against you, leave your offering there before the altar and go; first be reconciled to your brother"* (Matthew 5:23-24).

Scripture states that when Christians are at odds with one another, they should not settle their disputes through the courts. *"Does any one of you, when he has a case against his neighbor, dare to go to law before the unrighteous, and not before the saints? [2]Or do you not know that the saints will judge the world? If the world is judged by you, are you not competent to form the smallest law courts? [3]Do you not know that we will judge angels? How much more matters of this life? [4]So if you have law courts dealing with matters of this life, do you appoint them as judges who are of no account in the church? [5]I say this to your shame. Is it so, that there is not among you anyone wise who will be able to decide between his brothers and sisters, [6]but brother goes to law with brother, and that before unbelievers? [7]Actually, then, it is already a defeat for you, that you have lawsuits with one another. Why not rather suffer the wrong? Why not rather be defrauded?"* (1 Corinthians 6:1-7).

Instead of initiating a lawsuit, a three-step procedure for Christians to resolve their differences is set forth in Matthew 18:15-17: *"If your brother sins, go and show him his fault in private; if he listens to you, you have gained your brother. But if he does not listen to you, take one or two more with you, so that on the testimony of two or three witnesses every matter may be confirmed. And if he refuses to listen to them, tell it to the church; and if he refuses to listen even to the church, he is to be to you as a Gentile and a tax collector."*

Go in private. The party who believes he has been wronged needs to confront the other person in private with his claims. If the dispute remains unresolved, then:

Go with one or two others. The person who feels wronged should return with witnesses who can confirm facts or help resolve the dispute. If this is still unsuccessful, then:

Go before the church. The third step is mediation or arbitration before an impartial group in the church or perhaps a Christian conciliation service if this is available in your area.

The greatest benefit of following this procedure is not simply reaching a fair settlement of the dispute but practicing forgiveness and demonstrating love.

Eternity

On Monday, October 25, 1999, the news reported an unfolding story. Air Force jets following a Learjet from Orlando, Florida, were unable to communicate with its pilots. I learned later that two of my very close friends, Robert Fraley and Van Ardan, were on that Learjet as it carried them and professional golfer Payne Stewart to their deaths.

One of the most crucial perspectives for us to embrace when handling money is the reality of eternity. Robert and Van, in their mid-forties, lived with an eternal perspective. Robert had framed these words of Saint Augustine: "Take care of your body as though you will live forever; take care of your soul as though you will die tomorrow."

The Lord reveals in the Scriptures that there is a heaven and hell, that there is a coming judgment, and that He will grant eternal rewards unequally. God does this because He loves us. The Lord wants the best for us and wants to motivate us to invest our lives in such a way that we can enjoy an intimate relationship with Him now and the greatest possible rewards and responsibilities in heaven.

Our failure to view this present life through the lens of eternity is a hindrance of monumental proportions, robbing us of the ability to see our lifespan and our assets in their true light. Scripture urges us again and again to let the reality of our eternal future determine and shape our present life – and the use of our money and possessions.

People who don't know the Lord look at life as a brief interval that begins at birth and ends at death. Looking to the future, they see no further than their own life span. With no eternal perspective, they think, If this life is all there is, why deny myself anything?

Those who know Christ have an entirely different perspective. We know very well that this life on earth is brief. It's the preface, not the book. It's the trailer, not the movie. Yet this brief testing period will determine much of our experience in heaven throughout all eternity.

Aliens and Pilgrims

Scripture tells us several things about our identity and role on earth. First, *"Our citizenship is in heaven"* (Philippians 3:20), not on earth. Second, *"We are ambassadors for Christ"* (2 Corinthians 5:20), representing Him on earth. Imagine yourself as an ambassador working in a country that is generally hostile toward your own. Naturally, you will want to learn about this new place, see the sights, and become familiar with the people and culture. But suppose you eventually become so assimilated into this foreign country that you begin to regard it as your true home. Your allegiance wavers, and you gradually compromise your position as an ambassador, becoming increasingly ineffective in representing the best interests of your own country.

We must never become too much at home in this world or we will become ineffective in serving the cause of the kingdom we are here to represent. We are aliens, strangers, and pilgrims on earth. Peter wrote, *". . . Live out your time as foreigners here in reverent fear"* (1 Peter 1:17, NIV). Another Bible translation uses the words *"strangers and pilgrims"* (1 Peter 2:11, KJV).

Pilgrims are unattached. They are travelers – not settlers – aware that the excessive accumulation of things can distract them and bog them down. Material things are valuable to pilgrims, but only as they facilitate their mission. If we aren't thoughtful and careful, our possessions can begin to entrench us in the present world, acting as chains around our legs that keep us from moving in response to God. When our eyes are too focused on the visible, they will be drawn away from the invisible. *"So we fix our eyes not on what is seen, but on what is unseen, since what is seen is temporary, but what is unseen is eternal"* (2 Corinthians 4:18, NIV).

Pilgrims of faith look to the next world. They see their earthly possessions for what they are: useful for kingdom purposes but far too flimsy to bear the weight of trust. Thomas à Kempis, author of The Imitation of Christ, said it this way: "Let temporal things serve your use, but the eternal be the object of your desire."

Two truths will help us gain a proper perspective of our possessions.

1. WE LEAVE IT ALL BEHIND.

After John D. Rockefeller died, it was reported that his accountant was asked how much he left. The accountant's response was classic, "He left it all." Job said it this way, *"Naked I came from my mother's womb, and naked I shall return there"* (Job 1:21). Paul wrote, *"For we have brought nothing into the world, so we cannot take anything out of it, either"* (1 Timothy 6:7).

2. EVERYTHING WILL BE DESTROYED.

Earthly goods are destined to be destroyed or become dust. *"The day of the Lord will come like a thief. The heavens will disappear with a roar; the elements will be destroyed by fire, and the earth and everything done in it will be laid bare. Since everything will be destroyed in this way, what kind of people ought you to be? You ought to live holy and godly lives"* (2 Peter 3:10-11, NIV). The temporal nature of things should help us handle them with an eternal perspective.

Judgment

It's uncomfortable to think about judgment. However, because our Lord loves us so deeply, He wants us to realize what will happen in the future. For this reason, God revealed to us that we all will be judged according to our deeds.

- *"He has set a day on which He will judge the world in righteousness"* (Acts 17:31).
- *"They will have to give account to him who is ready to judge the living and the dead"* (1 Peter 4:5, NIV).

Notes

- *"Nothing in all creation is hidden from God's sight. Everything is uncovered and laid bare before the eyes of him to whom we must give account"* (Hebrews 4:13, NIV).
- *". . . everyone will have to give account on the day of judgment for every empty word they have spoken"* (Matthew 12:36, NIV).
- *"God will bring every deed into judgment, including every hidden thing, whether it is good or evil"* (Ecclesiastes 12:14, NIV).

The Bible teaches that all those who do not know Christ will be judged and sent to an unspeakably dreadful destiny. *"I saw a great white throne and him who was seated on it. . . . And I saw the dead, great and small, standing before the throne . . . Each person was judged according to what they had done. . . . Anyone whose name was not found written in the book of life was thrown into the lake of fire"* (Revelation 20:11-15, NIV).

You Can Know God

Realizing that we can know God personally changes everything. I was 28 years old when I started meeting with several young businessmen. It wasn't long before I was impressed by their business savvy. But more than that, I was attracted to the quality of their lives. I didn't know what they had, but whatever it was, I wanted it.

These men spoke openly of their faith in God. I had grown up going to church, but the religion I had seen modeled during those years meant nothing to me as an adult. I had concluded it was only a fairy tale until a friend described how I could enter into a personal relationship with Jesus Christ. He explained several truths from the Bible I had never understood before.

GOD KNOWS YOU PERSONALLY

The following passages are but a small sample of how personally the Lord is involved in your life:

- **God wrote every day of your life in His book before you were born.** *"Your eyes saw my unformed body; all the days ordained for me were written in your book before one of them came to be. How precious to me are your thoughts, God! How vast is the sum of them! Were I to count them, they would outnumber the grains of sand . . ."* (Psalm 139:16-18, NIV).
- **God made you in your mother's womb.** *"For you created my inmost being; you knit me together in my mother's womb. I praise you because I am fearfully and wonderfully made"* (Psalm 139:13-14, NIV).
- **God is constantly with you.** *"You have searched me, Lord, and you know me. You know when I sit and when I rise; you perceive my thoughts from afar. You discern my going out and my lying down; you are familiar with all my ways. Before a word is on my tongue you, Lord, know it completely"* (Psalm 139: 1-4, NIV).

- **God will personally wipe away every one of your tears in heaven.** *". . . God's dwelling place is now among the people, and he will dwell with them . . . God himself will be with them and be their God. He will wipe every tear from their eyes . . ."* (Revelation 21:3-4, NIV).

GOD WANTS YOU TO KNOW HIM PERSONALLY.

God desires a close relationship with each of us.

- *"For God so loved the world, that He gave His only Son, so that everyone who believes in Him will not perish, but have eternal life"* (John 3:16).
- *". . . I [Jesus] came so that they would have life, and have it abundantly"* (John 10:10).

Author Richard Foster said, "To think rightly about God is, in an important sense, to have everything right. To think wrongly about God is, in an important sense, to have everything wrong." For this reason, it is crucial for you to recognize how extravagantly God loves you.

Perhaps this example will help you understand the depth of His love. In the 1992 Olympics in Barcelona, Spain, Great Britain had a runner named Derek Redmond who had dreamed all his life of winning the gold medal in the 400-meter race. As the gun sounded for the semifinals, Derek knew he was running the race of his life. Then tragically, as he entered the backstretch, Redmond felt pain shoot up the back of his right leg. A torn hamstring sent him sprawling face down on the track.

Instinctively, Derek struggled to his feet in excruciating pain and began hopping on one leg toward the finish line. Suddenly a large man came bounding from the stands. Flinging aside security guards, he made his way onto the field and threw his arms around Derek. It was Jim Redmond, Derek's father. "Son, you don't have to do this," he said.

"Yes, Dad, I do," Derek assured him.

"All right then, let's finish this together," said the older man. And that's exactly what they did. With the son's head frequently buried in the father's shoulder, they made it to the end of the race as the crowd rose to its feet, weeping and cheering!

Derek Redmond did not win the gold medal in the Olympics. But he won something far more valuable. He walked away from the race with the memory of a father who was not only in the stands cheering, but who loved him too much to watch him suffer from a distance – a father who came down out of the stands and entered the race with him, staying beside him every step of the way.

We have a heavenly Father who watches us with eyes of love and affection. He is our Father-God who cared for us too deeply to stay in heaven, looking down on us, watching us fall and fail. Instead, He came down out of the stands and into our race in the person of His precious Son, Jesus Christ. And He is committed to staying in this race with us until we have safely crossed the finish line.

Notes

UNFORTUNATELY, WE ARE SEPARATED FROM GOD.

God is holy, which simply means He is perfect and can't have a relationship with anyone who is not perfect. My friend asked if I had ever sinned – done anything that would disqualify me from perfection. "Many times," I admitted. He explained that every person has sinned, and the consequence of sin is separation from God. *"All have sinned and fall short of the glory of God"* (Romans 3:23). *". . . your sins have cut you off from God"* (Isaiah 59:2, TLB). The diagram below illustrates the enormous gap that separates us from god. People try without success to bridge this gap through their own efforts, such as philosophy, religion, or living a good moral life.

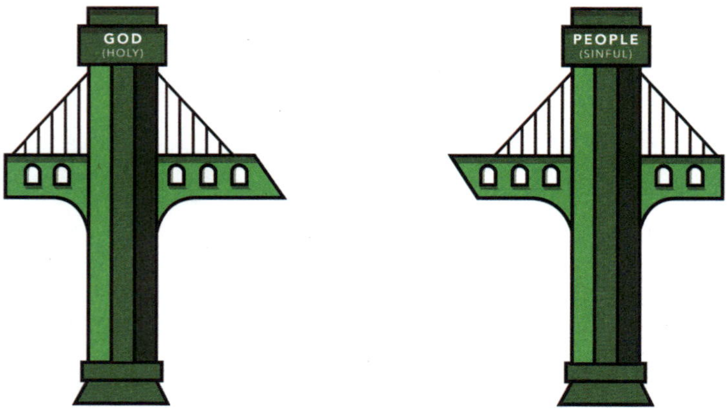

THE GAP BETWEEN GOD & PEOPLE

GOD'S ONLY PROVISION TO BRIDGE THIS GAP IS JESUS CHRIST.

THE UNION BETWEEN GOD & PEOPLE

The above diagram illustrates our union with God through Jesus Christ.

Jesus Christ died on the cross to pay the penalty for our sin, bridging the gap between God and us.

- *"Jesus said to him, 'I am the way, and the truth, and the life; no one comes to the Father except through Me'"* (John 14:6).
- *"God demonstrates His own love toward us, in that while we were still sinners, Christ died for us"* (Romans 5:8).

THIS PERSONAL RELATIONSHIP IS A GIFT FROM GOD.

My friend explained that by faith I could receive the free gift of a personal relationship with God. The transaction appeared inequitable. I had learned in business that a transaction happens only when both sides are convinced they are getting more than they are giving up. But now I was being offered a relationship with God, and it was free! *"It is by grace you have been saved, through faith – and this is not from yourselves, it is the gift of God – not by works, so that no one can boast"* (Ephesians 2:8-9, NIV).

I had only to ask Jesus Christ to come into my life to be my Savior and Lord. So I did! As my friends will tell you, I'm a very practical person; if something doesn't work, I stop doing it. I can tell you from more than forty-five years of experience that a relationship with God is real. And it is available to you through Jesus Christ. Nothing in life compares with knowing Christ personally. We can experience true peace, joy, and hope when we know Him. It's the only way you can enjoy a truly meaningful life and leave an eternally significant legacy.

If you want to know God and are not certain whether you have this relationship, I encourage you to receive Jesus Christ right now. Pray a prayer similar to the one I prayed: "God, I need you. I'm sorry for my sin. I invite Jesus to come into my life as my Savior and Lord and to make me the person you want me to be. Thank You for forgiving my sins and giving me the gift of eternal life."

You might have your finances in good shape, but without a relationship with Christ, it won't have any lasting value. If you asked Christ into your life, you have made the most important decision anyone could ever make. *". . . God has given us eternal life, and this life is in his Son. Whoever has the Son has life; whoever does not have the Son of God does not have life. I [John] write these things to you who believe in the name of the Son of God so that you may know that you have eternal life"* (1 John 5:11-13, NIV).

I urge you to find a church that teaches the Bible, one where you can begin to learn what it means to follow Jesus Christ.

Notes

JUDGMENT OF BELIEVERS

After they die, those who know Christ will spend eternity with the Lord in heaven, an unimaginably wonderful place. What we seldom consider, however, is that the entry point to heaven is a judgment.

Scripture teaches that all believers in Christ will give an account of their lives to the Lord. *". . . we will all appear before the judgment seat of God.. . . So then, each one of us will give an account of himself to God"* (Romans 14:10,12). The result of this will be the gain or loss of eternal rewards. In 1 Corinthians 3:13-15, we read, *"Their work will be shown for what it is, because the [Judgment] Day will bring it to light.. . . If what has been built survives, the builder will receive a reward. If it is burned up, the builder will suffer loss"* (NIV). Our works are what we have done with our time, influence, talents, and resources.

God's Word doesn't treat this judgment as just a meaningless formality before we get on to the real business of heaven. Not at all! Scripture presents it as a monumental event in which things of eternal significance are brought to light.

MOTIVATION AND REWARDS

Why should I follow God's guidance on handling money when it's so much fun to do whatever I please with it? After all, I'm a Christian. I know I'm going to heaven anyway. Why not have the best of both worlds – this one and the next? Though few of us would be honest enough to use such language, these questions reflect a common attitude.

The prospect of eternal rewards for our obedience is a neglected key to unlocking our motivation. The apostle Paul was certainly motivated by the prospect of eternal rewards. He wrote, *"I have fought the good fight, I have finished the course, I have kept the faith; in the future there is reserved for me the crown of righteousness, which the Lord, the righteous Judge, will award to me on that day"* (2 Timothy 4:7-8). The Lord appeals not only to our compassion, but also to our eternal self-interest. *"Love your enemies, and do good, and lend, expecting nothing in return; and your reward will be great"* (Luke 6:35).

UNEQUAL REWARDS IN HEAVEN

Some think, I'll be in heaven, and that's all that matters. But it's not that simple. On the contrary, Paul spoke about the loss of rewards as a terrible loss, and the receiving of rewards from Christ as a phenomenal gain.

Author Randy Alcorn states that "Not all Christians will have the same rewards in heaven." John Wesley said, "I value all things only by the price they shall gain in eternity." God's kingdom was the reference point for him. He lived as he did, not because he didn't treasure things but because he treasured the right things.

The greatest reward we can receive is Christ Himself and to hear His words, *"Well done, good and faithful [servant]. You were faithful with a few things, I will put you in charge of many things; enter into the joy of your master"* (Matthew 25:21). There are other rewards as well. I am especially motivated by the one to influence others for Christ.

- *"For what is our hope, our joy, or the crown in which we will glory in the presence of our Lord Jesus when he comes? Is it not you?"* (1 Thessalonians 2:19, NIV)
- *"my brothers and sisters, you whom I love and long for, my joy and crown"* (Philippians 4:1, NIV).

Can you imagine the incredible joy of meeting someone in heaven and learning that you had somehow influenced them to be there – throughout eternity – because of your prayers or the investment of your time and money?

God doesn't object to an investment mentality, rather He commands it, *"Lay up for yourselves treasures in heaven"* (Matthew 6:20, KJV). However, there is a fundamental question we must ask ourselves as we grow older. "Am I moving closer to the treasures I have laid up in heaven that will last forever, or am I moving away from the treasures I have stockpiled on earth that will become dust?"

Notes

Impacting Eternity Today

Our daily choices determine what will happen in the future. What we do in this life is of eternal importance. We only live on this earth once. *"It is destined for people to die once, and after this comes judgment"* (Hebrews 9:27). There is no such thing as reincarnation. Once our life on earth is over, we will never have another chance to move the hand of God through prayer, to share Christ with a friend who doesn't know the Savior, to give money to further God's kingdom, or to share with the needy.

Alfred Nobel was a Swedish chemist who made his fortune by inventing dynamite and other powerful explosives, which were bought by governments to produce weapons. When Nobel's brother died, one newspaper accidentally printed Alfred's obituary instead. He was described as a man who became rich by enabling people to kill each other on a massive scale. Shaken by this assessment, Nobel resolved to use his fortune to reward accomplishments that benefited humanity, including what we now know as the Nobel Peace Prize.

Let us put ourselves in Nobel's place. Let us read our own obituary, not as written by uninformed people, but as it would be written from heaven's point of view. Then let us use the rest of our lives to edit that obituary into what we really want it to be.

I loved playing Little League baseball as a young boy. We played on a huge field with towering fences in the outfield. Years later, shortly after my father died, I spent the day walking around my old hometown, reflecting on his life. When I visited the baseball field, I was shocked. It was so small! I could actually step over the outfield fences. While standing there, a thought struck me: Many of those things that seem so large and important to us today shrink to insignificance in just a few years.

When I am face-to-face with Christ and look back on my life, I want to see that the things in which I invested my time, creativity, influence, and money are big things to Him. I don't want to squander my life on things that won't matter throughout eternity.

What are the choices facing you now? How does an eternal perspective influence your decisions? Martin Luther said his calendar consisted of only two days: "today" and "that Day." May we invest all that we are and have today in light of that day.

Step Three:

Answer the Discussion Questions

What in the notes (and video) did you find revealing or interesting?

What in the notes challenged you the most?

What did you find revealing or challenging about the application worksheets in this chapter? Did you have any questions about the worksheets?

Chapter 5

Compass Commentaries

DAY ONE Perhaps the scariest aspect of a crisis is the moment we recognize that we have no control over the situation. We prefer to believe that we're always in control, in charge, directing the ship. But once circumstances get beyond what we can influence, it's scary!

One of the most important traits of a Christ-follower is accepting that we are not in charge. The Lord controls our circumstances, and we are to be faithful and obedient no matter what we face. We demonstrate that we believe in Jesus by trusting that His way is best. When we find ourselves in the middle of a crisis, there is often nothing better we can do than to be still, know that God is who He says He is, and listen for His voice. Ask Him what you are to learn from this experience. Review whether your own sin has led you to this point, and if so, confess and repent. Regardless, a crisis can be an event that draws you closer to Christ and strengthens your trust in His Lordship of your life.

DAY TWO We have referenced one concept quite often throughout this study, and it appears again in today's passage: wisdom! A wonderful display of wisdom is building our foundation upon the Word of God. This foundation – our faith in the one true God and its resulting belief system – is reflected in the knowledge that we need to be prepared for unseen events and the understanding that crises are inevitable in this life.

Because storms can occur in almost any area of our life, we need to be prepared on several fronts. Financially, we can prepare by reducing or eliminating debt, maintaining a reasonable savings balance, and giving generously so that money doesn't become our god. Relationally, we can treat others as more important than ourselves, making relational deposits into one another, and maintaining our relationship with Christ as the standard. Professionally, we should be diligent workers with impeccable integrity, honoring our employer as well as the Lord in all we do. None of these will eliminate life's storms, but they will help us weather them more effectively and honor God in the process.

DAY THREE A crisis can take us to the point of feeling totally abandoned by God. Nothing is further from the truth, however. God is always with us and will never forsake us. On this truth we should build our hope and gratitude: hope that we will be better prepared for the next challenge when it comes about, and gratitude to the Lord for the experience as well as the provision He gives to us. He is faithful and compassionate, loving us more than we can imagine.

Joy is not usually our initial emotion when a crisis hits. Yet that's exactly how we should react. Perhaps not so much for the challenge itself but for how the challenge will be used by God to develop our character. He is always in the process of building our perseverance, faith, wisdom, trust, maturity, and sufficiency. When we persevere under trials, we are proven to be worthy of the crown of life.

DAY FOUR The massive scope of eternity past and eternity to come can make our lives appear to be short and meaningless, a pretty depressing viewpoint. But the fact is that we all have the God-given ability to make a difference today that will make a difference for all eternity. As we invest in people, our family, friends, and even strangers, we share the love of Christ that influences where they will spend eternity – in the glorious presence of God or absent from His presence and every good thing it provides.

In addition to influencing the people that the Lord places in our inner circles, we can also impact the lives of people we have never met and probably never will meet this side of heaven. How can we do this? Through the investment of our financial resources, we can help those called to serve in foreign countries; doing the work to share the gospel; minister to the sick, poor, and homeless; and actively demonstrating the love of Christ.

While each of us can "number our days" by estimating how much longer we might expect to live, perhaps a greater challenge is to reflect on the previous six months or a year. Ask yourself what you have done to influence eternity for God's glory. If you don't like the answer to that question, make some better choices now!

DAY FIVE Someday, at a time we don't know, we will be taken from this earth and stand before the Lord to give an account of what we did with the skills and resources He gave us. Our works will be tested, and the only survivors will be those things done with a pure motive in Christ's love.

God's word reveals the standard by which we and our works in this life will be judged in eternity. Motives will be exposed, and nothing done with selfish intent or for personal benefit will amount to a hill of beans. If we did good things only to receive the recognition and applause of others, there will be no reward for us. But if we quietly went about our business and gave a cup of cold water to someone who was thirsty, and did it with the love of Christ, the reward will be great. Remember that the whys behind what we do can be more important than what we actually do. Let's make sure our motives please the Lord.

Chapter 6:

Finishing Well

All tools, videos, resources and electronic applications for this chapter can be found at ***compasstools.org***

THIS CHAPTER'S MEMORY VERSE:

Matthew 25:21

DAILY HOMEWORK:

Day One – Bible-Based

Day Two – Christ-Centered

Day Three – Prayer-Driven

Day Four – Holy Spirit-Led

Day Five – Discipleship-Focused, begin the Spiritual Goals Worksheet

Day Six – Watch the Build Your Finances God's Way video, Read the Notes, answer the discussion questions

BEFORE YOUR GROUP MEETING:

1. Memorize Matthew 25:21, (EHV). To prevent confusion when reciting the verse in a group setting, please memorize the version listed below.

> *"His master said to him, 'Well done, good and faithful servant! You were faithful with a few things. I will put you in charge of many things. Enter into the joy of your master'" (Matthew 25:21, EHV).*

2. Complete the Daily Homework.

Each day's homework is designed to take 20-30 minutes to complete.

3. Continue Tracking Your Income and Expenses

Bible-Based

PRAYER

Pray for the Holy Spirit's guidance as you begin reading passages of Scripture. Ask for clarity and insight as you engage in God's word.

SCRIPTURE READING

Read Hebrews 4:12-13.

"For the word of God is living and active, sharper than any two-edged sword, piercing to the division of soul and of spirit, of joints and of marrow, and discerning the thoughts and intentions of the heart. [13]And no creature is hidden from his sight, but all are naked and exposed to the eyes of him to whom we must give account" (ESV).

Read 2 Timothy 3:14-17.

"But as for you, continue in what you have learned and have firmly believed, knowing from whom you learned it [15]and how from childhood you have been acquainted with the sacred writings, which are able to make you wise for salvation through faith in Christ Jesus. [16]All Scripture is breathed out by God and profitable for teaching, for reproof, for correction, and for training in righteousness, [17]that the man of God may be complete, equipped for every good work" (ESV).

OBSERVATION

What do these passages say about...

God?

God's word?

Paul's final charge to Timothy?

6 - DAY ONE

Homework

SCRIPTURE READING

Read Hebrews 4:12-13.

"For the word of God is living and active, sharper than any two-edged sword, piercing to the division of soul and of spirit, of joints and of marrow, and discerning the thoughts and intentions of the heart. [13]*And no creature is hidden from his sight, but all are naked and exposed to the eyes of him to whom we must give account" (ESV).*

Read 2 Timothy 3:14-17.

"But as for you, continue in what you have learned and have firmly believed, knowing from whom you learned it [15]*and how from childhood you have been acquainted with the sacred writings, which are able to make you wise for salvation through faith in Christ Jesus.* [16]*All Scripture is breathed out by God and profitable for teaching, for reproof, for correction, and for training in righteousness,* [17]*that the man of God may be complete, equipped for every good work"* (ESV).

INTERPRETATION

What does it mean when God's word is referred to as *"living and active"*?

What does being *"complete, equipped"* look like?

How have you experienced God's word equipping you?

APPLICATION

How can being Bible-Based help you on your financial discipleship journey?

Write down one action point to do this week.

With God's help, I will . . .

PRAYERS FOR TODAY

This prayer section is for personal use and isn't meant to be part of the group discussion.

For you...

For your family and friends...

For those in your group...

Christ-Centered

PRAYER

Pray for the Holy Spirit's guidance as you begin reading passages of Scripture. Ask for clarity and insight as you engage in God's word.

SCRIPTURE READING

Read John 15:1-8.

"I am the true vine, and my Father is the vinedresser. [2]Every branch in me that
does not bear fruit he takes away, and every branch that does bear fruit he
prunes, that it may bear more fruit. [3]Already you are clean because of the word
that I have spoken to you. [4]Abide in me, and I in you. As the branch cannot bear
fruit by itself, unless it abides in the vine, neither can you, unless you abide in
me. [5]I am the vine; you are the branches. Whoever abides in me and I in him,
he it is that bears much fruit, for apart from me you can do nothing. [6]If anyone
does not abide in me he is thrown away like a branch and withers; and the
branches are gathered, thrown into the fire, and burned. [7]If you abide in me,
and my words abide in you, ask whatever you wish, and it will be done for you.
[8]By this my Father is glorified, that you bear much fruit and so prove to be my
disciples" (ESV).

OBSERVATION

What does this passage say about...

God?

Fruit?

Branches?

Homework

SCRIPTURE READING

Read John 15:1-8.

"I am the true vine, and my Father is the vinedresser. [2]Every branch in me that does not bear fruit he takes away, and every branch that does bear fruit he prunes, that it may bear more fruit. [3]Already you are clean because of the word that I have spoken to you. [4]Abide in me, and I in you. As the branch cannot bear fruit by itself, unless it abides in the vine, neither can you, unless you abide in me. [5]I am the vine; you are the branches. Whoever abides in me and I in him, he it is that bears much fruit, for apart from me you can do nothing. [6]If anyone does not abide in me he is thrown away like a branch and withers; and the branches are gathered, thrown into the fire, and burned. [7]If you abide in me, and my words abide in you, ask whatever you wish, and it will be done for you. [8]By this my Father is glorified, that you bear much fruit and so prove to be my disciples" (ESV).

INTERPRETATION

What does it look like to *"abide in me"*?

What would a branch that bears no fruit look like in your world today?

How have you experienced the Lord helping you to be fruitful?

APPLICATION

How can being Christ-Centered help you on your financial discipleship journey?

Write down one action point to do this week.

With God's help, I will . . .

PRAYERS FOR TODAY

This prayer section is for personal use and isn't meant to be part of the group discussion.

For you...

For your family and friends...

For those in your group...

6 - DAY THREE

Homework

Prayer-Driven

PRAYER

Pray for the Holy Spirit's guidance as you begin reading passages of Scripture. Ask for clarity and insight as you engage in God's word.

SCRIPTURE READING

Read Philippians 4:4-7.

"Rejoice in the Lord always; again I will say, rejoice. [5]Let your reasonableness be known to everyone. The Lord is at hand; [6]do not be anxious about anything, but in everything by prayer and supplication with thanksgiving let your requests be made known to God. [7]And the peace of God, which surpasses all understanding, will guard your hearts and your minds in Christ Jesus" (ESV).

Read Matthew 6:5-15.

"And when you pray, you must not be like the hypocrites. For they love to stand and pray in the synagogues and at the street corners, that they may be seen by others. Truly, I say to you, they have received their reward. [6]But when you pray, go into your room and shut the door and pray to your Father who is in secret. And your Father who sees in secret will reward you. [7]"And when you pray, do not heap up empty phrases as the Gentiles do, for they think that they will be heard for their many words. [8]Do not be like them, for your Father knows what you need before you ask him. [9]Pray then like this: "Our Father in heaven, hallowed be your name. [10]Your kingdom come, your will be done, on earth as it is in heaven. [11]Give us this day our daily bread, [12]and forgive us our debts, as we also have forgiven our debtors. [13]And lead us not into temptation, but deliver us from evil. [14]For if you forgive others their trespasses, your heavenly Father will also forgive you, [15]but if you do not forgive others their trespasses, neither will your Father forgive your trespasses" (ESV).

OBSERVATION

What do these passages say about...

Prayer?

How to pray?

God's response to our prayers?

Homework

SCRIPTURE READING

Read Philippians 4:4-7.

"Rejoice in the Lord always; again I will say, rejoice. [5]Let your reasonableness be known to everyone. The Lord is at hand; [6]do not be anxious about anything, but in everything by prayer and supplication with thanksgiving let your requests be made known to God. [7]And the peace of God, which surpasses all understanding, will guard your hearts and your minds in Christ Jesus" (ESV).

Read Matthew 6:5-15.

"And when you pray, you must not be like the hypocrites. For they love to stand and pray in the synagogues and at the street corners, that they may be seen by others. Truly, I say to you, they have received their reward. [6]But when you pray, go into your room and shut the door and pray to your Father who is in secret. And your Father who sees in secret will reward you. [7]"And when you pray, do not heap up empty phrases as the Gentiles do, for they think that they will be heard for their many words. [8]Do not be like them, for your Father knows what you need before you ask him. [9]Pray then like this: "Our Father in heaven, hallowed be your name. [10]Your kingdom come, your will be done, on earth as it is in heaven. [11]Give us this day our daily bread, [12]and forgive us our debts, as we also have forgiven our debtors. [13]And lead us not into temptation, but deliver us from evil. [14]For if you forgive others their trespasses, your heavenly Father will also forgive you, [15]but if you do not forgive others their trespasses, neither will your Father forgive your trespasses" (ESV).

INTERPRETATION

What does rejoicing in the Lord look like for you? What causes you to rejoice?

How does forgiveness impact our prayer lives?

How have you experienced God answering prayers in your life?

APPLICATION

How could being a Prayer-Driven person have an impact on your financial discipleship journey?

Write down one action point to do this week.

With God's help, I will . . .

PRAYERS FOR TODAY

This prayer section is for personal use and isn't meant to be part of the group discussion.

For you...

For your family and friends...

For those in your group...

6 - DAY FOUR

Homework

Holy Spirit-Led

PRAYER

Pray for the Holy Spirit's guidance as you begin reading passages of Scripture. Ask for clarity and insight as you engage in God's word.

SCRIPTURE READING

Read John 14:15-27.

"'If you love me, you will keep my commandments. [16]And I will ask the Father,
and he will give you another Helper, to be with you forever, [17]even the Spirit of
truth, whom the world cannot receive, because it neither sees him nor knows
him. You know him, for he dwells with you and will be in you. [18]I will not leave
you as orphans; I will come to you. [19]Yet a little while and the world will see me
no more, but you will see me. Because I live, you also will live. [20]In that day you
will know that I am in my Father, and you in me, and I in you. [21]Whoever has
my commandments and keeps them, he it is who loves me. And he who loves
me will be loved by my Father, and I will love him and manifest myself to him.'
[22]Judas (not Iscariot) said to him, 'Lord, how is it that you will manifest yourself
to us, and not to the world?' [23]Jesus answered him, 'If anyone loves me, he will
keep my word, and my Father will love him, and we will come to him and make
our home with him. [24]Whoever does not love me does not keep my words. And
the word that you hear is not mine but the Father's who sent me. [25]These things
I have spoken to you while I am still with you. [26]But the Helper, the Holy Spirit,
whom the Father will send in my name, he will teach you all things and bring to
your remembrance all that I have said to you. [27]Peace I leave with you; my peace
I give to you. Not as the world gives do I give to you. Let not your hearts be
troubled, neither let them be afraid'" (ESV).

OBSERVATION

What does this passage say about...

The Spirit?

The world?

Obedience?

Homework

SCRIPTURE READING

Read John 14:15-27.

"'If you love me, you will keep my commandments. 16And I will ask the Father, and he will give you another Helper, to be with you forever, 17even the Spirit of truth, whom the world cannot receive, because it neither sees him nor knows him. You know him, for he dwells with you and will be in you. 18I will not leave you as orphans; I will come to you. 19Yet a little while and the world will see me no more, but you will see me. Because I live, you also will live. 20In that day you will know that I am in my Father, and you in me, and I in you. 21Whoever has my commandments and keeps them, he it is who loves me. And he who loves me will be loved by my Father, and I will love him and manifest myself to him.' 22Judas (not Iscariot) said to him, 'Lord, how is it that you will manifest yourself to us, and not to the world?' 23Jesus answered him, 'If anyone loves me, he will keep my word, and my Father will love him, and we will come to him and make our home with him. 24Whoever does not love me does not keep my words. And the word that you hear is not mine but the Father's who sent me. 25These things I have spoken to you while I am still with you. 26But the Helper, the Holy Spirit, whom the Father will send in my name, he will teach you all things and bring to your remembrance all that I have said to you. 27Peace I leave with you; my peace I give to you. Not as the world gives do I give to you. Let not your hearts be troubled, neither let them be afraid'" (ESV).

INTERPRETATION

What does it mean when Jesus says "*whoever has my commandments and keeps them*"?

Why does God give us the Holy Spirit?

How have you experienced the Holy Spirit giving you insight, truth, or wisdom?

APPLICATION

How can being Holy-Spirit led help us on our financial discipleship journey?

Write down one action point to do this week.

With God's help, I will . . .

PRAYERS FOR TODAY

This prayer section is for personal use and isn't meant to be part of the group discussion.

For you...

For your family and friends...

For those in your group...

Discipleship-Focused

PRAYER

Pray for the Holy Spirit's guidance as you begin reading passages of Scripture. Ask for clarity and insight as you engage in God's word.

SCRIPTURE READING

Read Matthew 28:16-20.

*"Now the eleven disciples went to Galilee, to the mountain to which Jesus
had directed them. 17And when they saw him they worshiped him, but some
doubted. 18And Jesus came and said to them, "All authority in heaven and on
earth has been given to me. 19Go therefore and make disciples of all nations,
baptizing them in the name of the Father and of the Son and of the Holy Spirit,
20teaching them to observe all that I have commanded you. And behold, I am
with you always, to the end of the age"* (ESV).

OBSERVATION

What does this passage say about...

Jesus?

Disciples?

6 - DAY FIVE

Homework

SCRIPTURE READING

Read Matthew 28:16-20.

"Now the eleven disciples went to Galilee, to the mountain to which Jesus had directed them. [17]And when they saw him they worshiped him, but some doubted. [18]And Jesus came and said to them, "All authority in heaven and on earth has been given to me. [19]Go therefore and make disciples of all nations, baptizing them in the name of the Father and of the Son and of the Holy Spirit, [20]teaching them to observe all that I have commanded you. And behold, I am with you always, to the end of the age" (ESV).

INTERPRETATION

Why did some disciples worship Jesus and others doubt?

What does "*make disciples of all nations*" look like?

How have you experienced someone discipling you?

What has been your experience in discipling others?

APPLICATION

How can being Discipleship-Focused have an impact on your financial discipleship journey?

Write down one action point to do this week.

With God's help, I will . . .

SPIRITUAL GOALS WORKSHEET:

In this exercise you have the opportunity to draft a plan to help you on your Finishing Well journey by completing the Spiritual Goals Worksheet. Here are a couple thoughts to help you get started.

> Do not draw up a plan that is too ambitious to implement immediately.
>
> Select a person who will hold you accountable to apply these practices faithfully.
>
> If you are married, discuss these with your spouse. It is much easier to practice the disciplines if your spouse participates.

BIBLE READING

How often

How much time

Where

Bible Study Tool

PRAYER

How often

How much time

Where

Prayer Tool

CALLING

I sense the Lord calling me to...

Who

Where

How

When

DISCIPLESHIP

People who will help me on my finishing well journey:

Who ______________________________

Our Plan ______________________________

When we start ______________________________

People I will help on their finishing well journey:

Who ______________________________

Our Plan ______________________________

When we start ______________________________

Other practices to implement on your finishing well journey:

PRAYERS FOR TODAY

This prayer section is for personal use and isn't meant to be part of the group discussion.

For you...

For your family and friends...

For those in your group...

See Their Story...

See how the desire to finish well changed this top executive's life forever!

You can also watch these amazing stories at compasstools.org

Additional Tools for the Journey!

To help you on your financial discipleship journey, we have provided practical resources from a variety of people in the financial world. Visit us at **compasstools.org** to check out these resources.

Step One:

Watch the Video

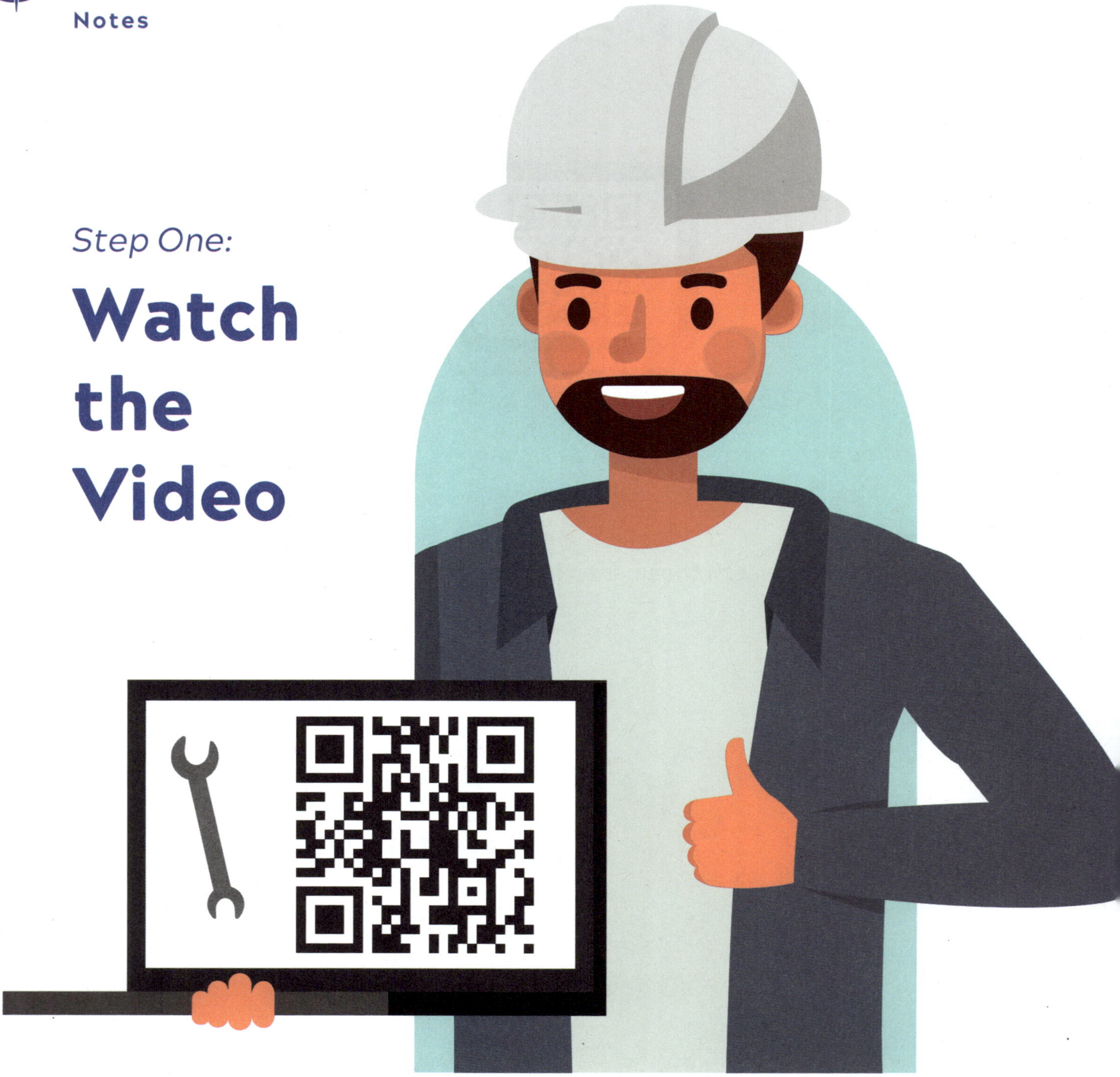

Open the camera on your phone to scan the QR code

OR

*Visit **compasstools.org** to view the video for this chapter*

Step Two:

Read the Notes

Not a fan of reading? You can listen to these notes at compasstools.org

Finishing Well

> *Can you imagine anything better than finishing well and having these words of Jesus ring in your ears throughout all eternity? "Well done, good and faithful servant . . . enter into the joy of your master" (Matthew 25:21, ESV).*
>
> *It sounds wonderful, but it can be a challenge. Of the 2,930 people mentioned in the Bible, we know significant details of only one hundred. And of those one hundred, only about one-third finished well. Most of the other two-thirds failed in the second half of their lives.*

Notes

Solomon is a classic example of someone who started out great but failed miserably later in life. Think about it: few people have started out as well and with more promise than Solomon.

- He was loved by God. "*. . . The Lord loved [Solomon] and sent word through Nathan the prophet that they should name him Jedidiah (which means beloved of the Lord)*" (2 Samuel 12:24-25, NLT).
- His father was King David, who authored most of the of Psalms and was described by God as "*a man after my own heart*" (Acts 13:22, NLT).
- Solomon made great choices early and was given more wisdom than any person. He wrote most of the book of Proverbs.

But then Solomon stopped following the Lord and descended into a life of disobedience. Deuteronomy 17 lists three things the kings of Israel were prohibited from doing.

- The king must not acquire great numbers of horses for himself or make the people return to Egypt to get more of them.
- He must not accumulate large amounts of silver and gold.
- He must not take many wives, or his heart will be led astray.

So, what does Solomon do?

- He acquires twelve thousand horses imported from Egypt.
- He amasses silver and gold for himself.
- He has seven hundred wives, and his wives lead him astray.

He was completely disobedient to the Lord. And the consequences were disastrous for Solomon, his family, and for the entire nation of Israel. Clearly, starting well does not guarantee that a person will finish well.

In your journey with the Lord, it's not how you start that matters. It's how you finish. The Christian life isn't a hundred-meter dash; it's a marathon. Long races don't require speed; they require determination and finishing power – fixing our eyes on the prize and finishing well.

Paul illustrates this from his own experience. "*. . . one thing I do: forgetting what lies behind and reaching forward to what lies ahead, I press on toward the goal for the prize of the upward call of God in Christ Jesus*" (Philippians 3:13-14).

Challenges to Finishing Well

To finish well, we need to invest our life to its fullest in serving Christ during our time on earth. To help us, we will address some of the most common reasons that followers of Christ do not finish well.

DISCONTENTMENT All too often, people are discontented with their lifestyles. First Timothy 6:8 issues this challenging statement: *"If we have food and covering (clothes and shelter), with these we shall be content."* Our culture has restated this verse to read, "If you can afford the finest food, wear the latest fashions, drive the newest automobiles, play with all the most up-to-date electronic gadgets, and live in a beautiful home, then you will be happy." Our consumption-oriented society operates on the assumptions that more is always better and that happiness is based on acquiring.

The word "contentment" is mentioned six times in Scripture, and five times it has to do with money. Paul wrote, *". . . I have learned to be content in whatever circumstances I am. I know how to get along with humble means, and I also know how to live in prosperity; in any and every circumstance I have learned the secret of being filled and going hungry, both of having abundance and suffering need. I can do all things through Him who strengthens me"* (Philippians 4:11-13, NASB1995).

Take note that Paul learned to be content. It wasn't automatic. It wasn't a slam dunk. Contentment didn't suddenly show up after Paul received Christ as his Savior. The fact is, none of us are born intuitively content; rather, we learn contentment.

There are three elements to the secret of contentment:

- Knowing what God requires of us in handling money and possessions
- Fulfilling those requirements
- Then trusting God to provide exactly what He knows is best

Note carefully that it's not just knowing these things that brings contentment; it's doing them. Once we have been faithful in the doing, we can be content in knowing that our loving heavenly Father will entrust the precise possessions He knows will be best for us at any particular time – whether much or little. Biblical contentment is not to be equated with laziness or apathy, nor does it exclude properly motivated ambition. In fact, I believe we should have a burning desire to be increasingly faithful stewards of the talents and possessions entrusted to us.

Biblical contentment is an inner peace that accepts what God has chosen for our present vocation, station in life, and financial situation. Hebrews 13:5 emphasizes this: *"Make sure that your character is free from the love of money, being content with what you have; for He Himself has said, 'I will never desert you, nor will I ever forsake you'"* (NASB1995).

Notes

COVETING Coveting means to crave another person's property, and it is prohibited throughout the Bible. The last of the Ten Commandments reads, *"You shall not covet your neighbor's house; you shall not covet your neighbor's wife or his male servant or his female servant or his ox or his donkey or anything that belongs to your neighbor"* (Exodus 20:17, NASB1995). Note the broad application: *"or ANYTHING that belongs to your neighbor."* In other words, we are commanded not to covet anything that belongs to anyone!

Greed is similar to coveting. *"But do not let . . . greed even be mentioned among you . . . Certainly you are aware of this: No immoral, impure, or greedy person – such a person is an idolater – has an inheritance in the kingdom of Christ, who is God"* (Ephesians 5:3,5, EHV). A greedy or covetous person is identified as an idolater.

Coveting and greed are among the most widespread sins of today. When I began studying what the Bible taught about money, I was overwhelmed by the extent of my own coveting. Ask the Lord to show you if you are guilty of coveting that which is another's. If so, ask the Lord to change your heart.

COMPARISON Some use comparison with others to justify spending more than they should. Many have suffered financially because they tried – but could not afford – to "keep up with the Joneses." Someone once said, "You can never keep up with the Joneses. Just about the time you've caught them, they go deeper in debt to buy more stuff!"

LIFESTYLE Romans 12:2 says, *"Do not be conformed to this world–this age, fashioned after and adapted to its external, superficial customs"* (AMP). We live in the most affluent culture in the history of the world, where we are constantly bombarded with manipulative advertising to prompt us to spend money. Advertisers usually stress the importance of image rather than function. For example, automobile ads rarely focus on a car as reliable, economic transportation. Instead, they project an image of status or sex appeal.

No matter what the product – clothing, deodorants, you name it – the message is communicated that the fulfilling, beautiful, wrinkle-free life can be ours if we are willing to buy it. Unfortunately, to some extent this media onslaught has influenced all of us. Author George Fooshee so aptly states, "People buy things they do not need with money they do not have to impress people they do not even like."

Every possession requires time and often money to maintain. Possessions can demand so much time or money that they distract us from our relationships with the Lord and our families. A quiet, simple life – with adequate time to invest in our most important relationships – is the safest environment for any marriage or family. As 1 Thessalonians 4:11-12 says, *"Make it your ambition to lead a quiet life and attend to your own business. . ."*

MARITAL INFIDELITY A local doctor was a generous and outspoken follower of Christ. His wife and four children also were committed to the Lord.

Then, the unthinkable happened. He became involved with a younger nurse at work, and the repercussions were horrendous. An emotional and highly contested divorce ensued after 40 years of marriage. The children chose sides and now refuse to communicate with one another. His Christian testimony in the community was decimated.

It is imperative for every husband and wife to be vigilant and construct guard rails to protect themselves from infidelity. Here are two guard rails to consider.

1. Never be alone with a member of the opposite sex

Yes, it can be inconvenient at times. Yes, it can be uncomfortable at times explaining the reason for this commitment. Yes, it can be effective!

2. Covenant with your eyes

When Job was defending his integrity, he said, *"I made a covenant with my eyes not to look lustfully at a young woman"* (Job 31:1, NIV). What we gaze upon becomes what we think about. What we think about becomes what we act upon.

These guardrails will go a long way in protecting you from marital infidelity and building an even closer relationship with your spouse.

Poverty, Prosperity or Stewardship?

Finishing well isn't determined by how much or how little you end up with. Some Christians embrace one of two extremes. On one end of the spectrum are those who believe that godliness can only occur in poverty. We learned earlier that a number of godly people in Scripture were among the wealthiest of their day. In the Old Testament, the Lord extended the reward of abundance to the children of Israel when they were obedient, while the threat of poverty was one of the consequences of disobedience. Deuteronomy 30:15-16 reads, *"I have set before you today life and prosperity, and death and adversity; in that I command you today to love the Lord your God, to walk in His ways and to keep His commandments . . . that the Lord your God may bless you"* (NASB1995).

We may legitimately pray for prosperity when our relationship with the Lord is healthy, and we have a proper perspective of possessions. *"Beloved, I pray that in all respects you may prosper and be in good health, just as your soul prospers"* (3 John 2). The Bible doesn't say that a godly person must live in poverty.

At the other end of spectrum lies the belief that all Christians who truly have faith will always prosper. This extreme is also in error. Joseph is an example of a faithful person who experienced

Notes

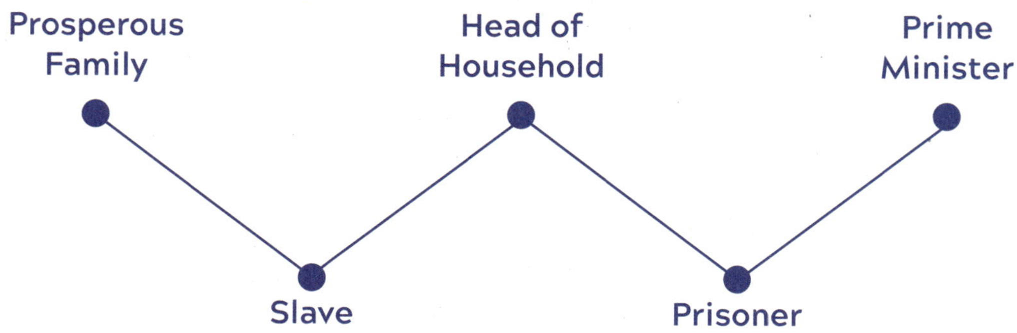

prosperity and poverty. He was born into a prosperous family, then was thrown into a pit and sold into slavery by his jealous brothers. While Joseph was a slave, his master promoted him to be head of his household. Later he made the righteous decision not to commit adultery with his master's wife, yet was thrown in jail because of that decision – and held there for several years! In God's timing, however, he was ultimately elevated to Prime Minister of Egypt.

Violating Scriptural Principles

Look again at Joshua 1:8. There is the requirement to do according to all that is written in the Bible. You may be giving generously but acting dishonestly. You may be a faithful employee but head-over-heels in debt. You may be completely out of debt but not giving. One of the biggest benefits of this study is that we explore what the entire Bible teaches about money. Those who don't understand all the requirements often neglect critical areas of responsibility unknowingly – and suffer financially.

Building Godly Character

Romans 5:3-4 reads, *". . . tribulation brings about perseverance; and perseverance, proven character."* Many godly people in the Bible went through periods when they were living righteously yet lost their possessions. David became a national hero after slaying Goliath. Here was a young man who served blamelessly, only to be forced to flee for his life from a tormented King Saul. Job lost his children and possessions in the space of a few moments, yet he was described as a *"blameless and upright man, fearing God and turning away from evil"* (Job 1:8). Paul learned the secret of contentment while being held captive in chains and suffering want, even though he was righteous.

Our Father knows us better than we know ourselves. In His infinite wisdom, He knows exactly how much He can entrust to us at any time without it harming our relationship with Him.

Our Dependence and His Discipline

A father was carrying his two-year-old child as he waded out into a lake. When they were close to shore, the child was unconcerned because of the apparent safety of the beach – even though the water was deep enough to drown him. He didn't understand his dependence upon his father. The farther they moved away from shore, however, the tighter the child held to his father. Like the child, we are always completely dependent upon the Lord to provide for us. However, we often don't recognize our dependence when we are experiencing the apparent security of financial prosperity. But when our possessions are few or none, it's easier to recognize our need and to cling to our heavenly Father.

Hebrews 12:6,10 tells us that, *"He punishes every son whom he accepts . . . for our good that we may share His holiness."* If we have sin in our lives or a wrong attitude toward money, the Lord may discipline us by allowing financial difficulties aimed at encouraging us to forsake our sin and return to Him with all our hearts.

The Mystery of God's Sovereignty

In Hebrews 11 we find Faith's Hall of Fame. In verses 1-35, we encounter a list of people who triumphed miraculously by the exercise of their faith in God. But in verse 36, the writer directs our attention to godly people who gained God's approval yet experienced poverty. God ultimately chooses how much to entrust to each person, and sometimes we simply can't understand His decisions.

Let's summarize: The Scriptures teach neither the necessity of poverty, nor the promise of uninterrupted prosperity. What the Bible teaches is the responsibility of being a faithful steward through all the ups and downs of life.

Before we leave the issue, it's important for us to understand the Lord's perspective on prosperity. The Lord evaluates true riches based on His spiritual value system, which is stated most clearly in Revelation. The godly poor are rich in God's sight. *"I [the Lord] know your tribulation and your poverty (but you are rich)"* (Revelation 2:9). Those who are wealthy yet do not enjoy a close relationship with Christ are actually poor. *"Because you say, 'I am rich, and have become wealthy, and have no need of anything,' and you do not know that you are wretched, miserable, poor, blind, and naked"* (Revelation 3:17).

The bottom line? True prosperity extends far beyond material possessions. True prosperity is gauged by how well we know Jesus Christ and by how closely we follow Him.

How to Finish Well

As we've learned, finishing well doesn't mean finishing with a perfect record. But it does mean learning from our mistakes, getting back on course, and pursuing the Lord with our whole heart. We need to work hard at building the kingdom of God as long as we are able – regardless of past failures. In the many years of Compass, we've seen people really struggle to finish well, and we've seen people flourish. We've noticed that the strong finishers have several key characteristics in common.

BIBLE-BASED

"All Scripture is God-breathed and is useful for teaching, rebuking, correcting and training in righteousness, so that the servant of God may be thoroughly equipped for every good work" (2 Timothy 3:16-17, NIV). Let's take a closer look at how Scripture has the ability to fully equip us on our Finishing Well journey.

There is simply no healthy Christian life apart from God's word. In the Bible, God tells us about Himself, enabling us to learn His ways and will. Only in the Scriptures do we find how to live in a way that truly pleases God.

When Jesus asked people about their understanding of the Scriptures, He often began with the words, "Have you not read?" He assumed that those claiming to be the people of God would have read the word of God. Unfortunately, this just isn't the case. A survey found that only 18 percent of Christians read the Bible every day, and 23 percent never do. So let's look at some ways we can break these trends and consistently be in God's word.

First, find the time. Perhaps one of the main reasons Christians never read through the entire Bible is its sheer length – it's BIG! At first glance it can feel overwhelming. But do you realize that you can read the entire Bible in 71 hours? Audio recordings prove it. In no more than 15 minutes a day you can read through the Bible in a year's time.

Another great practice is to find a Bible-reading plan. It's no wonder that those who simply open the Bible randomly each day soon drop the practice. Fortunately, there are some great Bible-reading plans available to help you stay consistent. Some Bibles are designed specifically to guide you through completing them in a year.

Each time you read, look for one phrase or verse to meditate on. Take a few minutes to think deeply about it. This will change your life. The Lord commanded Joshua, *"This book of the law shall not depart from your mouth, but you shall meditate on it day and night, so that you may be careful to do according to all that is written in it; for then . . . you will achieve success"* (Joshua 1:8).

Now, you may be thinking, "That's great for Joshua, but I've got a business or a household to run! I can't think about the Bible all day long. I've got decisions to make. It just isn't practical."

Let me assure you that meditation is the most practical thing in the world. Joshua didn't just sit around all day thinking about the Scriptures. He had two million people to manage. He was as busy, if not busier, than you are. So how does a busy person meditate on the Bible? Simple – read through a portion, and when a verse is especially meaningful to you, write it down. Take it with you, review it, and think about it during the day.

Finally, find a Bible study. Most of us will be way more consistent if we become involved in a Bible study. We need the encouragement and accountability of a group. And one of the greatest benefits of a group is developing close relationships with others who are also seeking to know the Lord better.

CHRIST-CENTERED

God's word is incredibly important in helping people finish well, but so is being Christ-centered. Since this may not be a term you hear every day, let's dig a little deeper into what it really means. It's actually pretty simple: if Jesus is the Lord of your life, you're going to do what He tells you to do. That's what it means to be Christ-centered.

When people surrender to the Lordship of Jesus Christ, they are acknowledging God's ownership and giving up their personal rights. This kind of obedience is a common theme we see among those who finish well. So, let's explore what it takes to be Christ-centered.

Our desire at Compass is threefold: helping people experience financial faithfulness, drawing them closer to the Lord, and encouraging them to surrender themselves to God. This includes recognizing that God owns it all, just as Psalm 24:1 tells us: *"The earth is the Lord's and everything in it"* (NIV).

Being Christ-centered isn't something we do just once; it is something we should strive to do every day, hour, and minute of our lives. It's a constant in the lives of those who finish well, and although it sounds challenging, there are several things we can do to make it a constant in our finishing-well journey.

A key factor in being Christ-centered is allowing the Lord to direct our paths. God is the only one who knows the direction we should take in our lives. Just as Israel was guided in the wilderness by the cloud and fire, and the apostles responded to Jesus when He said, "Follow me," we must constantly be sensitive to the direction of the Lord in our business, our relationships, our ministry, and our daily lives. And this applies not only to the big decisions we face but also our small everyday decisions as well.

Paul gives us a good example of being Christ-centered. *"For I resolved to know nothing while I was with you except Jesus Christ and him crucified. I came to you in weakness with great fear*

Notes

and trembling. My message and my preaching were not with wise and persuasive words, but with a demonstration of the Spirit's power, so that your faith might not rest on human wisdom, but on God's power" (1 Corinthians 2:2-5, NIV).

There is a lot of noise in this world on how to make the best decisions, how to be successful, and how to be the best you. Christ-centered people cover their ears to drown out this noise. They don't trust in the clever things of the world, but rather, humbly depend upon Jesus Christ to guide and direct their steps.

A second important factor in being Christ-centered is fruitfulness. A Christ-centered person recognizes that the fruitfulness of their lives is a direct result of their relationship with the Lord. John 15:1-5 tells us, *"I am the true vine, and my Father is the gardener . . . No branch can bear fruit by itself; it must remain in the vine. Neither can you bear fruit unless you remain in me. I am the vine; you are the branches. If you remain in me and I in you, you will bear much fruit; apart from me you can do nothing"* (NIV). The more obedient and dependent we are on the Lord, the more fruitful we will be in our ability to love and serve others.

PRAYER-DRIVEN

James 1:5 tells us, *"If any of you lacks wisdom, you should ask God, who gives generously to all without finding fault, and it will be given to you"* (NIV). Seeking the Lord's direction, provision, and protection through prayer must be a constant focus for us on our journey to finishing well. Prayer makes us more like Jesus as it shows us God's heart and reveals His wisdom. It is essential to us in understanding and doing His will.

If prayer could have been unnecessary for anyone, surely it would have been Jesus, the sinless Son of God. However, it was one of the dominant habits of His life and a frequent theme in His teaching.

Mark 1:35 tells us, *"Very early in the morning, while it was still dark, Jesus got up, left the house and went off to a solitary place, where he prayed"* (NIV).

Luke 6:12-13 tells us that *". . . Jesus went out to a mountainside to pray, and spent the night praying to God. When morning came, he called his disciples to him and chose twelve of them, whom he also designated apostles"* (NIV).

And Luke 5:16 tells us, *"But Jesus often withdrew to lonely places and prayed"* (NIV). This isn't something He did just on occasion; it was a normal part of His life.

Sometimes Jesus got up early in the morning to pray, sometimes He spent the whole night praying, and sometimes He would go off to a quiet place and pray. Regardless of when or where

He prayed, it is clear that even in the demands of His public ministry, Jesus consistently spent time alone with His Heavenly Father.

Throughout the history of the church, those serving in leadership have recognized the importance of prayer. Samuel Chadwick said, "The one concern of the devil is to keep Christians from praying. He fears nothing from our prayerless work, prayerless religion. He laughs at our toil, he mocks our wisdom, but he trembles when we pray."

One of the most important factors in true intimacy with the Lord is honesty in our prayer lives. As C. S. Lewis said, we should "lay before Him what is in us, not what ought to be in us." The Lord is thrilled that you are willing to come to Him as His child and spend time with Him, so come as naturally as you can. If you are hurting, share your pain. If you are confused, seek His guidance. If your joy is bubbling over, let it bubble over in praise. Being honest and transparent in your prayer time can take your prayer life and your relationship with the Lord to another level.

HOLY SPIRIT-LED

We cannot be truly Christ-centered, Bible-based, or Prayer-driven without being led by the Holy Spirit. Just as Jesus depended on the Holy Spirit to reveal the will of the Father to Him, we need to be completely dependent on Him to reveal God's will to us.

John 14:15-17 tells us, *"If you love me, keep my commands. And I will ask the Father, and he will give you another advocate to help you and be with you forever – the Spirit of truth. The world cannot accept him, because it neither sees him nor knows him. But you know him, for he lives with you and will be in you"* (NIV).

When we translate the Greek word for advocate, we see that it refers to someone coming alongside somebody, someone who plays the role of an encourager and urges people on. Our advocate isn't just some random spirit floating around; the Holy Spirit has a home, and that home is you. He literally lives in those who love the Lord – every believer.

Of all the gifts given to us, none is greater than the presence of the Holy Spirit. So, let's take a closer look at some of the ways the Holy Spirit helps us on our journey of finishing well.

One of the many ways that the Holy Spirit helps us is through insight. Think of it this way: have you ever had a verse you had read years earlier suddenly come to mind – exactly when you needed it most? That's not luck, and it's not a coincidence. It's the Holy Spirit prompting you with God's provision for that moment.

John 14:26 tells us, *"But the Helper, the Holy Spirit whom the Father will send in My name, He will teach you all things, and remind you of all that I said to you."*

In addition to insight from the past, the Holy Spirit gives us insight into the present. As we are reading and studying Scripture, it is the Holy Spirit who teaches us, guides us, and helps us to

Notes

understand the truth of God's word.

The Holy Spirit also teaches us to be more like Jesus. *"And we all, who with unveiled faces contemplate the Lord's glory, are being transformed into his image with ever-increasing glory, which comes from the Lord, who is the Spirit"* (2 Corinthians 3:18, NIV).

Although Moses got to experience God's glory on a mountaintop, the Holy Spirit gives us the opportunity to experience God's glory each and every day, no matter where we are!

Theologian Warren Wiersbe says it this way, "Moses reflected the glory of God, but you and I may radiate the glory of God. When we meditate on God's word and in it see God's Son, then the Spirit transforms us! We become more like the Lord Jesus Christ as we grow from glory to glory."

It is the Holy Spirit that equips us to be more like Christ, constantly transforming us and renewing us into His image.

The Holy Spirit is also the giver of gifts – gifts given to believers that are essential to the proper functioning of the Church. No one receives all the gifts: they're uniquely dispensed to God's people according to His plan for each person.

"Now there are varieties of gifts, but the same Spirit; and there are varieties of service, but the same Lord; and there are varieties of activities, but it is the same God who empowers them all in everyone. To each is given the manifestation of the Spirit for the common good" (1 Corinthians 12:4-7, ESV).

These gifts are given to us to equip us for the calling God has put on our lives. They aren't meant to be put on the shelf for a later date; they are given to us for the here and now, and for a purpose. So, I'd encourage you to think about how God is calling you and how you are using the gifts the Spirit has given you – for His glory.

DISCIPLESHIP-FOCUSED

Matthew 28:19-20 tells us, *"Therefore go and make disciples of all nations, baptizing them in the name of the Father and of the Son and of the Holy Spirit, and teaching them to obey everything I have commanded you. And surely I am with you always, to the very end of the age"* (NIV).

The word "disciple" essentially means "learner." The Great Commission, the last instruction Jesus gave, reflects His personal priority and greatest investment of time: making disciples by teaching them how to obey everything He commanded.

Although Jesus taught the multitudes, He focused on the few. Jesus knew that making disciples was crucial for succeeding generations to follow. The same Holy Spirit gives each member of the body different gifts, but all of us are commanded to make disciples.

A big part of the Finishing Well journey is being discipleship focused. This means examining how we are personally growing as disciples and also how we are making disciples by pouring our lives into others. So, let's explore some ways we can be discipleship focused.

One of the main characteristics of disciples is that they strive to imitate Jesus. Luke 6:40 tells us that *"A disciple is not above his teacher, but everyone when he is fully trained will be like his teacher"* (ESV).

When it comes to discipleship, the goal is to imitate the life of Christ. And in order to help believers grow as disciples, we must be willing not only to tell them how but also to show them how. Paul said, *"Be imitators of me, as I am of Christ"* (1 Corinthians 11:1, ESV). And in Philippians 4:9 he wrote, *"What you have learned and received and heard and seen in me – practice these things, and the God of peace will be with you"* (ESV). He not only gave verbal instructions to the believers, he also lived out his faith before them.

Another key characteristic of disciples is that they bear fruit. Let's look at what Jesus says in John 15:5. *"I am the vine; you are the branches. Whoever abides in me and I in him, he it is that bears much fruit, for apart from me you can do nothing"* (ESV).

As we grow in our discipleship journey, we should start producing fruit, the fruit of the Spirit: love, joy, peace, patience, kindness, goodness, faithfulness, gentleness, and self-control. This doesn't mean we have to be perfect in all of these areas, but it does mean that the fruit of the Spirit will become more apparent in our lives as we grow on our discipleship journey.

Multiplication is the goal when it comes to discipleship. Disciples make other disciples: they replicate themselves – they reproduce. They desire to see lives transformed and see people grow in their relationship with the Lord.

Jesus focused on growing His disciples, but He had a greater end in mind: He wanted them to reproduce themselves. In the Great Commission, Jesus passes the baton to them, telling them to go and make disciples of all the nations.

Disciples aren't supposed to just sit on what they've learned: they are commanded to share the gospel with others and teach believers to be imitators of Christ. Disciples go after people with God's love, sharing Jesus with them. They also pursue other believers, mentoring and encouraging them in their faith. Inevitably, a person who is finishing well is someone who is walking alongside others on their discipleship journey.

Notes

Now is the time!

At the risk of being misunderstood by some, I want to share an experience that has fueled my passion to help people learn and apply God's way of handling money. The year was 1977, and I was in the home alone when suddenly I was overcome by the Spirit of God and found myself prostrate on the floor, weeping.

While on the floor, the Lord revealed to me that during my lifetime our nation would experience economic upheaval and a very, very difficult time. God didn't show me precisely when this will occur or what it will be like, but there is no doubt that it will happen.

The financial crisis of 2008 and the Coronavirus pandemic that engulfed the entire globe, made it clear that the economies of the world are more fragile than most people imagine. So, what should you do to survive the coming economic storm?

We plead with you to become diligent in your efforts to get out of debt, give generously, budget, save and work as unto the Lord. In short, become a faithful steward. One of the best ways to demonstrate your love for your family and friends is to get your financial house in order and encourage others to do the same.

Thank you for spending this time with us. In closing, I'd like to leave you with a few thoughts that have been powerful motivators for me.

Nothing on this planet comes close to knowing Jesus Christ and living a life that pleases Him.

Leave your mistakes behind.

Be courageous.

Stay focused on Christ.

Never give up.

Jesus finished well when He said, *"I have brought you glory on earth by finishing the work you gave me to do"* (John 17:4, NIV).

Paul finished well when he said, *"I have fought the good fight, I have finished the course, I have kept the faith"* (2 Timothy 4:7).

Our prayer is that you will finish well, too. That you will complete the task the Lord has given you so that you will hear these words ring in your ears throughout eternity: *"Well done, good and faithful servant . . . enter into the joy of your master"* (Matthew 25:21, ESV).

Step Three:

Review the Tracking Tool Tips & Next Steps Sheet

Tracking Tool Tips:

We learned in the first chapter that we can't start well without being a faithful steward. This applies not only to how we start but also to how we finish. It's really hard to finish well if we aren't monitoring and keeping an account of all God has entrusted to us.

The *Tracking Tool Tips and Next Steps* document will give you suggestions on how to make adjustments as you track, including various ways to look at spending. It also offers budgeting tool recommendations to continue your financial discipleship journey!

Notes

As you are tracking, you may find that you need to make adjustments. This is totally normal and is part of the tracking process. Below are a few tips that you may want to consider as you make adjustments...

- Periodically get additional quotes for your insurance plans, such as home, life and auto. Before you make any changes, make sure you're comparing similar coverages and deductibles.
- Review any and all automatic payments that are deducted from your checking account or billed to your credit card. Ask whether you really need the service or should you cancel it. This could include things like gym memberships, subscriptions, social or club memberships, association dues, etc.
- Have a plan in place for what you will do with any unexpected income or cash gifts that you receive. How much will you give, what will you save, can you pay off some debts, how much might be left over to spend? Planning ahead will help you accomplish goals more quickly.
- Establish an amount that will determine when you will seek outside counsel or advice on what decision to make for non-budgeted purchases or expenditures. For example, if you determine that the amount is $250, anytime you consider a purchase of $250 or more, ask 2-3 friends or acquaintances, preferably those who know Christ, and do not have a financial interest in your decision, to help you think through the wisdom of making the purchase.
- Consider the net benefit of getting a second job. Would it cost more in transportation, clothing, childcare, etc. than you would bring home? Make a firm commitment to use any proceeds from a second income to give, pay off debt or fund an emergency savings account.

- Consider money saving coupons or sales for items you use and are going to need. This could include groceries, clothes, household items, etc. The key is to make sure you aren't purchasing an item simply because it is on sale or you have a great coupon, make sure it is used for things you need- if you don't use the products you're purchasing, then you're really just wasting money.
- Make sure you have an emergency savings account. Start with a goal of $1,000, then increase the amount to one month's living expenses, and finally to three month's living expenses. This should only be used for unexpected expenses such as accident repairs to cars or homes, medical emergencies, and other unexpected needs.

After 30 Days of Tracking

Once you have completed your 30 days of tracking, you can either continue using the tracking tool or check out our other recommended budgeting tools.

All of these tools are great, but do you want to know which one is the best? Simple, **the one you'll actually use.** Go to compasstools.org to find one that best fits your needs and use it to continue your financial discipleship journey.

Lights, Camera, Action!

Of all the things you can do to have an impact on others, few are more valuable and beneficial than telling your story. Telling people about the way God has moved and worked in your life can be a catalyst to someone growing in their marriage, their finances, and their relationship with the Lord.

Please share your story about how the Building Your Finances God's Way study has impacted your life. This online video platform allows you to put together a great video to encourage and motivate others. We are waiting to hear your story! Go to **compasstools.org** to share the impact this study has had on you.

Step Four:

Answer the Discussion Questions

What in the notes (and video) did you find revealing or interesting?

What in the notes challenged you the most?

What did you find revealing or challenging about the application worksheets in this chapter? Did you have any questions about the worksheets?

Chapter 6

Compass Commentaries

DAY ONE When we begin the journey as a follower of Christ, we probably know very little of what God expects from us. So where do we look? Everything, including being discipled by others, should be focused on God's word, the Bible. Through studying, memorizing Scripture, applying these principles to daily living, and prayer, the Bible will come to life and speak to us in every situation we experience. Its words convict us when we move away from God and reassure us of His loving desire to draw us closer. It is our source for wisdom, providing guidance for every single day of our lives

DAY TWO If you planted an orange tree, what would you expect to harvest within a couple of years – an apple? Of course not. You'd expect to be picking sweet, juicy oranges to enjoy for a season.

When branches become weak, you'd prune them off to improve the overall health of the tree. To maximize the production of the tree, you'd cultivate it and do everything possible to help it produce lots and lots of oranges. In the same way, Jesus reminds us that as Christ followers, He expects us to bear fruit. His fruit looks a bit different from an orange, though, because His fruit is the lives of other people.

As we draw closer to Him, understanding and obeying His word, we become like Him, the True Vine, bearing the same fruit He bears. We must recognize that we are only as productive as the strength of our dependence and trust in Him. When aspects of our life are unproductive, Christ prunes or disciplines us. Just as pruning a fruit tree ultimately produces more fruit, Christ's pruning and discipline in our lives enable us to accomplish His purposes for us. Pruning may not be pleasant in the short term, but it is necessary to produce not just more fruit, but much fruit!

DAY THREE One of God's greatest gifts to us is prayer that allows us to converse with Him anytime and anywhere. One of the important things to remember about prayer is that it is a two-way conversation. While we often think of it as a time to tell God everything that's on our minds, it's just as important that we spend time listening to what He may want from us.

Prayer should be our "go-to" response when we begin to feel worried or anxious about anything in our life. But presenting our wish list to Him should not dominate our time; we should also focus on rejoicing in Him and expressing gratitude. As we speak to God, He will calm our fears and assure us of His control over all circumstances and situations.

We've all heard and have been in awe of someone who prays with eloquence and passion, wondering what we have to do to pray like that. But Jesus reminds us that God sees our heart, mind, and soul when we pray, and these are much more important to Him than fancy words or phrases. Praying is speaking from the heart as we converse with the Lord. We give Him praise and adoration, acknowledge His sovereignty, confess, ask for forgiveness of our sins, ask for help in forgiving others, ask for safety and protection, and share our deepest thoughts with the Creator of the universe. What a great thing to experience throughout the day – every day!

DAY FOUR Can you imagine what Jesus' disciples were thinking when He told them that He would be leaving? Here they had given up their lives, families, and careers to follow Him, and Jesus was about to abandon them. Then He tells them part of His plan yet to be unveiled. They would not be left alone: He would give them an advocate, the Spirit of truth, the Holy Spirit. Did they have any idea what He was saying? Perhaps not at that moment, but they came to understand that Jesus was still with them, just in another form, and living within them!

The Holy Spirit enters our very being when we accept Christ as our Savior. As Jesus promised His disciples, the Spirit teaches us the ways of Christ, reminds us of what Christ has said, gives us wisdom and insight in our everyday activities, and calms our fears when we become anxious.

But the world does not experience the Holy Spirit or even understand who He is. He is an amazing blessing from God for those who know and love Jesus Christ personally.

DAY FIVE With all of the wonderful blessings God has given to us, do we have any responsibilities? How can we possibly repay Christ for what He has done for us in His ultimate sacrifice on our behalf? We can't. But we can express our love for Him by sharing His love with others. So, yes, we do have a responsibility, and it's called discipleship.

Jesus invited His disciples to follow Him. He spent time with them, taught them about His love for the world and how they could help the world experience His love. We have a similar opportunity and responsibility. We may never have the chance to travel the world like some of the great Christian teachers of our day, but we can talk about Jesus in our own homes and neighborhoods.

Once someone accepts Christ as their Lord and Savior, their journey is just beginning. They need to learn about God, learn to read and study the Bible, and figure out how they can apply God's truths to their own lives. The "figure out how" part is very difficult to do on their own, so it's beneficial to have someone experienced walk with them. That someone could be you.

The role of the disciple-maker is not to be a picture of perfection but to be real and authentic, acknowledging life's temptations and struggles. It also shows that living with Christ as the focal point is fulfilling, joyful, and rewarding. Each of us needs to be held accountable to live a Christ-centered life. Taking this journey with another like-minded person helps keep us on the path that Jesus has planned for us. We all can be disciples, who make disciples, who make disciples. This is what Jesus began over 2,000 years ago.

Continue the Journey

Congratulations on finishing the Building Your Finances God's Way financial discipleship study. We hope the Lord has had a significant impact on your financial discipleship journey through this study.

The financial discipleship journey is one that doesn't end until we hear the words *"well done, good and faithful servant."* We encourage you to continue on this journey in one of two ways.

Continue your journey by engaging in studies, tools, and resources that will help you grow. Visit us at ContinueGrowing.org to learn more.

Continue your journey by paying it forward and helping others grow. To learn more, visit us at HelpOthersGrow.org.

Thank you for the time and effort you have invested in this book. We pray the Lord will draw you ever nearer to Him as you continue to grow and help others grow.

Prayer Logs

In addition to the prayer sections for each day's homework, we have the Prayer Logs.

The Prayer Logs are designed to help you know how to pray for those that are in your group. End each class sharing answers to prayer requests and taking prayer requests. The requests need not be limited to financial concerns.

It is helpful if you have your prayer request completed in the Prayer Log before coming to your group discussion meeting. Prayer is a powerful thing, and we strongly encourage you to pray daily for the members in your group.

The Financial Discipleship App

In place of the prayer logs, you may want to use the prayer tool found in the Financial Discipleship App. The app allows you to create prayer groups, add prayer requests, see prayer requests from those in your group, and more!

Download on the App Store

GET IT ON Google Play

Prayer Log

Name: ______________________ Spouse: ______________________

Phone: ______________________ Children (ages): ______________________

E-Mail Address: ____

	Prayer Requests	*Answers to Prayers*
Chapter 1		
Chapter 2		
Chapter 3		
Chapter 4		
Chapter 5		
Chapter 6		

Long Term Prayer Request: ____

"Pray for one another" James 5:16

Prayer Log

Name: ______________________ Spouse: ______________________

Phone: ______________________ Children (ages): ______________________

E-Mail Address: ____

	Prayer Requests	*Answers to Prayers*
Chapter 1		
Chapter 2		
Chapter 3		
Chapter 4		
Chapter 5		
Chapter 6		

Long Term Prayer Request: ____

"Pray for one another" James 5:16

Prayer Log

Name: ______________________ Spouse: ______________________

Phone: ______________________ Children (ages): ______________________

E-Mail Address: ____

	Prayer Requests	*Answers to Prayers*
Chapter 1		
Chapter 2		
Chapter 3		
Chapter 4		
Chapter 5		
Chapter 6		

Long Term Prayer Request: ____

"Pray for one another" James 5:16

Prayer Log

Name: ______________________ Spouse: ______________________

Phone: ______________________ Children (ages): ______________________

E-Mail Address: ____

	Prayer Requests	*Answers to Prayers*
Chapter 1		
Chapter 2		
Chapter 3		
Chapter 4		
Chapter 5		
Chapter 6		

Long Term Prayer Request: ____

"Pray for one another" James 5:16

Prayer Log

Name: ______________________ Spouse: ______________________

Phone: ______________________ Children (ages): ______________________

E-Mail Address: ____

	Prayer Requests	*Answers to Prayers*
Chapter 1		
Chapter 2		
Chapter 3		
Chapter 4		
Chapter 5		
Chapter 6		

Long Term Prayer Request: ____

"Pray for one another" James 5:16

Prayer Log

Name: ______________________ Spouse: ______________________

Phone: ______________________ Children (ages): ______________________

E-Mail Address: ____

	Prayer Requests	*Answers to Prayers*
Chapter 1		
Chapter 2		
Chapter 3		
Chapter 4		
Chapter 5		
Chapter 6		

Long Term Prayer Request: ____

"Pray for one another" James 5:16

Prayer Log

Name: ______________________ Spouse: ______________________

Phone: ______________________ Children (ages): ______________________

E-Mail Address: ____

	Prayer Requests	*Answers to Prayers*
Chapter 1		
Chapter 2		
Chapter 3		
Chapter 4		
Chapter 5		
Chapter 6		

Long Term Prayer Request: ____

"Pray for one another" James 5:16

Prayer Log

Name: ______________________ Spouse: ______________________

Phone: ______________________ Children (ages): ______________________

E-Mail Address: ____

	Prayer Requests	*Answers to Prayers*
Chapter 1		
Chapter 2		
Chapter 3		
Chapter 4		
Chapter 5		
Chapter 6		

Long Term Prayer Request: ____

"Pray for one another" James 5:16

Prayer Log

Name: ______________________ Spouse: ______________________

Phone: ______________________ Children (ages): ______________________

E-Mail Address: ____

	Prayer Requests	*Answers to Prayers*
Chapter 1		
Chapter 2		
Chapter 3		
Chapter 4		
Chapter 5		
Chapter 6		

Long Term Prayer Request: ____

"Pray for one another" James 5:16

Prayer Log

Name: ______________________ Spouse: ______________________

Phone: ______________________ Children (ages): ______________________

E-Mail Address: ____

	Prayer Requests	*Answers to Prayers*
Chapter 1		
Chapter 2		
Chapter 3		
Chapter 4		
Chapter 5		
Chapter 6		

Long Term Prayer Request: ____

"Pray for one another" James 5:16